Terrorism : Reducing Vulnerabilities and Improving Responses

Terrorism : Reducing Vulnerabilities and Improving Responses

Avinash Bharti

CYBER TECH PUBLICATIONS
4264/3, Ansari Road, Daryaganj, New Delhi-110002 (India)
Ph.: 011-23244078, 011-43559448 Fax: 011-23280028
E-Mail: cyberpublicationsdelhi@yahoo.com
Website: www.cybertechpublications.com

TERRORISM : REDUCING VULNERABILITIES AND IMPROVING RESPONSES

Avinash Bharti

First Edition 2010

Published by :

G.S. Rawat for **Cyber Tech Publications**
4264/3, Ansari Road, Daryaganj, New Delhi-110002 (India)
Ph.: 011-23244078, 011-43559448 Fax: 011-23280028
E-Mail: cyberpublicationsdelhi@yahoo.com
Website: www.cybertechpublications.com

Printed at: Asian Offset Printers, Delhi-53

Preface

The threat of weapons of mass destruction — chemical, biological and nuclear — the risk that a Nuclear Power Plant (NPP) might be used as a radiological weapon has received much attention post-11 September 2001. While there is no danger of a nuclear-yield explosion if a NPP were attacked, a successful terrorist attack or sabotage attempt at a NPP containing a range of hazardous materials and facilities could cause the release of radioactive particles into the atmosphere. This would disperse radioactive contamination over a wide area. The contaminated area would thus become uninhabitable, with grave consequences for the environment, the economy and future generations.

Despite these threats, advances in science and technology are improving the nation's ability to prevent hazards from becoming disasters. Scientific breakthroughs and advanced technologies are being applied to every facet of hazard risk reduction, including precision storm modeling, earthquake shake tables, and innovative mitigation and risk communication techniques. These advances mean that natural and technological hazard events no longer inevitably lead to catastrophic disaster for the communities they threaten.

Scientific and technological advances developed in the arena of natural and technological disasters also can directly benefit terrorism preparedness and response. Addressing the threats posed by terrorism requires a close look at existing and emerging hazard risk-reduction techniques and tools. A common, all-hazards approach is necessary to effectively address all disaster risks—accidental, intentional, or natural.

—Author

CONTENTS

Chapter

1

Explaining Terrorism: A Psychosocial Approach

INTRODUCTION

Terrorism is a difficult topic. Its explanation may be biased by political assumptions and social prejudices. Policy makers and experts disagree about their theoretical perspectives. At a minimum, there are three approaches to studying terrorism: macrosociological, psychological, and psychosocial. Because the first two approaches have received more attention in past decades, this paper will discuss the third approach, which has gained more and more followers over the past few years (De la Corte, 2006).

Those researchers who subscribe to a macrosociological approach view terrorism as a reflection of various social dysfunctions or conflictive trends in the social system. In general, terrorism has been associated with several so-called "root causes" that have promoted other kinds of political violence such as riots and street protests, revolutions, civil wars, and international armed conflicts. Some of the possible root causes are poverty, authoritarian and repressive regimes, or cultural and religious practices. However, most of the studies that have analyzed the relationship among those sociological variables and terrorist campaigns are inconclusive (Crenshaw, 1995; Laqueur, 2003; Reinares, 2003; De la Corte, 2006; Newman, 2006). Classifying these sources is difficult because terrorism is usually promoted by minorities and the perspective of terrorists often involves a severe distortion of social reality. The most popular psychological explanations of terrorism involve disruptive or psychopathological personalities. While research is speculative, some researchers have tried to analyze terrorists by their propensity for violence or an inability to control their aggressive impulses. However, impulsive aggressiveness is not a common trait of terrorists.

According to biographical studies, people joining the same terrorist organisation have different motivations and personalities. Some common psychological attributes among terrorists are a lack of empathy with their victims, dogmatic or ideological mentality, or a simplistic or utopian worldview, (see Beck, 2003; De la Corte, 2006). However, one must consider that psychological profiles are based on information about the more fanatical and higher ranking members of terrorist organisations. While terrorist activity involves spreading one's ideology or carrying out attacks, it also requires strategic planning, logistical support, raising funds, and recruiting. Each of these activities usually requires people with different capabilities and varying psychological traits. Finally, it is not clear if the psychological attributes of the terrorists are fixed traits or attitudes induced by the experiences of the terrorist's life.

In sum, neither the individual psychology of terrorists, nor the social environments provide a complete explanation of why individuals become involved in terrorism. For this reason, more and more researchers are turning toward a psychosocial perspective in their studies.

First psychosocial principle: terrorism must not be seen as a syndrome but as a method of social and political influence

Social psychologists describe one's environment as the place where a person's behaviour is influenced by the social settings in which they live and their psychological predispositions. But first and foremost, it is a sphere of social influence, an area where people attempt to influence the behaviour and beliefs of other people. Therefore, the psychosocial perspective is not congruent with the widespread interpretation of terrorist attacks as a direct effect of any social or psychological determination, but viewed as several social interactive processes that take place both in both inter and intragroup environs. Moreover, many of these influential processes develop in a deliberate and strategic way. Often, terrorist organisations utilize an advertising technique similar to propaganda campaigns when promoting their cause. The idea is best describe by a well-known anarchist saying which defines terrorism as "propaganda by the fact".

Many minority groups conduct terrorist activities as a way to bring about social change. (Kruglanski, 2003). Usually, these groups represent beliefs and positions on political and religious issues which are not readily accepted by the majority. These terrorists are what some social psychologists define as "active minorities" (Moscovici, Mugny and Perez, 1991; Moscovici, 1996). According to research conducted by experimental social psychologists, minorities attempt to gain influence by persuading majority members to consider their point of view. Effective persuasion depends on the minority member's ability to clearly communicate their positions over several different occasions. Through such persistence, a minority may be able to change or influence the majority position. Terrorism is not much different from this process because the spreading of fear or terror through violence has a communicative dimension. Remember the relationship between terrorism and propaganda: after all, terrorist violence is a means to direct people's attention to certain problems (real, exaggerated or fictitious) and publicize the terrorist's political or religious demands.

Second principle: the attributes of terrorists are shaped by processes of social interaction

As a whole; social psychologists are predisposed to explain the psychological characteristics of individuals a result of several processes of socialization and social interaction. This ideal also applies to the mental attributes of terrorists. Previously, some researches suggested that the process of joining a terrorist group was heavily influenced by the prevailing political and social environment shared by friends and relatives. Obviously, growing up in an environment marked by radical ideas and values could lead one to a join terrorist group which embraces the same ideas and values. For example, many members of Euskadi Ta Askatasuna (ETA), Red Brigades or Irish Republican Army (IRA) were born and raised in families respectively attached to the subculture of Basque nationalist (Reinares, 2001; Romero, 2006), Irish Catholic (Lee, 1983) or Italian radical left-wing (Della Porta, 1990).

In other cases, joining a terrorist organisation is the result of making contact and relationships with people who embrace extremist political or religious ideas. Sageman (2004) states that personal paths, interactions, and choices may lead young Muslims to become radical jihadists. According to that research, the act of joining a jihadist organisation such as al-Qaeda stems from the individual making an unintentional friendship with a person who has radical jihadists' views. In the sample of 168 subjects who were investigated by Sageman, 68% said friendship was the main influencing factor contributing to joining jihadist groups. In about 14% of the cases, one joined a jihadist organisation because of familial bonds. The two other explanatory variables also dealt with socialization experiences prior to involvement in terrorist activity: 1) experiences related to education in certain *madrassas* or Koranic schools (8% of the members of the sample,) or 2) assiduous participation in the activities of certain radical mosques. The psychosocial perspective also emphasizes the importance of "secondary socialization" processes in which terrorists become involved after joining a radical organisation. It should be noted that some experts have found significant similarities between the indoctrinative method of sectarian groups and those that are used inside terrorist organisations (Rodriguez, 1992; Della Porta, 1998; Sageman, 2004; De la Corte, 2006). In any case, there is no doubt that the activities and lifestyles developed inside terrorist organisation shape the mentality of its members, intensifying their commitment to such organisations, and preparing them to engage in criminal activities.

Third principle: terrorist organisations can be analyzed by analogy with other social movements

Many terrorist organisations can be closely related to cycles of political mobilization and mass protests against states that take place from time to time (Tarrow, 1989; Gonzalez Calleja, 2003). Very often, terrorist campaigns are the result of a long radicalization process of certain political or religious movement. When those movements lose their social influence, they tend to split off and form different groups. Sometimes, extremists in those groups adopt terrorism as its preferred method of social influence (Reinares, 1998; De la Corte, 2006).

One aspect that terrorist organisations share with ordinary political or religious movements is the central role played by psychological processes of collective identification. Typically, terrorist organisations present themselves as the defenders of the values and interests of an ethnic or religious community (see Javaloy, Rodriguez and Espelt, 2003). As Social Identity Theory predicts, the self-identification of terrorists as members of a much larger community will help them to fulfil their goals; see table 1 (Tajfel, 1984; Turner, 1991; Javaloy, Rodriguez and Espelt, 2003; Taylor, 2003).

Table 1: *Psychosocial effects and relationship to social identity*

Effect	Explanation
Depersonalization	Terrorists tend to perceive themselves as interchangeable members of an organisation. This motivates terrorists to give preference to the interests and goals of the organisation
Social cohesión	The collective identity shared by members of terrorist organisation promote positive relationships among them, which increases intragroup cohesion and cooperation
Conformity, obedience	The greater identification with the terrorist organisation, the greater identification with the norms which rule the members' behaviour. Therefore, a reduction in disobedience and challenging the orders of their leaders.

Bipolar worldview	Identifying with their organisation and reference community motivates terrorist to develop negative prejudices about people from other communities. The world is divided between us and them. The responsibility of problems and injustices suffered by the terrorist's reference community may be attributed to another community who could play a scapegoat role.

Fourth principle: terrorism only is possible when terrorists have access to certain resources

Resource Mobilization theory (McCarthy and Zald, 1973; McAdam, 1982) states that the probability of the emergence of any social protest movement depends not only on the opportunities offered by the social situation, but also by the capability of the movement to "mobilize" certain basic resources. Specifically, a terrorist campaign requires materials (money, technology and others), people (militants, collaborators, supporters) and symbols (clearly linked to the ideologies that motivate terrorist acts) (Waldman, 1997). It is important to note that a majority of a terrorist's time and effort is dedicated to obtaining the above resources. In order obtain these primary resources, terrorist may engage in predatory activities such as theft, extortion, kidnapping or various legal and illegal businesses (see Bovenkerk and Chakra, 2004; Ward, 2004). To obtain their human resources, terrorist organisations design unique methods of radicalization, recruitment strategies, and training programs (De la Corte, 2006).

Fifth principle: the decision to begin and sustain a terrorist campaign is always legitimized by an extreme ideology

Terrorism would not be possible without the existence of an extreme ideology that provides meaning and justification for the people who plan, execute, and support the violent actions. Ideology here refers to a system of extremist beliefs and values that are shared by a terrorist organisation and its allies. When the terrorist's ideology is rooted in the traditions and history of their reference community (for example, the Palestinian community for Hamas or the Basque people for ETA), it is possible that ideology also earns the acceptance of many individuals and other groups not involved in terrorist activity.

Table 2: Arguments and beliefs which legitimize terrorism

Ideological resources	Psycho-social functions
Arguments and beliefs that identify and criticize certain social injustices, offences, or threats that affects a terrorist's reference community	• Activation of feelings of frustration and moral outrage
Arguments and beliefs that identify a collective enemy as responsible for such injustices, offences or threats and insults. Those arguments and beliefs configure a stereotype which devalues the enemy image even to the point of dehumanization	• Transference of responsibility related to terrorist attacks • Inhibition of empathetic reactions toward victims • Activation of feelings of hatred and desires for revenge
Arguments and beliefs that describe a positive social identity shared by terrorists and their reference community	• Identification of terrorists with the interests and values of their reference community
Arguments and beliefs that define: 1) collective goals linked with the values and interests of the terrorist's reference community; 2) violence as the only effective method to achieve those collective goals	• Legitimization of violence by their presumed political, social, or religious consequences
Arguments and beliefs which predict a future state in which terrorists would have reached their collective goals through violence.	• Increase in the efficacy expectations associated with terrorist activity

As stated by Krunglanski (2002), the latter is important because the more people who share a similar point of view to that of the terrorists, the greater the potential for violence. Several investigations have been undertaken regarding the nature, contents, and functions which characterized the ideologies of different terrorist organisations. One study found similarities in the ideologies of ETA (Sabucedo, Rodriguez and Fernandez, 2002; Sabucedo, Blanco y De la Corte, 2003), the Colombian guerrilla *Fuerzas Armadas Revolucionarias de Colombia* (FARC), the paramilitaries group called Autodefensas Unidas de Colombia (AUC) (Sabucedo et al., 2005) and the jihadist propaganda and the message of al-Qaeda's leaders (De la Corte, 2005; De la Corte and Jordan, 2007). Overall, the research has found at least five elements shared by all these ideological discourses. Table 2 lists these elements and describes their psychosocial functions.

Sixth principle: every terrorist campaign involves strategic goals but the rationality which terrorists apply to their violence is imperfect

According to the most influential theoretical model in contemporary social sciences, individuals, organisations and social movements usually behave like rational actors (Coleman, 1990; Rosenberg, 1995). A rational actor only chooses those actions that he considers as the most effective means to attain his objectives or satisfy his preferences. In its original version, Rational Choice Theory assumed that people always try to behave as rational actors and that human rationality tends to be almost perfect.

In other words, it was understood that the actions undertaken by rational actors were the most effective according to the real situations in which they operate. Certainly, it seems that terrorist perceived themselves as rational actors. Many terrorist organisations have been able to introduce changes into their strategies in order to adapt themselves to changing situations and to react to their opponents (State, social audiences, etc). Some authors have interpreted those adaptations as a substantial proof of the terrorist's rationality (Crenshaw, 2001).

However, and contrary to suggestions which come from the first version of Rational Choice Theory, many investigations have showed that the rationality which guides human behaviour is rather limited and imperfect (Kahneman and Tversky, 1982; Elster, 1984; Simons, 1995). This paper will discuss only two aspects of the concept of human rationality (for a broader review see De la Corte, 2006). First, no individual or collective actor is really able to anticipate perfectly or realize *a posteriori* the complete sum of consequences that could be produced by their own actions.

Therefore, many of the forecasts and assessments conducted by terrorists will not be completely accurate. Second, the emotions (anger, desire for revenge, hatred, etc.), ideological motives, and other psychological elements could influence the terrorist's subjective perspective in the sense to distort their expectancies and their reflections about the result of their violent actions. Various studies suggest that terrorists tend to overestimate their chances of success and sometimes have problems recognizing the ineffectiveness of their actions. Indeed, those biases are typical among the members of many non-violent protest movements (San Martin, 2005). Moreover, sometimes terrorists may underestimate the negative reaction that their most brutal attacks could provoke among their own actual or potential supporters (Bandura, 2003). Finally, the scientific literature shows that, if individual actors' rationality tends to be limited and imperfect, the rationality of collective actors (groups, organisations, social movements, institutions, etc.) becomes even more problematic.

Seventh principle: the activity of terrorists partly reflects the internal features of their organisations

The chances of terrorists acting in a rational way are not only limited by their individual psychological attributes, but also by the characteristics of their organisations. Research in the psychology of groups and organisations offers knowledge highly relevant in this regard (Blanco, Caballero y De la Corte, 2004). There exist at least two kinds of terrorist organisation attributes that affect their activities.

The first has to do with the organisational structure, and the second one is relating to group dynamics. The structure of any organisation is equivalent to the formal pattern of social relations that are established among their members depending on certain roles and norms. There are two main structures of terrorist organisations (De la Corte, 2006). The first type is a more or less hierarchical one, as in the case of terrorist groups such as the IRA or the Italian Red Brigades. The second structure is much less hierarchical and much more flexible and decentralized. It corresponds to terrorist groups composed by multiple cells which usually operate almost autonomously. The small jihadist networks which today operate in various parts of the world offer the most obvious examples of this second type. The hierarchical structure involves stronger leadership and control over the organisation and ensures a greater compliance to the operational guidelines and order which emanate from the highest positions in the organisation. In turn, the less hierarchical structures are more difficult to dismantle because the neutralization of some cells or networks does not necessarily result in irreparable harm. According to Arquilla and Ronfeldt (2003), many contemporary terrorists have adopted more flexible organisational models which also are better adapted to the strategic and tactical demands of transnational terrorism campaigns.

Regarding group dynamics inside terrorist organisations, we need to be aware of the decision-making process. Many experimental studies have shown that human groups tend to polarize attitudes and decisions to a greater extent than individuals. Sometimes this group polarization effect promotes highly risky actions (Myers, 1978). Terrorist cells exhibit the same conditions which facilitate group polarization. For instance, during certain periods, terrorists tend to reduce drastically their contact with people who do not embrace their similar extremist ideology. Furthermore, terrorists are frequently subject to strong discipline. Both factors also could promote 'groupthink'. The social psychologist Ervin Janis (1972) coined that expression to define the dynamic of interactions which have caused some serious decision-making mistakes made by important political or military committees during the last century. Several researchers have applied the concept of groupthink to their explanations of different cases of terrorism.

Other group aspects that facilitate terrorist activities concern: the norms and roles to which terrorists use to adjust their behaviour; the influence exerted by group leaders; and the material benefits and psychological rewards associated with the terrorist's militancy. Finally, research on social influence, persuasion and changing attitudes show that reasons which people use to justify some of their actions are actually only developed after such actions haven take place (see Briñol, De la Corte and Becerra, 2001). Aronson (1972) coined the term "retrospective rationality" to design this tendency which has been demonstrated by several experiments. Furthermore, the same trend has been identified as a thought pattern frequently applied to justify collective and organisational actions (Pfeffer, 1998). In a similar way, some of the "reasons" that terrorists use to justify their activity could be mere rationalizations. Alonso and Reinares have found evidence that supports the rationalization hypothesis in their studies of IRA (Alonso, 2003) and ETA terrorism (Reinares, 2001).

CONCLUSIONS

This paper has offered some clues which can be used to characterize a social psychological approach to the explanation of terrorism. In addition, this approach provides some suggestions to future research and analysis of the following key issues: 1) the socio-political environment, social relations, and the primary socialization processes that could promote the radicalisation of and enlistment in terrorist organisations; 2) the relationship between terrorist organisations and broader political or religious movements; 3) the recruitment processes and indoctrination techniques applied by terrorist organisations; 4) the structure of terrorist organisations and their group dynamics, and 5) the discourses and ideological principles that some leaders and ideologists developed and propagate in order to legitimize their criminal activities and garner support from their reference communities.

Chapter

2

Home-grown Terrorism: Issues and Implications

Recently, much attention has been devoted to the 'home-grown' nature of Islamist terrorism in Western countries. This term permeates headlines, various reports and national psyches. It has been described as the "new face of terrorism," and the "main [terrorist] threat" faced by the West. However, it is a term that carries with it certain assumptions and implications that should be clarified so the public may gain a greater understanding of contemporary threats to national security. This article examines key connotations of home-grown Islamist terrorism in an effort to assess the validity of the term and draw attention to the need for more careful specification of meaning in its application.

First, it is necessary to clarify the scope of reference. 'The West' is a very broad expression generally understood to include Australia, Canada, Western Europe, and the United States. Of course, these countries share social and political dimensions that make them comparable; however, each also has their own unique history and profile that must be taken into account when assessing individual 'home-grown' issues. Each country's immigration history and related cultural identity affects the extent to which Muslims in the West have become integrated into their 'host' societies. Hypothetically, the less integrated and more socially isolated, the greater potential for feelings of disillusionment and resentment, which may significantly increase the likelihood of one turning to terrorism

Thus, it is argued that Western European countries (their own differences notwithstanding) are far more at risk to home-grown Islamist terrorism (HGIT) than the US due in large part to a history of lax immigration and asylum laws. These policies are contributory factors behind the large number of –often unskilled and therefore deprived- Muslim immigrants to enter countries like Britain and Spain and in combination with nationalistic cultural nuances these conditions are thought to have fostered marginalisation and segregation. By contrast the US's 'cultural melting pot' and 'land of opportunity' ethos are thought to have fostered far more integrated Muslim populations that are more likely to positively identify with their host nation and to reject collective explanations for personal adversity, relative or otherwise.

Australia and Canada have been posited as lying somewhere between these two extremes. Like America, immigration has been integral to the growth of their populations, but like Europe they have maintained liberal asylum policies and social benefit systems, which may attract the 'wrong' kind of immigrants. While such claims may at times seem blunt and sweeping, it is apparent there are differences between Western countries that may at times be more relevant than their similarities. The present paper represents a brief overview of relevant matters, but for the purposes of more country-specific in-depth analyses, such differences would necessarily take on greater significance.

Working definitions of terrorism require a degree of common sense and an appreciation of the relativity of labelling. The use of politically/religiously justified violence against non-combatants by sub-state groups or organisations is a key part of the globally accepted definitions. Specifically, Islamist terrorism is inspired by Salafi/Wahhabi ideology and championed by al-Qaeda and similar organisations across the globe. 'Home-grown' Islamist terrorism as a term seems to be largely taken for granted as being self-evident without being specifically defined.

Usage of the term tends to focus on where perpetrators are from and whether they receive international organisational support.

Each of these elements carries implications for the practice of terrorism, which allow the definition of HGIT to be broken down into several facets. Stricter definitions of HGIT would require that attempted/successful terrorists:

- Were born and/or spent most of their lives in the West
- Were radicalised within their Western home countries
- Have trained and achieved attack-capability in their Western home countries
- Have planned/carried out attacks in their Western home countries
- And are lacking direct foreign (non-Western) international support or control

While it may be rare for any one group of terrorists to fulfil all of these criteria, certain key overlapping themes commonly appear in definitions of HGIT. Notable aspects include the nationality of the terrorists and the country of radicalisation in relation to the targeted country. Also highlighted are the country of "jihadisation" and preparation involved in attack (including training, planning and procurement of materials and weapons) and the level of international influence or cooperation at each stage (including ideological communication, training, operational advice and logistical support).

What seems like a simple straight-forward piece of terminology, is in fact, a moniker laden with assumptions and implications. It is therefore important to assess the veracity of prescribed attributes of HGIT, which revolve around a central theme of change and development. If HGIT represents a 'new' manifestation of the ongoing terrorist threat, what exactly is new about it? In order to answer this question it is necessary to further explore the who, when, what, where, how, and why of terrorism.

Who and when relate to terrorist profiles- who commits acts of radical Islamist terrorism and at what point in their lives do they choose to do so? The heterogeneity of terrorists "makes it difficult, if not impossible, to effectively profile [them]"; however, it is still possible to make general observations that aid in assessing the nature of HGIT. Prior to September 11th, it was suggested that "U.S. Customs personnel should give extra scrutiny to the passports of young foreigners claiming to be "students" and meeting the following general description: physically fit males in their early twenties of Egyptian, Jordanian, Yemeni, Iraqi, Algerian, Syrian, or Sudanese nationality, or Arabs bearing valid British passports, in that order. These characteristics generally describe the core membership of Osama bin Laden's Arab "Afghans"...who are being trained to attack the United States with WMD."

The inclusion of possible British passports reflects recognition that mujahedin had been establishing themselves throughout Europe since the early 1990's. However, more recent profiles clearly emphasise Western nationality as being a likelihood, rather than a possibility, of one attacking a target in the West. Summarizing the characteristics of the terrorists behind five plots from 2004 to 2006 Silber & Bhatt describe those responsible as being male Muslims below the age of 35 and local residents/citizens of Western liberal democracies, a profile repeated in their analysis of groups throughout the United States. It also noted that these men are often second or third generation inhabitants as opposed to recent immigrants. They generally also had 'ordinary' backgrounds and included recent 'converts' to Islam among their numbers. Along similar lines, Leiken & Brooke report that of a sample of 373 terrorists charged, convicted, or killed in Europe and North America between 1990 and 2004, 41% were Western nationals. Such observations are almost certainly the least contestable aspect of HGIT, indeed they are the very basis for the term as a recognition of the evolution of the threat posed by terrorism in the West from 'exogenous' to 'endogenous.' Who carries out attacks is of course very much related to the Where of Islamist terrorism.

While Islamist terrorists were responsible for the first World Trade Centre bombing of 1993, and a group of French-born militants acting for the Armed Islamic Group (GIA) were responsible for the 1995 spate of bombings in France, the consensus is that Europe and the West have now emerged as primary targets, as well as bases of operation. This is reflected in the apparent graduation of terrorist networks in the West as they have moved beyond logistical support and *dawa* to carry out attacks, as evidenced by the steady stream of uncovered plots since 9/11. For purposes of assessing the home-grown element of terrorism, it is notable that in addition to radicalisation, it appears that the internet and camping trips are utilised for training purposes within the West. This means that, at least theoretically, a terrorist group could emerge and reach attack capability without ever leaving their home country, although foreign travel seems to occur more often than not.

Returning briefly to the profile of HGIT, further developments seem to suggest that terrorists are getting younger and females are playing an increasingly important role. Taarnby Jensen states "it is now possible to radicalise and recruit very young Muslims in much more diverse settings than previously" and the Dutch General Intelligence and Security Agency (AIVD), describes the radical pool of potential and emerging terrorist recruits as "youngsters" between the ages of 16 and 25. They also note "the growing participation of young women in local jihadist networks." Such findings reflect a growing awareness and accessibility of radical Islamist messages in the West, propagated via successful attacks and the dissemination of related (often online) propaganda.

However, in terms of assessing the nature of HGIT, it is also important to note that seemingly wider dissemination goes hand in hand with a degree of bastardization as new audiences input their own knowledge and experience into the basic ideological 'us versus the formula popularised and re-expressed countless times in the wake of 9/11. Thus, the Hofstad group's ideological and operational innovation demonstrates active reconstruction and interpretation of the Islamist terrorist cause (although interestingly this 'innovation' –focussing on local issues and opting for targeted assassination- is reminiscent of terrorist approaches in the pre-Global jihad era).

The 'cultural dilution' of militant Salafism is exemplified by the observation that "Many youngsters from the Muslim-majority ghettoes of various European cities adopt several behaviors typical of Western street culture, such as dressing like rappers, smoking marijuana and drinking alcohol, yet watching jihadi videos and having pictures of Osama bin Laden on the display of their cell phones." Whether or not increasingly popular, distorted and diverse interpretations of Islamist terrorist ideology will eventually detract from the potency of the overall cause, their existence confirms and re-emphasises a truly home-*grown* phenomena.

Consistent with recognition of Western input into the overriding anti-Western campaign are assertions as to the autonomy of HGIT groups. This brings us to the what, how, and why of terrorism and relates to both the genesis of terrorist activity (radicalisation and jihadisation) and the physical acts involved (preparation and execution of attacks). The radicalisation of a minority of young Muslim men of differing backgrounds in Western countries seems to have traditionally been viewed as a direct result of the presence of foreign 'recruiters,' usually in the form of experienced jihadis and sheiks operating out of established "centres of gravity" such as London's Finsbury Park mosque, part of an extensive international network established in the post-Afghan jihad era.

However, accounts of contemporary processes of radicalisation and jihadisation tend to emphasise spontaneous group interaction, bottom-up "grass roots" adoption of militancy and "only marginal ties to structured terrorist groups" indicating a lack of organisational support or control. These developments have lead HGIT groups such as the 7/7 bombers to be regarded as 'self-starters' and have been widely attributed to the ""decentralization of Al Qaeda" [caused by post-9/11 counter-terrorism measures] or the growth of Salafism as a social movement." Spontaneous group interaction and bottom-up recruitment have nevertheless been important throughout the life of the 'global Salafi jihad' and although societal conditions have changed,(including growth of the Internet, greater public awareness of Islamist terrorists' cause, and a more restrictive security environment),basic patterns of radicalisation still share certain key features.

Thus, while Taarnby Jensen draws attention to differences in the profiles of recent Danish terrorists as being younger, raised and radicalised within Denmark, and of questionable organisational affiliation, his description of the 'Glostrup' cell follows a very familiar sounding trajectory.

This small group of friends spontaneously formed in and around mosques and grew extremely close to each other before eventually rejecting the mosques as too moderate. Group meetings continued in more private settings and they established associations with known radicals as they sought to pursue terrorist activities, in this case abroad in Bosnia. This closely resembles descriptions of the basic patterns of radicalisation, which capture underlying social-psychological processes at the heart of extremism and seem to be widely applicable to various Islamist terrorist groups over the years.

Whether or not the role of autonomy in the past has been under-emphasised, it seems generally accepted that HGIT groups today are significantly more independent, and as a result, more amateurish when they progress to the operational stage because they must rely on their own resources and initiative to gain the knowledge and skills required. Nevertheless, the existence and nature of (international) ties to external groups, networks, or organisations remains a poorly understood area of concern, sometimes tainted with rumour or speculation, and perhaps at times too easily dismissed as a thing of the past. Commenting on the Operation Crevice trial of UK-based would-be bombers arrested in March 2004 the Deputy Assistant Commissioner of the Metropolitan police remarked upon evident links between the UK group and al-Qaeda in Pakistan as well as links to the US and Canada, "What this case and others in the future will show is that we are dealing with a threat posed by interlinked networks of terrorists." Likewise, Australian Parliament reported in 2006 that recent experience of Islamist terrorism showed that it "has an international dimension, in the sense that perpetrators are likely to receive training or get financial support from sources in other countries". Jonathan Evans, the Director General of MI5, reported this year that a "development in the last 12 months has been the extent to which the conspiracies here are being driven from an increasing range of overseas countries."

Given the highly social nature of Islamist terrorist activity and the apparent importance of status systems as well as the sustained popularity of jihadi combat zones within radical Islamist subcultures it seems likely that 'official' affiliation will often be sought and achieved to varying degrees. It is therefore prudent not to think of HGIT as a homogenous phenomenon, but instead a continuum encompassing "a whole spectrum of realities, positioned according to the level of autonomy of the group." Along such lines, Hoffman15 identifies four levels of al-Qaeda, including the remaining core central staff (still representing the biggest potential threat) various organisational affiliates, 'al-Qaeda locals' who have established links to al-Qaeda, and finally the 'al-Qaeda network' with no organisational links. The why of terrorism is possibly the most difficult question to answer. While isolated individuals may crop up who are experiencing some form of psychopathology, there is nothing to indicate that perpetrators of HGIT on the whole are more likely than terrorists of the 'past' or than the world's general population to be suffering from mental illness. Although it is beyond the scope of this paper to explore the full range of explanations for why people take to terrorism, suffice to say there are multiple, interacting factors that make it more or less likely one will do so.

Thus, for example, at the individual level experience of personal adversity or change might contribute to decisions that lead to terrorist involvement whilst at the societal and global level political grievances and worldly events can have a profound impact on groups and individuals. A common thread which seems to tie these levels of explanation together is a process of social identification. Thus what both personal and global circumstances share is the power to lead individuals to identify with a certain social category, in this case the perceived Muslim *umma.*

What then drives individuals beyond identification and empathy towards violent action is rooted in spontaneous group dynamics and continued exposure to violent ideology, which together act to narrow down the gamut of acceptable identities and to define related scripts for action. It is extremely difficult to say whether antecedents of HGIT are any different from 'imported' terrorism. Terrorists born in Middle Eastern or other countries may have been more likely to have been involved in violent political conflicts or to have experienced oppression first hand growing up. Therefore, terrorist militancy, while still extreme, would be an extension of an existing almost innate and more 'real' identity.

Conversely the adoption of terrorist identities by 'purely' home-grown participants born and raised in the West appears to have a strong reactionary or deliberately rebellious nature as they consciously reject Western identities that they are geographically born, if not raised into. Along these lines, Roy has asserted that "To convert to Islam today is a way for a European rebel to find a cause; it has little to do with theology" and Durodié has suggested that acts of home-grown terrorism are "akin to the Columbine high school massacre," finding their basis in cultural nihilism. An interesting related implication is that there may have been a change in expectations about what it means to get involved in radical and militant Islam. Hence Silber & Bhatt remark that "there is no longer any illusion as to what the adoption of jihadi-Salafi ideology means" and Taarnby Jensen observes that individuals drawn to radical mosques "often know exactly which interpretation of Islam they want to hear."

If such claims are accurate, it is possible to make a distinction between earlier generations of Islamist terrorists and their home-grown 'descendants' based upon their social identities. Relatively speaking, in earlier generations an identity congruent with the cause preceded or went hand in hand with some form of frustration and desire to act, whilst in later generations 'frustration' precedes adoption of an identity which enables action. From this perspective, the radical Islamist ideology behind HGIT is more of a vehicle for expression rather than a cause of violence per se, which therefore implies that in the absence of such an ideology groups and individuals would presumably find some alternative avenue of expression.

A potential danger with this line of reasoning; however, is the possibility of underestimating HGIT as it paints a picture of home-grown terrorists as something less than the genuine article, (and tendencies toward underestimation would be exacerbated if the disruption caused by counter-terrorism efforts has been inflated). There may well be many 'wannabes' and 'amateurs' among the ranks of Islamist terrorists, but they are still committed to killing. As evidenced by racial tensions and violence in the Netherlands following the murder of Theo Van Gogh, it does not take a huge number of casualties to have a significant impact on society.

Furthermore the 'decentralised' or dispersed network structure attributed to contemporary Islamist terrorism, (seemingly therefore integral to HGIT), in conjunction with the apparent growth in the number of terrorists holding Western passports, is thought to be evidence of increased difficulty in detecting their activities. Such a perspective is given credence by the AIVD who have acknowledged that "The emergence of these local cells, some of which interact with members of international veterans networks, has complicated the anticipated threat for the near future, especially since such locally operating cells can easily blend in with the society in which they live, which makes it more difficult to identify them." Conversely, heightened counter-terrorism measures (for instance, France alone has arrested some 1422 people on terrorist charges since 2002) have increased chances of detection. This fact, along with the significant number of successfully foiled plots, seems to suggest that –pending an exceptional group of terrorists- overall, the odds remain stacked in the favour of the security services. Of course, the maxim remains that terrorists only have to succeed once. Given that there has been a marked increase in radical Islam, what may be the true difficulty for security services is the problem of false positives, or being confronted with a haystack of potentially dangerous radicals that demand attention, sometimes at the expense of being able to distinguish the truly 'jihadized' terrorists.

There is more than meets the eye to 'home-grown' Islamist terrorism, and yet, it is widely referred to without clarification. It is undeniable that "Islamist terrorism can no longer be regarded as an external threat, but rather as a threat rooted in and aimed against the Western society itself." This is reflected in the increasing popularity of radical Islam within various Western countries and the obvious willingness of a minority of Western citizens and residents to perpetrate acts of terrorism in their home countries in the name of 'Islam.' References to HGIT have helped draw attention to 'endogenous' elements of a pervasive global Islamist struggle, whereby processes of radicalisation, jihadisation, and preparation for attack all take place within the West.

This recognition has helped to focus the efforts of various security agencies, policy makers, and analysts alike as Western societies are now scrutinised as much if not more than their Middle Eastern or North African counterparts in the search for 'answers' to terrorism. However a closer, yet still brief, examination of underlying assumptions has highlighted the fact that contemporary Islamist terrorism in the West does not appear to be an entirely distinct manifestation from previous decades and is both varied and complex. Invoking unqualified reference to HGIT with the advent of each new plot uncovered runs the risk of overemphasising homogeneity.

Groups of terrorists do seem to share common patterns of development as individuals come together, radicalise and decide to take action but there appears to be considerable variation both within and between these groups. In particular levels of international support and cooperation may have been underemphasised as foreign links are often uncovered and the nature and role of 'autonomy' (ideological, financial, and operational) is poorly understood. By taking a much more systematic approach to the analysis and cross-comparison of groups of terrorists in and out-with the West rather than relying on anecdotal evidence it will be possible to describe with more confidence the existing range of HGIT, which in turn will increase pattern-recognition and chances of prediction of future trends.

In addition, qualified and consistent usage of terms such as 'home-grown' has the potential to aid research into terrorism because researchers and authors of open source materials both mutually influence each other's work. Finally, Islamist terrorism is a diverse and dynamic phenomenon. Researchers must remain sensitive to change and development but also continuity in order to be able to accurately capture and understand the progression of its various manifestations.

GLOBAL POVERTY, INEQUALITY, AND TRANSNATIONAL TERRORISM

Among politicians and political figures within the media and throughout the general public, the idea that transnational terrorism is a predictable consequence of global poverty and the unequal distribution of global wealth remains quite popular. This belief rests on an essentially reasonable premise: If citizens of a country are denied the means to satisfy their basic human needs, are deprived of access to reasonable economic opportunities, or are faced with glaring levels of socioeconomic inequality; they will become hopeless and enraged and may view political violence as an acceptable means for redressing their grievances. Because political moderation and trust in the established system to address society's problems rest upon a healthy and prosperous economy, economic distress increases the appeal of radicalism in the eyes of ordinarily reasonable and moderate people.

Linking terrorism and wealth distribution is also politically attractive because it prompts a straightforward policy response to the problem and aids policymakers in creating political support for that policy response. If poverty and inequality cause terrorism; world leaders, media figures, analysts and ordinary people can embrace a causal framework through which something can be done to stop terrorism.

Concluding that terrorism is caused by bad conditions - rather than by "bad people" or other abstractions - facilitates a concrete policy response. Furthermore, because of the prevailing belief that poverty, inequality, or poor economic developments are causes of terrorism, politicians are able to harness this belief to build political support behind antipoverty policies. Politicians may use these beliefs to communicate two very strong messages:

(1) one can do something to reduce or even stop terrorism; which is to reduce or eliminate global economic want; and

(2) to continue to ignore global poverty or inequality is to continue to place the world and its citizens in mortal danger.

Indeed a very wide range of public figures have communicated these very messages, including President George W. Bush, former President Bill Clinton, former U.S. Secretary of State Colin Powell, former Secretary General of the United Nations Kofi Annan, and Nobel Laureate Desmond Tutu.

Reducing or eradicating global poverty or what former U.S. President Bill Clinton referred to as the "dark side of globalization" – the yawing gap in wealth between the industrialized and the developing countries – is, without question, a worthwhile objective for policymakers. But will it lead to a reduction in transnational terrorism? A spate of recent scholarship suggests that it will not.

To date, there is no evidence that that convincingly demonstrates that countries with low levels of economic development, high rates of unemployment, poor rates of economic growth, high levels of income inequality, and high levels of malnutrition have higher levels of terrorism. It is also not the case that perpetrators of terrorist attacks are more likely to be poor themselves, have low levels of education, high rates of unemployment, or to hail from impoverished countries. Moreover, these findings seem to stand up whether they are derived from individual, group, subnational, regional, or cross-national studies.

A Global Analysis

Are poverty and international inequality predictors of terrorism when looked at from a global perspective? Are changes in levels of global poverty and changes in the distribution of global wealth related to fluctuations of transnational terrorist activity? For several reasons the unique nature of transnational terrorism makes a global analysis, rather than a country-specific or cross-national examination, particularly useful. First, the country locations of transnational terrorist attacks may not be linked to the socio-economic conditions that produce terrorism in the first place.

Rather, countries attacked by transnational terrorists might be selected on the basis of local security dynamics, the international prominence of the target, the likelihood that local media will cover the attack, or the softness of the target. Second, as globalization progresses, domestic political economies are more likely to be affected by global processes, leading in turn, to a general globalization of socio-economic and political conflict. Transnational terrorism is more likely to be a reaction to these globalized conflicts. Finally, the theory of blowback posits that transnational terrorism is a counter-reaction to change in global hegemony, both security and economic hegemony, and resistance to dominant paradigms, one of which may be the current structure of the international economic system. A global study, in which the entire international system is the unit of analysis, is well positioned to capture the most important economic forces that are popularly argued to cause transnational terrorism.

This brief research note examines transnational terrorism by employing a global perspective using data on transnational terrorist attacks derived from Terrorism Knowledge Base (TKB) provided by the Rand Corporation and the Memorial Institute for the Prevention of Terrorism. The TKB collects open source data on transnational terrorist attacks – defined as attacks in which the perpetrator(s) and the victim(s) come from different countries – for the years 1972 to the present day and is regarded as a reputable and reliable database.

The analysis compares annual total rate of transnational terrorist attacks in the world to two other variables that encompass the popular focus on global poverty and inequality of wealth distribution. First, attacks are compared to the annual percentage of the world's population designated as 'in poverty' by Chen and Ravallion, though figures are available only from 1982. Second, attacks are compared to the annual gross domestic product differential between those countries designated as "high income" verses those designated as "low income" by the United Nations Development Program.

Results

However, a closer examination of the annual rate of attacks yields an interesting pattern. There are five peaks of transnational terrorist attacks – in 1976, 1982, 1985, 1991 and 2004. There is a significant decrease at the end of the 1990s, with 2000 representing the nadir. The 1980s is the most active period for transnational terrorism, and this corresponds with the observations of many qualitative studies of global terrorism. The most dramatic spike in attacks occurs between 2001 and 2004, largely due to the increased terrorist activities within Iraq. Between 2003, the start of the U.S. invasion and occupation of Iraq, and 2006, an average of 36.6 percent of all transnational attacks occurred within Iraq. In 2004, transnational attacks in Iraq accounted for 61.3 percent of total worldwide attacks for the year. Iraq after 2003 is an outlier, producing a large percentage of total attacks at the end of the time-series. When these attacks are excluded from the data, the results show a somewhat different picture.

Conclusion

Clearly these results do not provide compelling evidence that global poverty and global inequality are precipitants of terrorism – certainly not of the type that could support the rather confident assumptions underlying much of the policymaking world's statements about the root causes of transnational terrorism. But, they do provide the possibility that economic development could play a part in antiterrorism efforts by demonstrating that transnational attacks co-vary with levels of total people in poverty in the world. Further empirical investigation is required to determine the validity of this preliminary finding.

The results do yield some more unambiguous points of interest to researchers who use quantitative data on terrorism to explain its root causes. First, global measures of absolute level of development, such as the percentage of people living in poverty, might bear a different relationship to transnational terrorism than relative measures, such as the global distribution of wealth, even though policymakers tend to lump both of them together as precipitants of terrorism.

Second, researchers must consider outliers' effects because they have potentially important consequences for the overall pattern of transnational terrorism. It is possible that short-term and geographically isolated conditions, such as the invasion of Iraq and the disruptions that resulted due to sudden regime-change in that country, can distort the overall picture and mask more universal predictors of transnational terrorism. Finally, there is value in using a global view – an analysis that uses the entire world as a unit of analysis – in quantitative analyses of transnational terrorism. This method could be particularly useful in conjunction with single-case or cross-national analysis.

Chapter

3

Terrorism and the 'Invisible'

Much of the fear terrorism evokes is connected to its invisible character. Unlike states tied to fixed geographical locations, terrorists have, as is frequently said, "no return address." The organizations are clandestine, the members melt into the general population, and "sleeper cells" may lie dormant for long periods waiting for the opportune time to strike. Although the weapons terrorists actually employ are visible enough – bombs, box-cutters, and the like – governments and citizens are often obsessively concerned about tools and tactics they might use, particularly those with means of dispersal that are invisible: biological, chemical, and radiological. Thus, fear of the unseen, both in terms of perpetrators and methods, provides contemporary terrorism with a particularly sinister edge.

Yet it is not automatically clear what it means to say that something is "invisible." This article employs the term in a broader sense than its common usage. Here, it refers not merely to what cannot be seen, but to anything that cannot be detected by the unaided senses.

The dangers connected to invisible terrorism are those that are either produced intentionally by terrorists or believed by potential victims to be produced intentionally. Thus, the invisible dangers associated with terrorism may be real, in the sense that they reflect the actions of actual terrorists and weapons; or they may rest on false attributions, for example, the frequently cited but specious link between Sadaam Hussein and the September 11th hijackers.

Terrorists can secure intentional invisibility through four principle means: organizational secrecy; secret communications; technical invisibility; and crowd invisibility. Organizational invisibility occurs through such well-known means as cellular organizations; the careful vetting of recruits; tests of loyalty; and other techniques through which secret societies of many kinds have historically maintained their boundaries against spies, informants, and surveillance.

Similarly, secret communications within clandestine groups has a long history. Much of it involves forms of encryption, ranging from the primitive to the sophisticated. Some organizations have kept secrets from their own members through internal hierarchies with differential levels of knowledge. This creates a form of invisibility even within the organization, to the extent that the organization as a whole may attempt to be invisible vis-à-vis the outside world, while creating degrees of invisibility within, depending upon what has been revealed to different classes of members.

The more hostile the relationship between a group and the larger society, the less adequate these techniques will be for maintaining invisibility. Where terrorists are concerned, therefore, one often finds two additional modalities, technical invisibility and crowd invisibility.

Technical invisibility refers to invisibility that systematically seeks to defeat the human senses and the attempts of authorities to artificially enhance them. Especially since September 11th, terrorists and governments compete; the former seeking to conceal, the latter seeking to unmask. Airport screening has become increasingly elaborate and with more attention being given to technologies that can detect minute quantities of dangerous chemicals and biological agents. Large cities are also using closed-circuit television to monitor public spaces. Research continues for ever subtler ways to detect behavioral cues that might separate terrorists from innocent members of the public. But however much the technology of detection has advanced, it has not produced the desired results. Neither governments nor the general public believe that all terrorists or weapons can be detected, or that the threat of a major attack can be reduced to something approaching zero. To that extent, terrorists are perceived as having maintained some degree of technical invisibility. Each new attack validates the perception.

Terrorists may utilize crowd invisibility, a condition encapsulated by the well-known phrase, "hiding in plain sight." When the qualities that differentiate individuals can no longer be detected, as in a crowd, one person seems very like another. This is true by extension whether the class is made up of airline passengers, luggage, or shipping containers. Small differences cease to be noticeable in large groupings made up of superficially similar members.

Differences become of great importance if some members of a class are more dangerous than others. In that case, their ability to melt into a population and take advantage of crowd invisibility becomes an acute problem. Among the alternatives are either to carefully examine each member of the class, a laborious process, or to find some technology that ferrets out those that present dangers. Much of the attention given to the technological extension of the senses to defeat technical invisibility is also driven by the dilemma of crowd invisibility. To an extent, then, the two forms of invisibility are often linked. The challenge is to distinguish the particular suitcase, passenger, or shipping container that matters from all the rest, an enterprise that seeks to frustrate both technical and crowd invisibility. The same may hold true for so-called "sleeper cell," whose members live conformist and superficially blameless lives, melting into the environment. This sub-group maintains a functional invisibility until such time as they are activated, unless members falter in their conformity to the community's mores.

While these modalities are intentionally chosen by groups with hostile intent, putative targets may also identify invisible dangers where none in fact exist. These are cases of attributed invisibility. They occur in three principle ways: through over-inclusive classes, belief in conspiracy theories, and as a result of false or fragmentary intelligence.

Over-inclusive classes occur as a variant of the crowd invisibility problem. In this case, however, because observers' difficulties are compounded by situations in which there is contact between groups with dissimilar cultures or belief systems, there is a strong likelihood that dangers will be invented as opposed to being recognized. At least one side, and sometimes both, will be burdened by substantial ignorance of the other. As a result observers lack the ability to correctly interpret behavior and intentions, and are likely to impute risk and danger where none exists. In such a condition of ignorance, the entire observed group may seem both sinister and partially "invisible" due to its opaqueness to outsiders. This invisibility and particularly the associations of dangers with an amorphous "other" will be amplified when some of its practices cannot be publicly viewed because they take place behind the doors of homes, houses of worship, or other facilities. The effect of observers' ignorance is to project danger on the other based on their own fears rather than on clear evidence.

Conspiracy theories are a more straight-forward form of attributed invisibility, because they offer a world-view built around imagined secrets. They do so because the conspiracist makes three cardinal assumptions: that nothing happens by accident; that everything is connected; and that nothing is as it seems. Thus the visible world, seen naively through the senses, is said to hide the real but invisible workings of evil. With the theory as a template, the conspiracist can then, as it were, "decode" the clues available in the visible world. Indeed, one can imagine situations in which both terrorists and their potential victims conceptualize each other through mirroring conspiracy theories, each imputing invisible perpetrators and weapons to the other.

Fragmentary or erroneous intelligence provides a clearer case. The cliché metaphor of "connecting the dots" presumes that enough pieces of valid information exist to construct an accurate representation. However, not all of the information may be valid, or there may be too few pieces from which to produce a coherent narrative. Whether or not it is possible to determine the validity of the information, the temptation may be to interpolate enough potential "facts" to create a plausible picture, but one which will presumably be consistent with pre-existing prejudices and expectations, including expectations about invisible perpetrators and weapons.

It remains only to emphasize that the fear invisibility engenders in potential victims is not lost on terrorists, who recognize that invisibility can be manipulated as a weapon. While the obvious advantage of invisibility is avoiding detection, there are two additional benefits. The first is the likelihood that potential targets will significantly over-estimate terrorists' numbers and capabilities. Such mis-estimations were commonly made by nineteenth-century governments facing dissident secret societies, and there is little reason to think that this tendency has ceased. The second and more subtle effect, alluded to in much of the preceding, is the fear generated by the invisible. For those who live in a culture imbued with a materialist and scientific ethos, the presence of unseen dangers is particularly disturbing. They fill the world with mysterious and malevolent forces, transforming benign environments into, to use the geographer Yi-Fu Tuan's evocative phrase, "landscapes of fear."

The Modern Terrorist Threat to Aviation Security

During this busy holiday season, much is being said by pundits and policymakers about the potential vulnerabilities of today's global aviation system. While no specific threats have been reported, there is a widespread fear based upon an extensive history of attacks, ranging from hijackings and in-flight bombings to surface-to-air missile Most recently, authorities from the Saudi Arabian interior ministry arrested 172 suspected terrorists in April 2007 after uncovering a plot to hijack several airplanes and fly them into oil facilities and other critical infrastructure targets in that country.

In the summer of 2006, law enforcement agencies foiled a plot to simultaneously detonate homemade bombs on at least 10 U.S. airliners while en route from London to the United States (US). According to U.S. Homeland Security Secretary Michael Chertoff, the suspects planned to smuggle a relatively small amount of homemade liquid explosives onboard disguised as sports drinks. "If they had succeeded, there could have been thousands of lives lost and an enormous economic impact with devastating consequences for international air travel." Fortunately, arrests in Pakistan led United Kingdom (UK) and US officials to a British Muslim terrorist cell, which disrupted the attack on American targets. Airports in the United States and the UK were put on red alert (meaning a potential attack could be imminent), and all liquids were banned from carry-on luggage. Furthermore, numerous suspects were questioned, including 24 British-born Muslims and seven Pakistanis. Government authorities tested the explosive liquids and established a three ounce liquid limit for carry on items to eliminate the possible risk. To date, passengers are still restricted when bringing liquids onboard and those rules may remain in place forever.

Following this attempt to carry out simultaneous suicide attacks on commercial aircraft, U.S. airports remained on high alert for nearly a year. Among law enforcement professionals, the plot resulted in a heightened awareness of the creativity and innovative thinking of today's terrorists. Thus, when officials discovered an Arabic-language video clip on the Internet in October 2007 illustrating how to convert a remote-control toy car into a detonator for a bomb, Transportation Security Administration officers nationwide stepped up their scrutiny of passengers carrying remote-control toys aboard airplanes. Indeed, we should not be surprised in the future when other ordinary items that passengers would expect to carry on board without difficulty are suddenly given additional scrutiny because new intelligence indicates they could possibly be used in a terror plot. This dimension of creativity and innovation is a hallmark of the most lethal terrorist groups.

In truth, terrorists—at least the most sophisticated and lethal ones—learn from each other and are continually devising new and creative ways to wreak havoc and murder. Attacks which have not yet occurred, but for which we are ill-prepared, could include using an aircraft's in-flight oxygen circulation system to infect the passengers and crew with biological pathogens or unleashing a deadly chemical agent in the cockpit that renders the pilot and crew unconscious and causes the plane to crash. One could imagine a rash of in-flight food poisonings or attempts to corrupt signals from the air traffic control system in order to re-direct planes into each other or crash land in low-visibility conditions.

During the October 2007 "toy car scare", additional scrutiny was initiated in part due to intelligence, but also because—as one federal official noted—remote-control toys might have been used already by terrorists in Sri Lanka and India. Overall, as Bruce Hoffman recently observed, we should anticipate that terrorists are constantly searching for new vulnerabilities and adapting and adjusting to our countermeasures.

Another form of vulnerability stems from the contemporary aviation environment. This ever-expanding global system has seen increases in (1) the number of airplanes in the sky carrying passengers and cargo, (2) the size of these airplanes (like the new Dreamliner), and (3) the number of locations to which one can now fly. Terrorists—much like criminals, insurgents and other violent non-state actors—exploit vulnerabilities in the systems they target, and these systems are only as strong as their weakest link. Thus, as the commercial aviation system becomes more globally interconnected, the overall impact of these measures at U.S. airports has an important, but relatively minor impact on the aviation sector worldwide.

While airports in Europe and North America responded to the rash of hijackings and bombings during this period, many other countries—particularly in Africa and Asia—found it difficult to impose most of these costly security measures, thus providing vulnerabilities that could be exploited. The globalized aviation system, which includes numerous developing countries, is vulnerable and plagued with substandard security capabilities, corruption, bribery, and weak governance. Additionally, the Internet provides worldwide access to all types of information that could be useful to terrorists, including flight schedules, specific details and diagrams of both aircraft and airports, and reports of successful terrorist tactics and countermeasures developed by governments.

In a related area of concern, the nature of our response to the global threat to aviation relies on the strength of the partnership between governments and the private sector and how involved each want to be in diminishing the threat. In general, the aviation sector is driven by free market competition. Thus, airlines must maintain an emphasis on convenience and cost-savings; making investment in costly security measures relatively difficult. Among governments, we have seen bloated bureaucracies, a lack of intelligence sharing, and an overarching tendency to implement security policies in response to an attack that has already occurred, rather than embracing measures that might prevent an attack from occurring.

Beginning in the late 1960s, increasingly robust layers of security measures were put in place in response to hijackings. Yet, after four decades, the aviation sector was still vulnerable, as demonstrated by the events of September 11, 2001. Since then, we have seen additional security layers such as reinforced cockpit doors, armed pilots, increased presence of air marshals, and an overall increased awareness of the threat worldwide. Therefore, the post-9/11 security environment may be one in which the threat to aviation is lower than it has been in the past, but in-flight bombings are still a possibility.

On August 24, 2004, at approximately 11pm local time, two Chechen females, Satsita Dzhebirkhanova and Amanta Nagayeva , carried out separate suicide bombings on a Siberia Airlines flight and a Volga-Avia Express flight. Chechen field commander Shamil Basayev claimed responsibility for the bombings in an open letter published on the Chechen separatists' websites less than a month later. The letter noted that the bombings had cost his organization roughly $4,000—a small price to pay for killing 89 people.

Responding to events is insufficient; modern aviation security requires preventive measures. While these new measures may inconvenience passengers and create some inefficiency, they will increase the breadth and depth of intelligence gathering and sharing worldwide. Additionally, government officials should no longer underestimate the adaptive nature of terrorists. Terrorism is a form of asymmetric warfare, where the statistically weaker enemy will try to attack its stronger opponent in ways they do not expect.

The threat posed by innovative enemies requires a robust government response that does more than harden targets. In addition to examining the potential capabilities of terrorists to do harm to others by targeting airplanes and airports, we must commit ourselves to the study of terrorist ideologies, strategies, and motivations. We must educate both law enforcement and intelligence agencies in all countries about how our enemies might try to "game the system" and exploit new, perhaps even hidden, vulnerabilities in aviation security. Only then will we be able to respond to the threat with greater sophistication and success.

Chapter

4

Nato's Military Concept for Defence Against Terrorism

BACKGROUND

The 11 September 2001 terrorist attacks against the United States demonstrated both the capability of a determined enemy and the vulnerability of Alliance members to large-scale terrorist attacks. NATO's Article 5 declaration and subsequent operations demonstrated the Alliance's resolve to deal with this threat.

On 18 December 2001, NATO Defence Ministers tasked the NATO Military Authorities to prepare a Military Concept for Defence Against Terrorism for approval by the North Atlantic Council. The NATO Military Authorities requested political guidance from the North Atlantic Council and following receipt of the necessary guidance, submitted their Concept for approval. The Concept was approved by the North Atlantic Council in permanent session and then endorsed by Heads of State and Government at the Prague Summit on 21 November 2002.

CONCEPT DEVELOPMENT

The major guiding principles in the development of the Concept were:

- The Washington Treaty.
- The 1999 Alliance Strategic Concept.
- The NATO threat assessment on Terrorism.

- The Political Guidance provided by Council, which stipulated that NATO's actions should:
    - o Have a sound legal basis and fully conform to the relevant provisions of the UN Charter and all relevant international norms, including those concerned with human rights and humanitarian requirements.
    - o Help deter, defend, disrupt and protect against terrorist attacks or threat of attacks, directed from abroad against populations, territory, infrastructure and forces of any NATO member state, including by acting against these terrorists and those who harbour them.
    - o Act, on a case-by-case basis, if requested, in support of the international community's efforts against terrorism.
    - o Provide assistance to national authorities in dealing with the consequences of terrorist attacks, particularly where such attacks involve the use of Chemical, Biological, Radiological and Nuclear (CBRN) weapons.
    - o Work on the assumption that it is preferable to deter terrorist attacks or to prevent their occurrence rather than deal with their consequences and be prepared to deploy as and where required to deal with particular circumstances as they arise.

Threat Assessment

NATO's Military Concept for Defence Against Terrorism was developed to defend against the threat identified in NATO's Threat Assessment on Terrorism. This assessment concluded that:

- Although religious extremism is likely to be the source of the most immediate terrorist threats to the Alliance, other motivations for terrorism could emerge from economic, social, demographic and political causes derived from unresolved conflicts or emerging ideologies.
- In addition, although state sponsorship of terrorism is currently in decline, political circumstances could lead to its

rise, providing terrorists with safe havens and considerable resources.

- Although the predominant form of terrorist attack remains the creative use of conventional weapons and explosives, terrorist groups are expected to strive for the most destructive means available, including Weapons of Mass Destruction.

MILITARY OPERATIONS

Overview

The Concept identifies four different roles for military operations for Defence against Terrorism. In each of the four roles, Force Protection (FP) is an essential consideration. The 4 roles are:

- Anti Terrorism, essentially defensive measures.
- Consequence Management, which is dealing with, and reducing, the effects of a terrorist attack once it has taken place.
- Counter Terrorism, primarily offensive measures.
- Military Co-operation.

Force Protection

Force Protection must be a fundamental part of any military plan aimed at defending against terrorism. As total Force Protection is probably unachievable and unaffordable, even in the most benign of environments, Military Commanders must balance the risk to their forces against their mission objectives and decide on the appropriate level of force protection to employ. Their decisions will be influenced by up to date threat assessments.

Anti Terrorism

Anti-Terrorism is the use of defensive measures to reduce the vulnerability of forces, individuals and property to terrorism. Although nations have the primary responsibility for the defence of their populations and infrastructures, there is a role for the Alliance if a nation requests support. Timely and accurate intelligence is an essential requirement in successful deterring and protecting against terrorist attacks. Allied Anti Terrorist actions could include:

- Sharing of intelligence.
- NATO-wide standardised threat warning conditions and defensive procedures
- Assistance in air and maritime protection.
- Assistance to a nation wishing to withdraw its citizens or forces from an area of increased terrorist threat.

Consequence Management

Consequence Management is the use of reactive measures to mitigate the destructive effects of terrorism and is the responsibility of national civil authorities, but the Alliance could provide a wide range of military support, such as:

- Robust planning and force generation processes to rapidly identify and deploy the necessary specialist assistance. This could include, for example, the immediate assistance to civil authorities in the areas of: Chemical Biological, Radiological and Nuclear defence; engineering; and management of Displaced Persons.
- The creation of an Alliance Registry of capabilities which are available at short notice to support national efforts.
- The establishment of a training and exercise co-ordination capability for development of multi-national response capabilities.
- The Euro-Atlantic Disaster Relief Co-ordination Cell could provide the necessary nucleus to enhance co-ordination between NATO and affected nations.

Counter Terrorism - General

Counter terrorism is offensive military action designed to reduce terrorists' capabilities. Allied nations agree that terrorists should not be allowed to base, train, plan, stage and execute terrorist actions and that the threat may be severe enough to justify acting against these terrorists and those who harbour them, as and where required, as decided by the North Atlantic Council. Counter terrorist operations will be mainly joint operations and some units specifically trained in Counter Terrorist operations might be extremely effective. Furthermore, winning the trust of the local population through Psychological Operations and Information Operations is vital. The Concept addresses two broad roles for NATO's involvement in Counter Terrorist operations:

- NATO in the lead.
- NATO in support.

Counter Terrorism - NATO in the lead

The Concept states that in order to carry out successful Counter Terrorism operations, NATO must have adequate Command and Control and intelligence structures, as well as forces trained, exercised and maintained at the appropriate readiness levels. While the capabilities needed to successfully execute Counter Terrorist operations are largely a subset of those needed to carry out more traditional joint operations, the manner in which the conflict will be fought will be different. Therefore the following planning aspects need special attention:

- Procedures and capabilities that support accelerated decision cycles, in order to be successful in detecting and attacking time sensitive targets in the Counter Terrorist environment.
- Access to flexible and capable Joint-Fires, ranging from precision-guided stand-off weapons to direct conventional fires.
- The need for more specialised anti-terrorist forces.

Counter Terrorism - NATO in support

The North Atlantic Council has decided that, on a case-by-case basis, the Alliance might agree to provide its assets and capabilities to support operations in defence against terrorism, undertaken by or in co-operation with the European Union or other International Organisations or coalitions involving Allies. Possible support for the

European Union or other International Organisations will be based on relevant arrangements agreed between NATO and the organisation concerned. In this context, NATO's support options could include the following:

- A role as coalition enabler and interoperability provider.
- The ability to back-fill national requirements. An example of this was when NATO deployed to the United States in order to free US Airborne Warning and Control Systems (AWACS) to deploy to Afghanistan.
- Forward deploying of forces in support of the broader coalition efforts. An example of this was the deployment of NATO maritime forces to the eastern Mediterranean.
- The expression of political and military commitment.
- Practical support as manifested by Host Nation Support and logistic assistance, including over flight and basing rights.
- The use of NATO's operational planning and force generation capabilities to plan a mission and generate a force for a coalition of like-minded NATO members, and also help to support and sustain that operation.

Military Co-operation

There have been many discussions, in many organisations, about options to counter the threat posed by terrorism. A common theme in these discussions has been that military action alone will not be enough to deal with the terrorist threat and that military operations should be coordinated and implemented in a coherent manner with diplomatic, economic, social, legal and information initiatives.

Within most NATO nations, civil authorities, such as the police, customs and immigration authorities, finance ministries, interior ministries, intelligence and security services, are the primary agencies involved in dealing with terrorism and military forces will need to operate in support of, and in close coordination with all these agencies. The Concept therefore states that NATO must harmonise its procedures and efforts with civil authorities within nations in order to maximise its effectiveness against terrorism.

NATO regularly confers with the major international organisations such as the United Nations, the Organisation for Security and Cooperation in Europe, and the European Union. In addition, NATO has several programmes that can facilitate co-ordination outside the Alliance. These include the Partnership for Peace, the NATO/Russia Council, the NATO/Ukraine Commission and the Mediterranean Dialogue.

The Concept notes that the trust, transparency and interaction already developed through these relationships serve as an excellent vehicle for the further co-ordination of measures to combat terrorism and recommends that they should be further explored.

REQUIREMENTS FOR IMPLEMENTING THE CONCEPT EFFECTIVELY

Capabilities

The Concept identifies a number of essential capabilities that will be required to successfully implement it. These capabilities are:

- Effective Intelligence.
- Deployability and Readiness. Once it is known where the terrorists are or what they are about to do, military forces need the capability to deploy there. Due to the likelihood that warnings will be received only at very short notice, forces need to be at a high state of readiness.
- Effective Engagement. Forces need to be able to engage effectively. This means precision-guided weapons and weapons able to reduce the risk of collateral damage.
- Force Protection. There is a constant requirement for Force Protection to ensure Alliance forces' survivability.
- CBRN Defence. Given the possible terrorist use of CBRN weapons, CBRN defence equipment needs to be given a high priority.

Procedures

In addition to the capabilities described above, the Concept identifies certain procedures that need to be developed or enhanced. These include:

- Identifying Alliance vulnerabilities and how to protect them appropriately.
- Developing an overarching international strategy for defence against terrorism.
- Developing appropriate arrangements for providing support to the relevant civil authorities.
- Reducing the availability of weapons of mass destruction, and small arms and mines, for terrorist use, including through Arms Control, Disarmament and Non-Proliferation procedures.
- Making Alliance decision making as effective and timely as possible in order that, given the very short warnings that are likely for terrorist activity and intentions, Alliance forces can be deployed and employed appropriately.

CONCLUSIONS

The principal conclusions of the Concept are:

- NATO and its member nations face a real threat from terrorism and countering this threat will, in most circumstances, be time critical.
- Nations have the primary responsibility for defence of their populations and infrastructures; therefore NATO should be prepared to augment nations' efforts.
- There are 4 roles for NATO's military operations for defence against terrorism. These roles are Anti-Terrorism; Consequence Management; Counter-Terrorism; and Military Cooperation. NATO's Counter Terrorism operations could be either with NATO in the lead, or with NATO in support. Force Protection needs to be considered in all military operations to defend against terrorism.

- The Alliance needs to be prepared to conduct military operations to engage terrorist groups and their capabilities, as and where required, as decided by the North Atlantic Council.

DEFINITIONS

Definitions to clarify terms used in MC 472 are listed below. Where the definition contains agreed language, the source is indicated in brackets.

- Anti-Terrorism: Defensive measures used to reduce the vulnerability of forces, individuals and property to terrorism, to include limited response and containment by military forces and civil agencies.
- Asymmetric Threat : Threat from unconventional methods and means that attempt to circumvent or negate an opponents' strengths whilst exploiting his weaknesses, with potentially disproportionate effects.
- Consequence Management: Reactive measures used to mitigate the destructive effects of attacks, incidents or natural disasters.
- Counter-Terrorism: Offensive measures used to reduce the vulnerability of forces, individuals and property to terrorism, to include Counter-force activities and containment by military forces and civil agencies.
- Explosive Ordnance Disposal : The detection, identification, on-site evaluation, rendering safe, recovery and final disposal of suspected unexploded ordnance. It may also include explosives ordnance which has become hazardous by damage or deterioration. (AAP-6)
- Explosive Ordnance Reconnaissance: Reconnaissance involving the investigation, detection, location, marking, initial identification and reporting of suspected unexploded explosive ordnance, by explosive ordnance reconnaissance agents, in order to determine further action. (AAP-6)

- Force Protection: All measures and means to minimize the vulnerability of personnel, facilities, equipment and operations to any threat and in all situations, to preserve freedom of action and the operational effectiveness of the force.
- Information Operations: In the military aspects, INFO OPS are co-ordinated actions to influence decision-making of adversaries in support of the Alliance overall objectives by affecting their information, information-based processes and systems while exploiting and protecting one' s own. (MC422/1)
- Joint Fires: Fires produced during the employment of forces from two or more components in co-ordinated action towards a common objective. Joint Fires are weapon effects from joint operations and include, but are not limited to, weapons effects from such operations as joint suppression of enemy air defences (J-SEAD) and naval surface fire support (NSFS) provided to assist air, land, amphibious, or special operations forces, joint air operations, joint manoeuvre operations, and joint interdiction operations. (AJP3)
- Psychological Operations: Planned psychological activities designed to influence attitudes and behaviour affecting the achievement of political and military objectives. (AAP-6)
- Terrorism: The unlawful use or threatened use of force or violence against individuals or property in an attempt to coerce or intimidate governments or societies to achieve political, religious or ideological objective (AAP-6)
- Weapons of Mass Destruction: Weapons that are capable of a high order of destruction and/or being used in such a manner as to destroy or incapacitate large numbers of people or livestock.

Chapter

5

Terrorism and the Private Sector

The threat of terrorist attacks in the United States is highly uncertain, but, since September 2001, there has been a heightened awareness of a greater potential for attacks across the nation. Although there have been no large terrorist attacks in the United States since September 11, 2001, subsequent attacks elsewhere, such as those in Bali in 2002, Madrid in 2004, and London in 2005, suggest that the risk of terrorism has increased internationally and that it remains a serious concern. The public sector has taken on the primary response to this increased risk of terrorism. The U.S. Department of Homeland Security and associated federal, state, and local government efforts have focused on critical counterterrorism strategies such as increasing border security, strengthening intelligence operations, and improving emergency response (e.g., Riley et al., 2005; LaTourrette et al., 2006).

Complementing these public sector efforts, the private sector is exploring potential steps that may be appropriate for it to take to further address the threat of terrorism. Facilities in which large numbers of people are present in high concentrations, such as office buildings, auditoriums, and shopping centers, are attractive targets for terrorists. Owners and operators of such facilities are therefore becoming increasingly concerned about their exposure to terrorist attacks and how they may reduce their risk.

While some research has begun to examine private-sector efforts to reduce their risk from terrorism (e.g., Briggs, 2002; The Bellwether

Group, Inc., 2005) and how government policy might be used to increase the level of terrorism security in the private sector (e.g., Dixon et al., 2004; Carroll et al., 2005; Farmer, 2004), the options and appropriate role of the private sector in contributing to terrorism security efforts merit further attention.

SHOPPING CENTERS AS TERRORIST TARGETS

Terrorists have repeatedly targeted shopping centers in particular. Since 1998, over 60 terrorist attacks at shopping centers have occurred throughout the world. A statistical analysis of important characteristics of these attacks is presented in Chapter Two. It is noteworthy that attacks have occurred at shopping centers in 21 countries, including those in Western Europe and North and South America. Within the United States, shopping centers have been identified as potential terrorist targets, with specific warnings about attack threats at shopping centers in West Los Angeles in April 2004 and again in Columbus, Ohio, in June 2004. While no actual attacks occurred in either case, the Los Angeles warning prompted the deployment of over 100 local and federal law enforcement officials to local shopping centers, leading to widespread panic and disruption (Yang, 2004).

In terms of their potential role as terrorist targets, shopping centers present numerous challenges for security. Shopping centers are distributed throughout the United States, both in areas that are considered high risk for terrorist attack (e.g., prominent cities or areas with iconic targets) and in areas that are not (e.g., rural or suburban areas). This wide distribution makes prioritizing security efforts difficult. Shopping centers also allow unimpeded access to the public and attract a wide cross-section of the nation's population. In addition, most people have access to alternative venues for their shopping needs and can therefore avoid shopping centers without suffering undue hardship. Shopping centers therefore differ markedly from facilities like airports, which provide an essential service with few alternatives. For this reason, shopping center customers and tenants may not tolerate the expense and inconvenience of increased security. In addition, shopping center operations are governed by a complicated ownership and decisionmaking structure consisting of, among others, property owners and managers, tenant retailers, on-site employees, contract security, and customers. This multistakeholder structure increases the difficulties of implementing security and other risk-reduction measures. Finally, as with any competitive private-sector business, shopping centers may have a difficult time justifying investment in reducing the seemingly remote risk of terrorism. Because shopping centers remain attractive targets for terrorists, stakeholders are beginning to consider increased security measures. In light of the security challenges discussed above, understanding methods for reducing the risk of terrorist attacks in shopping centers is therefore an important topic for public policy analysis.

Study Motivation and Objective

In light of continuing concerns about the risk of terrorist attacks at shopping centers and the uncertainties and complexities involved in reducing that risk, the RAND Corporation undertook a study to examine vulnerabilities to terrorist threats at shopping centers and to assess security options that could be implemented to reduce these vulnerabilities. The primary objective of the study was to identify and prioritize security options that could help reduce the risk of terrorist attack losses at commercial shopping centers.

The intention is not to recommend which specific security options should be implemented immediately, but rather which security options make the most sense in terms of cost and effectiveness against particular threats. Decisions about which options to implement and when to implement them will depend on how perceptions about the absolute risk of terrorist attacks at shopping centers evolve in a changing threat environment over time. Some stakeholders could choose to implement some of the security options analyzed in this report immediately, but many of the options may not be feasible or appropriate under current conditions. If the terrorist threat in the United States increases over time, then the security options and priorities identified in this report provide a basis upon which to plan for increasing security as the risks increase.

Study Approach

Our analysis is built largely around a modeling approach in which the estimated effectiveness of specific security options in reducing the risk of particular terrorist attack scenarios is weighed against the costs of implementing those options. The basic elements of the model are a set of attack scenarios, estimates of the relative likelihoods and the consequences of each scenario, a set of potential security options, the cost of each option, and the likely effectiveness of each option in each scenario.

These inputs are drawn from multiple sources, including a survey of terrorist attack statistics in shopping centers and in general throughout the world. For a given risk outlook, the model provides a prioritized list of security options and the cumulative decrease in relative risk and the cumulative cost as each option is implemented. We also examine some security issues outside the model framework. These include preparing "standby" postures that facilitate the rapid implementation of security options, some aspects of structural design criteria, considerations for special events, and the importance of addressing terrorism both at the facility level and at the company or industry level.

Study Scope

Although we use the general term *shopping center*, our analysis is restricted to centers with a common corridor connecting tenants (*malls* in the terminology of DeLisle, 2005). We do not consider centers in which most tenants are accessed directly from a parking lot or street (*open-air centers*), although we do consider outdoor *malls*. We apply our model of terrorist scenarios and security options to three specific shopping centers: an outdoor shopping center with underground parking (Center A), a large indoor center surrounded by surface parking (Center B), and an urban center at which many customers enter from the street and from public transportation (Center C). The specific centers span a range of important shopping center characteristics, such as size, parking arrangements, indoor versus outdoor, and urban versus suburban.

This set of centers was chosen to help understand the extent to which different access and design characteristics influence the prioritization of security options and to provide a more generalizable test of the risk-reducing effects of security options in shopping centers. In addition, our analysis considers individual center-level security options only—it does not cover company- or industry-wide steps.

While we do consider differences in the physical design characteristics of the three centers, we do not consider any variations in the exogenous threat of terrorism that may exist among the centers (e.g., from being located in higher-risk cities). Finally, we consider the threat from terrorism only and do not consider benefits to nonterrorism security concerns or indirect negative implications of security options (e.g., customer resistance). We do provide a qualitative estimate of these implications, some of which may have an important influence on decisionmaking.

HISTORICAL TRENDS IN TERRORISM

Predicting Terrorism Risk from Historical Trends

In this chapter, we summarize recent (1998–2005) historical trends in terrorism. In particular, we characterize the relative frequency of different types of terrorist attacks and the consequences of those different types of attacks. Our analysis examines both terrorist incidents in general and terrorist incidents specifically targeting shopping centers. The objective is to inform estimates of the relative likelihoods and consequences of the terrorist attack scenarios we examine in our risk modeling.

Making assessments about future likelihood or consequences of particular terrorist attacks is an elusive undertaking. One approach is to examine recent historical evidence of what types of attacks terrorists have been conducted and what the consequences of those attacks have been. There is considerable debate about the extent to which historical trends in terrorism can be used to predict terrorism risk in the future (e.g., Willis et al., 2005; Grossi and Kunreuther,

2005; Sauter and Carafano, 2005; Haimes, 2004). Compared with other risks (e.g., automobile accidents), there are limited statistical data about terrorist attacks from which to parameterize terrorism risk rigorously in terms of relevant variables such as target type, weapon type, and geographic location.

Extrapolation from historical trends is also difficult because terrorist organizations are known to evolve and adapt as security and counterterrorism efforts are implemented (e.g., Jackson et al., 2005a, 2005b). A related uncertainty is the difficulty in predicting how terrorism, which so far has occurred largely outside the United States, will evolve if it becomes a more common threat in the United States. In short, no golden rule says that terrorists will continue to choose targets or carry out attacks in a similar manner as they have in the recent past. However, we must begin by characterizing data from recent incidents and then determine which, if any, of the parameters estimated are likely to be different today and in the future.

Data

We used data from the RAND–National Memorial Institute for the Prevention of Terrorism (MIPT) Terrorism Incident Database.1 Observations were restricted to those that occurred between January 1, 1998, and December 31, 2005, because we are interested in assessing morerecent consequences of terrorist incidents. We eliminated observations in which an attack was interrupted or aborted. We also eliminated attacks that occurred in Iraq after March 2003. While attacks in Iraq might be considered acts of terrorism, we do not think that they appropriately characterize the risk facing potential targets outside Iraq.

This analysis included a total of 12,831 observations. Some of the observations do not report data for specific parameters. For example, for analyzing the average number of fatalities by weapon type, only 9,614 observations report the number of fatalities. That analysis excluded observations with missing data. The RAND-MIPT Terrorism Incident Database does not specify car or truck bomb as a weapon type. The weapon field for attacks using car or truck bombs is categorized simply as explosives. For our purposes, we believed that it was useful to analyze car bomb incidents as a specific weapon type. Car bombs have the potential to deliver a much higher explosive yield than, say, a backpack, package, or pedestrian suicide bomb, and security measures relevant to them are very different. Therefore, we used the description field to identify incidents that involved a car or truck bomb.

When it was concluded from the terrorist incident description that a car or truck bomb was clearly used, we classified the weapon type as a car or truck bomb. It is important to note that this process may not result in the identification of every car and truck bomb incident. For example, a car bomb incident may appear in the database that does not include the phrase "car bomb" in the description field. However, this process does pull out instances in which it is clear from the description that a car or truck bomb was used. Additionally, we compared the differences between terrorist incidents against any target with those against shopping centers.

To do this, we first separated incidents that had occurrences of the words "mall" or "shopping center" in the description field. Then we examined the descriptions to ensure that the incident did target a shopping center or mall (e.g., some descriptions made reference to a previous attack by the same group that targeted a mall; such incidents are not be included here). Between 1998 and 2005, 62 incidents met the previously discussed inclusion criteria and clearly targeted a shopping center based on the description. Short descriptions and other data fields from the shopping center attacks are listed in Appendix A.

Weapon Types Used in Terrorist Attacks

A key consideration in prioritizing efforts to address the risk of terrorism is understanding the relative frequency of different weapons used by terrorists. Different security measures address different weapon and attack types, and an overall security approach needs to be based on an expectation about what sorts of incidents are most likely. In this section, we first examine data for all incidents that meet the inclusion criteria described previously to understand the relative frequencies with which different weapons are used. We then compare the results for all incidents with those targeting shopping centers to determine whether there are differences in the weapons terrorists use when attacking malls or shopping centers.

The results for all incidents show that terrorist attacks are dominated by nonsuicide explosives (i.e., placed bombs), which make up nearly 50 percent of all terrorist attacks in our sample. Nonsuicide explosives are a factor of 2 more common than firearms, the next most common weapon. Together, nonsuicide explosives and firearms constitute about 75 percent of the attacks, with the remaining weapon types combining to make up the remaining 25 percent. Note that fewer than 0.5 percent of the attacks used chemical or biological weapons.

When looking at the subset of incidents targeting shopping centers, we find that the results are even more strongly dominated by nonsuicide explosives, which make up 71 percent of the attacks. In fact, every weapon type that involves explosives (i.e., nonsuicide explosives, suicide explosives, and car bombs) represents a larger fraction of incidents at shopping centers than of terrorist attacks in general. As a result, over 90 percent of terrorist attacks at shopping centers are conducted with explosives.

A consequence of this bias toward explosives is that the second most common attack type at shopping centers is suicide bombings, making up 15 percent of attacks. This contrasts with the results for all incidents, where suicide bombings are the sixth most common attack type, at 1.7 percent. Attacks with firearms, on the other hand, are negligible at shopping centers compared to attacks in general.

In summary, this analysis indicates that explosives are far and away the most common weapon used by terrorists from 1998 to 2005 and that this preference is particularly strong when targeting shopping centers. Compared with attacks overall, attackers targeting shopping centers are far less likely to use firearms and far more likely to use suicide bombs. The lower incidence of firearms attacks at shopping centers can readily be understood when considering how firearms are used in terrorist attacks. Inspection of the description field for firearms attacks in the database indicates that the majority of such incidents involve targeted political assassinations, roadside ambushes, or sieges on small villages. In this light, firearms attacks in indoor facilities such as commercial businesses or government offices are expected to be rare.

The reason for the higher incidence of suicide bombings in shopping centers is less clear, but probably reflects the bias of such attacks toward targets that allow unimpeded access and have high population densities. If recent historical trends are a good predictor of terrorist weapon choices, these data provide us with an estimate of the relative likelihood of various weapon types that might be used against malls or shopping centers. We use this evidence to guide our estimates of likelihood of the various scenarios we include in our model.

CONSEQUENCES OF TERRORIST INCIDENTS

In addition to the likelihoods of different attack types, understanding the consequences of terrorist incidents is important for assessing risk and allocating resources to reduce this risk. The primary consequences of terrorist attacks are casualties and property damage. Other important consequences include business interruption, liability, and indirect economic impacts. While all of these consequences can be substantial, most are rarely documented and are difficult to estimate. The RAND-MIPT Terrorism Incident Database records consequences in terms of injuries and fatalities. Although casualties reflect only part of the total consequences, they are arguably the single metric of greatest concern. To characterize the consequences of past terrorist attacks, we examined the number of fatalities produced by incidents as a function of weapon type used.

Our analysis indicates that casualty numbers from terrorist attacks span a substantial range but are heavily skewed toward low values. Figure 2.2 shows the distribution of fatalities from attacks using all types of explosives. This distribution indicates that, while bombs can cause large numbers of fatalities, such incidents are exceedingly rare. Out of 4,800 records, only 24 (0.5 percent) had more than 30 fatalities. Ninety percent of the attacks resulted in two or fewer fatalities, and 75 percent resulted in no fatalities. The data indicate that, on average, terrorist bombings yield 1.2 casualties. Distributions for other attack types show similar strong skewing toward low fatalities.

Given the very wide range in the number of fatalities that can occur from a given attack type, it is difficult to characterize fully the results with a single statistic such as the average. For our risk modeling, however, we are interested in estimating the most likely casualty outcomes of different attack types and in distinguishing the likely outcomes of different attack types. For this purpose, the average number of fatalities is an appropriate measure.

An important finding from this analysis is that suicide attacks are significantly more lethal than nonsuicide attacks. The mean number of fatalities for suicide explosive attacks (i.e., pedestrian suicide bombers) is more than seven times greater than that for attacks using nonsuicide explosives (i.e., placed bombs). The difference for car bombs is even more pronounced, with suicide car bombs being more than a factor of 10 more lethal than nonsuicide car bombs, although the distribution for suicide car bombs is much more dispersed. This difference in lethality between suicide and nonsuicide bombs probably reflects two distinguishing features. The first is that, compared with placed bombs, suicide bombers are better able to choose the best location and time to detonate to maximize the casualties. The second is that suicide bombers generally intend to kill victims, while nonsuicide bombers sometimes target property only and purposely avoid victims.

The most notable difference appears to be for attacks using nonsuicide explosives, where the average number of fatalities for attacks against shopping centers is double that for all incidents. However, this is driven by a single incident that had 28 fatalities. If we exclude this observation, the average fatality number drops to 1.2 with a standard error of 0.4. Suicide attacks at shopping centers are significantly more lethal than nonsuicide attacks, analogous to the case for all incidents.

Modeling the Effect of Security Options on Terrorism Risk

We used a quantitative modeling approach to help identify and prioritize potential security options that a shopping center could implement to reduce the risk of terrorism losses. A systematic modeling approach was chosen to help contend with the great uncertainty and complexity inherent in addressing terrorism risk. Estimates of the level of terrorism risk and the effectiveness of various security options in reducing that risk are subjective and sensitive to the assumptions built into the model. In addition, the large number of potential attack scenarios and security options that must be considered make it difficult to keep track of cumulative effects, interdependencies, and mutual exclusivities. A modeling approach has the advantage of applying consistent rules and treating input parameters systematically. This generates results that are internally consistent, can be linked to specific parameters, and can be tested for their sensitivity to particular assumptions.

In our analysis, we borrow from the theoretical logic of rational-choice models of offending and situational crime prevention strategies (Clarke, 1983). This theoretical model applied to terrorism assumes that the decisionmaking process is rational and that terrorists considering an attack on a shopping mall consider the risks of their actions. We assume that terrorists are rational actors and consider the risks and rewards of their actions. These risks are assumed to flow from a consideration of the likelihood that terrorists think they can be successful in their planned attack and the consequences of their attack (e.g., number of people killed). Therefore, efforts to minimize the likelihood of a terrorist attack on a mall should focus on options that reduce the opportunities for terrorism. This study focuses on specific terrorist event scenarios and how the risk of these events can be "manipulated" through variations in the management of security and design characteristics of shopping centers that limit their attractiveness as terrorist targets.

Modeling Approach

The overall modeling approach involves incrementally reducing the risk from terrorism by sequentially implementing security options. The overall terrorism risk is the sum of the individual risks of different attack types that are intended to span the range of attacks that may occur at a shopping center. Different attack types are characterized in terms of 17 specific terrorism scenarios. The model selects security options according to their effectiveness at reducing risk and their cost and estimates the reduction in overall risk with each option.

Prioritizing Security Options

Given a set of scenarios, security options, security option costs, and deterrence, denial, and mitigation effectiveness values for each option in each scenario, the model prioritizes the selection of security options based on a cost-effectiveness algorithm. Security options are selected sequentially in such a way that each selection generates the greatest reduction in risk for the lowest cost. Starting with a baseline risk value (i.e., no options implemented), the optimum option is selected and implemented.

The overall risk is then recalculated with that option in place, and a new optimum option is selected from the remaining pool of options. Some options are mutually exclusive (e.g., unarmed security guards and armed security guards) and are therefore prohibited from being selected together. This process is repeated until all options have been selected or a maximum spending budget has been reached.

Model Inputs

This section summarizes the various input parameters used in the security options model. Each subsection discusses the rationale for the parameters chosen, data sources, and uncertainties. Input parameters were also informed by site visits to each of the three shopping centers examined in this report. Site visits comprised discussions with center operators, engineers, and security managers, along with tours of systems and individual components essential to security, such as entrances, parking facilities, loading docks, service halls, and roofs. It is important to acknowledge that the parameters that contribute to terrorism risk are highly uncertain and therefore difficult to estimate.

Our estimates of scenario likelihoods are informed by statistical analysis of past terrorist attacks, but there is substantial uncertainty as to whether historical trends are good predictors of future attacks. The consequences of the various scenarios we consider are also informed by past terrorist attacks and, while they are better understood than likelihoods, are still subject to uncertainty stemming from details of individual attacks that are complex to predict and beyond the resolution of this analysis. And the effectiveness of a particular security option in a given scenario is also often difficult to estimate, either because its technical effectiveness is uncertain or because its effectiveness depends on scenario details that have not been modeled (e.g., will a terrorist appear to be a customer or attempt to impersonate an employee?).

We also tested the sensitivity of our estimates to a varying set of assumptions. These analyses, which are discussed in the Modeling Results section below, illustrate how the rankings of security options vary with the various parameters used to define risk.

Attack Scenarios

We examined 17 terrorist attack scenarios in this analysis. The scenarios were drawn from analysis of past terrorist attacks at shopping centers and elsewhere as well as discussions with shopping center operators and security contractors about particular concerns and vulnerabilities.

Scenarios fall into three general categories based on the weapons used: firearms, explosives, and chemical or biological. The scenario set includes the most common terrorist attack modes, as well as several modes that are less commonly employed or that have never occurred. Although it is impossible to predict with any certainty how a terrorist strike may occur, the selected set is intended to span the range of attack types of general concern and the range of vulnerabilities present in commercial shopping centers.

Scenario Likelihoods

The first major component of risk is event likelihood. The more likely an event is, the more often it will occur over the long term. Scenarios with higher likelihoods will therefore occur more often and have higher overall losses. Because risk represents an estimate of expected loss, higher likelihood translates into higher risk.

We treated the overall terrorist threat to shopping centers as uniform at all centers. In reality, exogenous factors may cause the threat to be higher at particular centers. However, such factors are elusive and often evolve with time, so our analysis did not take into account differences in scenario likelihoods stemming from different threat environments that may exist among the three centers. Where necessary, however, we excluded particular scenarios at a specific center if the physical design of that center made the particular scenarios impossible (e.g., a car bomb in an underground parking lot is not an option in a center with no underground parking).

As noted above, we restricted our estimates to relative likelihoods, or the likelihood of a particular scenario occurring relative to the likelihoods of other scenarios. The relative likelihood assigned to each scenario was estimated based on our analyses of the frequency of use of different weapons in past terrorist attacks at shopping centers. Likelihoods for 10 of the 17 scenarios were taken directly from these historical frequency data. From these data, for example, we estimated that a terrorist attack at a shopping center is most likely to involve a placed bomb. Likelihoods for the remaining scenarios were estimated in two ways.

First, likelihoods for attacks perpetrated by an insider (i.e., tenant employees, contractors, and delivery people) were assumed to be one-tenth the likelihood of the same attack being perpetrated by an outsider. Second, likelihoods for three scenarios were estimated based on the frequencies for similar scenarios for which we had likelihoods estimates: The hostage taking was assigned the same likelihood as the commando attack, the sniper attack was assigned a likelihood 2.5 times greater than that of the commando attack, and the suicide truck bomb likelihood was estimated from the nonsuicide truck bomb frequency multiplied by the ratio of suicide and nonsuicide car bomb frequencies.

Values are normalized to a 0–1 scale so that they will be equally weighted with consequences in the risk calculations.

Because attack likelihoods are so poorly understood, they are the most uncertain parameters in our analysis. We examined the sensitivity of our findings to this uncertainty in two ways. In the first, we developed three likelihood profiles that reflect different basic assumptions about terrorist intentions and capabilities.

The profiles differ in the assumptions made about two factors. The first is the likelihood of attacks involving terrorist suicide relative to the likelihood of a similar type of attack not involving suicide (e.g., a car bomb in an unoccupied car compared with a suicide car bomb). The second is the likelihood of attacks being led or assisted by insiders relative to the likelihood of the same type of attack being conducted by outsiders.

It is also informative to explore how the rankings of security option selected by the model respond to independent changes in the likelihoods of individual scenarios. Different security options are effective against different scenarios, so the ranking of options is expected to be sensitive to large changes in likelihoods.

We therefore conducted a second analysis to determine how much the likelihoods can be varied before the option rankings begin to change significantly. This analysis, which is described below, shows that likelihoods can be varied independently by as much as a factor of 10 before the rankings of security options begin to change.

Scenario Consequences

The second major component of risk is event consequence. Because risk is a measure of expected loss, the greater the consequences of an event, the greater its risk. As discussed in Chapter Two, there are several types of potential consequences of terrorist attacks, including casualties, property damage, business interruption, liability, and indirect economic impacts. However, as also mentioned, most of these consequences are difficult to estimate, particularly given that casualties are generally the only consequence metric recorded in historical terrorism data.

For this analysis, we have modeled terrorist attack consequences in terms of two components: fatality count, which is intended to reflect the human loss component, and the amount of time a center would be shut down after an attack, which is intended to reflect the economic loss component of terrorist attacks. Because our analysis examines relative likelihoods and, therefore, relative risks, including separate estimates of well-correlated components does not help distinguish the relative risks of different scenarios and thus adds no value to the analysis.

Fatalities

The numbers of injuries and fatalities in terrorist attacks are very sensitive to details such as the relative locations of weapons, structures, and victims; the population density in the affected area; and structural characteristics of any buildings involved. Our scenarios do not stipulate this level of detail, and we have not attempted to tailor fatality estimates precisely to the multitude of possible outcomes of a given scenario. Rather, fatalities for each scenario were estimated from the historical fatality data for terrorist attacks on shopping centers using associated weapon types.

The average number of fatalities resulting from attacks using a particular weapon was assumed to reflect the most likely outcome of that type of attack and thus the appropriate value to use in our risk modeling. The value for *placed bombs* was taken from *explosives (nonsuicide)*, the value for *pedestrian suicide bomber* was taken from *explosives (suicide)*, the value for *vehicle bomb outside* was taken from *car bomb (nonsuicide)*, and the value for gunfire attacks (scenarios 1–5) was taken from *firearms*. Based on the data for all incidents, the value for the *truck bomb in loading* scenarios was taken from *truck bomb* and the value for *car bomb in mall—crash in from street* was taken to be 10 times the value for *vehicle bomb outside.*

The value for the *car bomb in parking* scenarios was assumed to be the same as for *vehicle bomb outside.* Note that, for a vehicle bomb in an underground parking lot or loading dock, there is no obvious reason that a suicide attack would lead to more fatalities than would a nonsuicide attack, so the fatality values for suicide and nonsuicide attacks are the same. Finally, fatality values used for biological and chemical weapons are 10 times higher than those observed in the historical data for all incidents in order to reflect potential improvements in terrorist capabilities with these weapons. Note that, despite using higher fatality estimates, the likelihoods of chemical and biological attacks are sufficiently low that they have negligible influence on the overall risk.

Values are normalized to a 0–1 scale so that they will be equally weighted with likelihoods in the risk calculations.

Downtime

Downtime is a measure of the time that part or all of a shopping center would remain closed following a terrorist attack. Very few data reporting closure durations or property damage are available for past terrorist attacks. Consequently, we developed a fairly coarse five-point scale that attempts to account for such activities as clean-up, investigation, reconstruction, and decontamination.

In contrast to high-rise office buildings, shopping centers generally have very low height-to-footprint ratios, making total structural collapse highly unlikely. Thus, it would be very difficult for even a very large explosion to result in an entire center remaining shut down for an extended period. Given the uncertainties regarding decontamination methods and standards, an anthrax attack may require a particularly long downtime. An equal weighting is used because we find no a priori justification for alternate weighting schemes. One major impediment to devising a more sophisticated weighting approach is that it is difficult to compare the value of a casualty loss with that of loss from property closure or damage. In principle, casualty losses can be converted into dollars using estimates of insurance coverage, lost productivity, or other estimates of the statistical value of a life. However, such conversions are controversial and, given the lack of precision in our fatality and downtime estimates, not warranted in this analysis. We have examined the effect of alternate weightings in our sensitivity analysis (see below) and find that option rankings are quite insensitive to consequence weighting factors.

Baseline Relative Risk Estimates

Using these inputs, the baseline relative risk values for each scenario calculated (where no security options are implemented and so *Dt*, *Dn*, and *Mt* are each zero). This figure illustrates that placed bombs dominate the overall risk, primarily because the likelihood of this type of attack is so much higher than for any other scenario.

Security Options

We have examined the effectiveness of 39 security options in our analysis. Several criteria were used to arrive at the final set of security options included. Many options were chosen based on established and emerging security approaches used in other environments (e.g., airports; see Stevens et al., 2004).

Options were also designed in response to consultation with mall operators and security contractors. Finally, some options were selected or tailored to address particular vulnerabilities to the various scenarios that exist in a shopping center operational environment. For example, to cover insider and outsider threats separately, customer entrance checkpoint options are divided into two sets—one for the hours during which the center is open to the public (when outsiders have access) and another for the hours during which it is closed to the public (when only insiders have access). The options considered target individual facilities—our modeling focuses on deterring, denying, or mitigating terrorist attacks at a given center and does not consider implications for other centers within a company or across the industry. For example, a security option that causes a potential terrorist to choose a different target is considered entirely effective because it has deterred an attack at the center of interest.

The options we consider in our modeling cover operations, technology, staffing, and management, but exclude major design and construction issues. Although property development and redevelopment are important aspects of the shopping center industry, design and construction go beyond the scope of our analysis and our expertise. Several government agencies have developed guidance in this area and we include in Chapter Four a brief summary of this topic. The security options we used in our analysis are listed in Table 3.6. For each option, we include a brief explanation, along with the options with which it is mutually exclusive.

Mutual exclusivity occurs when options provide essentially redundant capabilities (e.g., explosives detectors and explosives dogs) or when one option includes another (e.g., customer entrance checkpoints include security personnel and so are mutually exclusive with security guards at entrances).

Option Effectiveness

Each option was assigned values for its effectiveness at deterring, denying, and mitigating each of the 17 scenarios. In some cases, the distinctions between deter, deny, and mitigate can be ambiguous. For clarity, we use the following definitions in apportioning effectiveness between deter, deny, and mitigate: An attack scenario is deterred if no attempt is made at the facility. Examples of deterrence include background checks, checkpoints, and security patrols. An attack scenario is denied if an attack attempt is not successful, where attack success is defined for different scenario types as follows: for firearms, at least one shot is fired in the intended location; for explosives, the explosive is detonated where intended; for chemical or biological weapons, the agent is released. Examples of denial include checkpoints, bollards, and threat awareness training.

An attack scenario is mitigated if the consequences of a successful attack are reduced. Examples of mitigation include emergency response, security patrols, and chemical and biological agent detectors. Note that many options are effective in more than one of these three categories.

Effectiveness values vary between 0 and 1, with 0 indicating no effectiveness and 1 indicating complete effectiveness. Effectiveness values estimates were informed by multiple factors, including the effectiveness of technologies, theories of deterrence and situational crime prevention (Clarke, 1983; Shapland, 1995), research on the effect of environmental modifications on workplace violence (Mair and Mair, 2003), and research discussing prior terrorist attacks (Lesser et al., 1999; Jackson et al., 2005b). In many cases, a security option's effectiveness was uncertain and analytical judgment was employed. Estimates of the effectiveness of the different options were made in the context of two important aspects of terrorism risk in commercial shopping centers.

First, shopping centers are numerous, are largely interchangeable in terms of their attractiveness as targets, and generally allow unimpeded access. Stated differently, the opportunities for terrorist attacks in shopping centers are ubiquitous. Second, terrorists are expected to conduct substantial planning and surveillance and will try to avoid situations in which they may get caught. As a consequence of these aspects, reducing terrorism risk in commercial shopping centers hinges strongly on deterrence.

Strong denial effectiveness is less important than in nominally higher-security environments (e.g., federal government buildings) because deterrence is more effective in sending a terrorist planning to attack a shopping center to an alternate center (or comparable soft target) than in sending a terrorist planning to attack a federal building to an alternate federal building. Mitigation, or reducing consequences of a successful attack, is even less effective, primarily because the majority of terrorism risk comes from explosive attacks. Outcomes of large terrorist bombings indicate that the chances for saving lives after a terrorist bombing are minimal. In an analysis of 29 terrorist bombings that produced 30 or more casualties, Arnold et al. (2004) found that 94 percent of the fatalities in these events occurred immediately at the site or in transport to a hospital. If rapid medical attention were an important factor in saving people with life-threatening injuries, we might expect a higher fraction to survive longer before dying.

An implication of the high value of deterrence for our modeling is that the perceptual deterrence effectiveness of any option is always greater than the denial effectiveness of that option. The threshold for deterrence might increase if terrorism security were widely implemented at soft targets. In this situation, terrorists would have no easy alternatives and might attempt attacks that they would not have attempted if less secure targets were available. Under such conditions, the deterrence effectiveness values used in this analysis might need to be raised to reflect this new environment. However, the United States is currently far from these conditions. A single set of effectiveness values was used for all three shopping centers examined in this study. While the centers differ in important ways, these differences are accounted for in our analysis by including or excluding particular scenarios and security options in our modeling (e.g., outdoor centers have no common area air system and so air filters cannot be used).

Option Costs

Security option costs were estimated in terms of a total annual cost, regardless of which stakeholder (e.g., center owner, tenants, employees) would ultimately bear that cost. In particular, as noted above, we assume that implementation of security options includes anchor tenant facilities. Costs comprise primarily labor and equipment. Other cost elements include staff time (for training), lost rental income (from rental space used for security purposes), and minimal construction, installation, and maintenance requirements. We do not include the effects of economic inflation or depreciation in our estimates. Equipment costs were estimated from quotes from vendors. In general, equipment costs were amortized over 10 years.

Most commercial shopping centers undergo significant redevelopment about this often, at which point equipment may be replaced or upgraded. The service life of a few items (e.g., escape hoods) is less than 10 years, and, in such cases, an appropriately smaller value was used. Labor costs are estimated based on an average security staff salary of $10 per hour (U.S. Bureau of Labor Statistics, 2005); higher values were used for some positions requiring special training (equipment operators and dog handlers). For example, the cost of security checkpoints at customer entrances depends on the number of entrances.

COLLATERAL BENEFITS AND DETRIMENTS OF SECURITY OPTIONS

The security options analyzed in this study were chosen for their ability to reduce the risk of specific terrorist scenarios. However, the options also have some important collateral benefits and detriments. Some of the options have collateral benefits in terms of their effect on other security concerns. On the other hand, several of the options are likely to have a negative impact on the conventional shopping center operational environment, such as impeding customer access. The impacts of such collateral effects may be important considerations in security decisions.

However, these impacts are very difficult to characterize because they may include both logistical (e.g., time lost waiting at a security checkpoint) and psychological (e.g., concern about the risks of terrorism in shopping centers) aspects. Consequently, we did not include quantitative estimates of collateral effects in our risk modeling. Rather, we present a simple qualitative tabulation of collateral benefits and detriments associated with each security option that accompanies the prioritized list of options.

Each option was assessed for collateral impact in five categories. Non–terrorism-related security benefits include aiding loss prevention and reducing workplace violence. Operational detriments include impeding customer access, inconveniencing employees, and negative psychological impacts. The assessment simply indicates in which benefit and detriment categories each option is judged to have an impact—we made no attempt to assess the magnitude of the impact of any option in any category. The Modeling Results section presents collateral impact assessments associated with each of the prioritized security options for each center.

Modeling Results

Our analytical model generates a prioritized list of security options, the cumulative reduction in risk as each option is added, and the cumulative annual cost as each option is added. Each figure shows the prioritized list of selected security options, with the priority decreasing from top to bottom. The figures also show the cost for each security option, the cumulative cost of the options up to any point in the list, and the cumulative relative risk at any point achieved by implementing the options up to that point in the list. These results are also listed in tabular form in Tables B.4–B.6.

General Findings

The modeling results for the different centers share several common characteristics that reflect some important general conclusions about terrorism security at commercial shopping centers that can be drawn from our analysis. Based on our model and assumptions, implementing security options can substantially decrease the terrorism risk at a shopping center: We find that if all the security options considered in this study were implemented, the risk of terrorism could be reduced by a factor of 20.

The prioritization of security options is similar for the different centers. Eight of the top 10 options for each of the three centers are the same, and few options are shifted by more than two positions among the three centers. This result is discussed further below. The prioritization of security options is strongly driven by the risk of bomb attacks. Because bomb attacks dominate the overall terrorism risk, the model selectively chooses options that address bomb attacks. Most of the risk reduction occurs with the highest priority options.

The cumulative risk drops steeply with the initial options, then decreases more gradually as additional options are added. We find that 95 percent of the total reduction achievable with all options is provided by the first six to ten options (the high-priority set). Most risk reduction occurs with less expensive options; the average cost of each of the options in the high-priority set is 20–35 percent of the average cost of all the options. This result is discussed further below.

Differences Between Centers

As noted above, the prioritized list of security options is similar for the different centers examined. This reflects the fact that the analyses for each center are based on the same set of scenarios and security options and that the same security option effectiveness values were used for each center. Security option costs differ substantially between centers, but most costs correlate with center size, so option costs tend to scale uniformly between centers and thus have little effect on the relative priority of different options. The differences in option priorities among the three shopping centers stems mainly from the inclusion or exclusion of particular scenarios or options that are unique to these centers. For example, Center A is an outdoor center for which dispersal of biological or chemical agents is ineffective. Scenarios 15–17 (anthrax or chemical release) and options 34–39 (air filters and anthrax and chemical detectors) are therefore excluded from the prioritization analysis for Center A.

COSTS AND EFFECTIVENESS OF PRIORITIZED SECURITY OPTIONS

The annual costs of the candidate security options range from $550 for option 25 (*more clearly label exits*) at Center C to nearly $5 million for option 11 (*dogs at entrances, open hours*) at Center B. The model algorithm prioritizes the security options according to their cost-effectiveness. Since costs do not necessarily correlate with effectiveness, the model preferentially selects the less expensive, more effective options. Consequently, the average cost of each option in the high-priority set is only 20–35 percent of the average cost of all the options.

The total annual cost of the high-priority set of options is $1.1 million at Center A, $2.0 million at Center B, and $0.4 million at Center C. For comparison, typical annual common area maintenance costs are $15 to $20 per square foot (Field and Bodamer, 2005), or $15 million to $20 million per year for a 1 million–square-foot center. The most cost-effective option at all three centers is *suspicious package reporting* (option 2). Its value stems from the ability to take advantage relatively easily of the surveillance capability of the large number of customers in a shopping center. As with most other options, the greatest strength of this option is as a deterrent—if a terrorist group knows that an unattended bag or package will be reported swiftly, it will choose another target or choose another method to attack the same target.

Note that the model does not necessarily select options in the order of their individual cost-effectiveness. This is because the model algorithm recalculates the overall risk after each selected option is implemented and then selects the option that is most cost-effective at reducing the risk from that point. Previously selected options will have already reduced some of the risk for various scenarios, which could potentially decrease or even nullify the incremental effectiveness of a remaining option. In other words, the cost-effectiveness of any option depends on which options have already been implemented.

In terms of pure effectiveness (i.e., setting aside cost considerations), the most effective options entail security screening at customer entrances—*dogs at entrances, open hours* (option 11), *search bags, open hours* (option 6), *mandatory coat and bag check, open hours* (option 7), *metal detectors and search bags, open hours* (option 8), and *trace detector portals at entrances, open hours* (option 10). Note that some options in this group are mutually exclusive. Security screening at customer entrances is the most effective approach because it is very good at preventing bomb attacks, which constitute the majority of the terrorism risk (see Figure 3.2). However, security screening is also an expensive approach, because it requires staff and, in some cases, equipment at every entrance. Because of their high cost, the highest any of these options rank in the three centers is fifth.

Collateral Impacts of Security Options

In general, cumulative collateral impacts (either negative or positive) do not correlate with the prioritized rank of the security options. Although these collateral impacts are not considered when the model prioritizes the security options, they may be helpful for decisions about which options to implement or about the details of how an option is implemented. Screening checkpoints, in particular, could have strong negative collateral impacts if they cause people to wait in line to enter a shopping center or parking lot. We have examined the effect of screening checkpoints on line formation by using a simple queuing theory model. The queuing model calculates the wait time at a checkpoint as function of the arrival rate of people or cars and the number of security checkpoints in operation.

Analyses were conducted for a manual search of bags at customer entrances and for a manual search of vehicles entering a parking garage. Search times were assumed to be 30 seconds per bag at customer entrances (and we assume that half the people entering have bags that require searching) and 1 minute per vehicle. Arrival rates (30 people per minute and 17 cars per minute) are based on daily average rates for Center A during peak customer traffic times (mid-December). Peak arrival rates during the busiest part of the day could be as much as double the daily average rate. On the other hand, arrival rates at slower times of year could be less than half the rates in December.

These two effects will tend to offset each other, so the rates we examine approximate typical values for this center. The lowest value shown for the number of servers in each figure (eight for customer entrances and 18 for vehicle entrances) is the minimum number of checkpoints needed to prevent the line from growing to infinite length. The results show that nine checkpoints for searching bags at customer entrances is sufficient to keep the wait time under 1 minute. Vehicle screening, however, requires a minimum of 18 checkpoints, which could be infeasible. Note that analyses made with this model are only approximate, since they assume a steady arrival rate and do not allow for natural fluctuations in arrival rates. In particular, lower numbers of servers may suffice if arrival rate variations allow a backlog of excess arrivals in one time interval to be "made up for" in a subsequent lower-traffic time interval.

Sensitivity to Model Parameters

The security option rankings generated in our analysis depend on certain assumptions, and it is informative to examine the sensitivity of the rankings to the various parameter values. In this section, we examine the sensitivity of the results to different input parameters. This provides a measure of how much security option rankings change when we vary our estimates of likelihoods and other assumptions.

Likelihood Estimates. Because different security options are effective against different scenarios, the option rankings selected by the model depend on the relative likelihoods of the scenarios. To understand how sensitive the rankings are to changes in likelihoods, we conducted an analysis to determine how much the likelihoods could be varied before the option rankings began to change significantly. We used a Monte Carlo simulation6 to calculate the frequency with which each option was assigned a particular rank, since the likelihood values for each scenario were varied independently. Based on this analysis, we found that the option rankings did not begin to change appreciably until likelihoods were varied by more than a factor of 10. This indicates that the security option rankings determined by the model are insensitive to uncertainties of a factor of 10 in the scenario likelihoods. That the results are insensitive to such a large range in likelihood values may seem surprising, but can be understood in light of the fact that the likelihood for the different scenarios span a range of 5,000.

Results for the Monte Carlo analysis for Center A, which are typical of all centers. This figure shows distributions of the individual rankings for each of the top six options considered. The peak of each distribution corresponds to the rank for that option when using fixed likelihoods. For example, option 21, which is ranked third when using fixed likelihoods, ranks first in 0.5 percent of the model runs, ranks second in 4 percent of the runs, ranks third in 92 percent of the runs, and ranks fourth or higher in 2 percent of the runs as the likelihood values are varied.

Likelihood Profiles. To examine further the effect of likelihood values on our results, we also varied the conditions so that future attack likelihoods depart from historical trends. For this analysis, we developed alternate likelihood profiles in which the relative likelihoods of suicide attacks and insider attacks are increased by a factor of 10 relative to the historical base case. A positive value for a given option indicates that the rank of that option has moved up in the list in the indicated likelihood profile relative to the base case profile. A negative value indicates that it has moved down in the list. A zero value indicates that it has remained in the same position.

The changes in ranking of various options under the alternate likelihood profiles can generally be understood in terms of the differential effectiveness of options for suicide and insider attacks. For example, option 21, *search carts/kiosks daily*, is effective against insider attacks only, so it moves up five positions under the high insider profile.

Consequence Weighting. We also examined the effect of alternate weightings of fatalities and shopping center downtime on the rankings of security options. This analysis indicates that the option rankings are less sensitive to the relative weightings of fatalities and downtime than they are to likelihood profiles. This appears to result from the fact that the dynamic range of both consequence metrics is small compared with the dynamic range of the likelihood values: Fatalities vary by a factor of 25 among the scenarios, while likelihoods vary by a factor of 5,000. Thus, security option rankings are less sensitive to changes in consequences than they are to changes in relative likelihoods.

Results for Heightened Threat Conditions

Thus far, our model results have addressed conditions under which there is no specific heightened threat of a terrorist attack. Here we examine how the model can be used to prioritize security options under such conditions. A heightened terrorist threat at shopping centers could occur in two ways. One is a general increased terrorist threat nationwide, in a particular local area, or for shopping centers in particular. In this situation, the overall likelihood of an attack is higher, but there is no specific information to indicate that a particular weapon or scenario is planned. Consequently, the likelihoods for all scenarios would increase uniformly and there would be no effect on the relative prioritization of security options. Note, however, that more options would need to be implemented to reduce the risk to the same level as when no heightened threat condition exists.

The other way in which the threat level could increase is if authorities indicated that they had reason to believe that terrorists were planning specific scenarios or planning to use particular weapons. In this case, the relative likelihoods of the various scenarios would change, which could have a strong effect on the optimal prioritization of security options. We have examined three cases in which particular weapon types are identified as the likely threat. In each case, we exclude all scenarios that do not use the given weapon type, effectively raising the likelihoods of the identified weapon type. Results are presented for Center B.

Comparison with the results for the case when all scenarios are included shows that the results for explosives scenarios only are generally quite similar to results for all scenarios. The top four options are identical, and the ranks of most other options change by only a few positions. This similarity reflects the overall high risk of explosives scenarios relative to other types of scenarios. The higher risk for explosives means that the explosives scenarios dominate the overall risk, and so options effective against explosives are selected preferentially even when other scenario types are included.

Firearms. Results for the case when only scenarios using firearms are included. In contrast to the case for explosives, the prioritized options for firearms scenarios are markedly different from those for all scenarios. Twelve of the options in the allscenario case, including the top four options, are not selected when the scenarios are limited to firearms only. In addition, three options are selected in the firearms-only case that were not selected in the all-scenario case. These differences reflect the fact that the effective options in firearms attacks are generally different from the effective options in explosives attacks; enhancing the risk of firearms attacks by excluding explosives attacks results in a large shift in security option priorities.

Chemical and Biological Weapons

Results for the case when only scenarios using chemical and biological weapons are included. As would be expected, there are substantial differences between these results and the all-scenario case, both because the chemical and biological scenarios are quite different from the explosives scenarios and because several options (34–39) are specific to chemical and biological weapons. However, it is worth noting that the highest-priority risk reduction option is a traditional security approach of searching kiosks daily, which is also a high-priority option under normal conditions.

Our analysis shows that implementing about 10 security options that span a range of approaches and that deter, deny, or mitigate a range of potential terrorist threats can substantially reduce the terrorism risk at commercial shopping centers.

The majority of these options involve traditional security approaches, such as installing bollards at pedestrian entrances, searching bags, encouraging suspicious package reporting, and searching vehicles. Although there are some differences in the order of the high-priority options selected for different centers, overall the prioritizations of security options for the different centers examined in this report are similar.

The similarity among centers ultimately reflects the fact that shopping centers generally share a similar set of vulnerabilities to terrorism and lend themselves to the same types of security options to reduce the terrorism risk. Qualitatively estimated collateral impacts of high-priority options are likely to influence security decisions. A simple queuing model applied to a modest-sized center indicates that customer entrance security checkpoints could easily be implemented with minimal wait times but that vehicle screening at parking entrances may result in substantial wait times. The total annual cost of the high-priority options (those that generate 95 percent of the total possible risk reduction) ranges from $0.4 million to $2.0 million at the three centers examined. Prioritization results are largely insensitive to the relative weighting of fatalities and center downtime and are moderately sensitive to variations in likelihood estimates. Results are most sensitive to variations in which scenarios are included, which could vary if authorities indicate an increased likelihood of attacks using a specific weapon type.

ADDITIONAL COMPONENTS OF TERRORISM SECURITY AT SHOPPING CENTERS

The model presented in Chapter Three prioritizes the security options considered under assumptions about likelihood and consequence of varying types of attacks and effectiveness of options. There is a wide spectrum of nuanced strategies and implications that this model does not attempt to characterize yet that are important considerations. This chapter discusses some perspectives that the model does not address, but nonetheless may be important for guiding decisionmaking about reducing terrorism risk at shopping centers.

Standby Considerations

Some of the high-priority security options identified in our modeling may be appropriate to implement immediately. Indeed, some shopping centers have begun implementing terrorism security strategies that include some of the options identified in this report.

On the other hand, stakeholders may choose not to implement many of the security options unless the terrorism threat conditions were to change for the worse. If the risk of terrorist attacks were to increase rapidly, e.g., if periodic attacks began occurring in the United States, it would be important for shopping center operators to be in a position to implement additional security options quickly. The security options identified in this report cannot leap immediately from concept to implementation.

Much consideration will have to be brought to each option to develop a suitable implementation plan. This section discusses some things that center operators could do now to facilitate the implementation of security options.

Preparing for Future Acquisitions

Some of the security options require physical assets (e.g., metal detectors) that shopping centers may not already possess. Many of the options will require substantial changes in security operations and staffing levels. Some will require light construction. All options will require some level of public relations effort to educate tenants and customers about new procedures. All these steps could be facilitated by contacting suppliers and prepositioning agreements with specific vendors for assets that might be needed in the future. This would increase how quickly shopping centers could respond to a particular threat environment to continue operations.

Data Collection Opportunities

The model does not take into account every consideration that management would have to weigh for each security option. Many of these considerations are very site specific and would be exceedingly difficult to build into a general model. For example, inspecting the vehicles of all patrons parking at the facility could require more inspection stations than there are entrances to a garage. This is a physical constraint that particular shopping centers face, which is not represented in the model. Similarly, a decisionmaker cannot make a sound judgment as to whether a particular site can inspect every vehicle entering a parking structure without knowing something about projected volume of vehicles entering. Decisionmakers must have access to detailed data in order to make sound judgments, estimate costs accurately, and develop implementation plans. An effort to collect relevant data ahead of time would enable management to determine whether and how to implement various security options in particular environments when the need arises.

Modeling Opportunities

Implications of many of the security options could be explored further using site-specific data mentioned above. Queuing theory could be applied to several of the security options considered. More sophisticated queuing models could elucidate optimal strategies for specific sites. Such models would allow decisionmakers to determine the appropriate number of stations needed and define efficient staffing schedules. Queuing models have been successfully used in a variety of industries to optimize operations.

Psychological Implications

Implementation of some of the security options may have a negative psychological impact on shopping center customers and employees. For example, requiring shoppers to go through a screening checkpoint imposes a disutility that might turn away the consumers on the margin.

It is difficult to project how consumers will react to measures taken to increase security. Much will likely be determined by the public's perception of the risk environment at a particular point in time. For example, after September 11, 2001, the public accepted increased security measures at airports that might have been met with more resistance earlier.

There may be strategies that shopping centers could design to mitigate the psychological impact of shoppers. Such strategies should seek to communicate to consumers that facilities have taken appropriate security measures while still providing a permissive environment for shopping.

Structural Design Considerations

The security options considered in this report exclude major design and construction issues. In some cases, the risk of bomb attacks can be mitigated by means of structural design approaches. Given that property development and redevelopment are important aspects of the shopping center industry, structural design and construction options may be useful approaches. In this section, we summarize some guidance available from government agencies regarding structural hardening (physically strengthening a structure) and building standoff zones. This material is provided for informational purposes only and has not been reviewed for accuracy or effectiveness. As described in Chapter Two, explosives are the most common weapon used in terrorist attacks. Notable examples include pedestrian suicide bombers in Israel and vehicle bombs at the Murrah building in Oklahoma City, Khobar Towers in Saudi Arabia, and the U.S. embassies in Kenya and Tanzania.

The blast from explosives affects structures and the people inside them in multiple ways. People can be injured or killed by the blast pressure, by being propelled into walls or objects, and by fragments created and propelled by the blast wave. Fragments can come from glass and structural materials as well as from shrapnel placed around the bomb. Blast can also cause localized damage to a structure, knocking down walls and columns and causing sections of a building nearest the explosion to collapse. The effects of a particular bomb depend on its size and the distance it is detonated from the building.

In shopping centers, bombs can also damage merchandise, equipment, and real property. Bombs can lead to revenue losses for the merchants and the shopping center owner by forcing the closure of a portion or even the entire facility.

A bomb's effects can be amplified many times over if the blast from a bomb causes a structure to undergo a progressive collapse, where an initial local structural failure spreads to other elements in the structure, resulting in collapse that is much larger than the explosive would have caused on its own (Federal Emergency Management Agency, 2003a). The collapse of the two World Trade Center buildings in 2001 illustrates the amplifying effect that progressive collapse can have on casualties and property losses. Many of the deaths and injuries in the Oklahoma City bombing were in the zone of progressive collapse (Mallonee et al., 1996). Structural mitigation measures can be broken into two basic groups: those that keep the bombs away from the structure or critical elements of the structure and those that harden the structure, making it more resistant to the effects of a bomb.

Standoff

The most effective mitigation measure for bomb attacks is to keep bombs as far away from the structure as possible. This is accomplished by establishing a standoff distance between a structure and potential bomb detonation locations. This approach takes advantage of the fact that the blast effects from a bomb decrease rapidly with distance. It is possible to create standoff zones to some extent for truck and car bombs at shopping centers where access can be restricted. But this can be difficult in urban areas if a shopping center adjoins city streets and sidewalks.

Exterior Standoff. U.S. Department of Defense (2003) guidance for military facilities mandates standoff distances of 80–150 feet for inhabited buildings. This guidance was developed primarily for sleeping quarters and office buildings. The topology of shopping centers provides comparatively greater protection to the occupants from bombs detonated outside of the structure. There generally are not many windows facing outside, and the storefronts face the internal common area rather than the road or parking areas. Moreover, the areas closest to the exterior of the structure tend to be storage areas and service hallways, where the density of people is very low. This topology means that the standoff distance needed for a shopping center is likely to be smaller than that needed for an office building.

Interior Standoff. The open nature of shopping centers creates risks that are less common in office buildings—the public can simply walk into the common area where the density of people is the highest. Keeping package bombs and pedestrian bombers out of a shopping center is thus difficult, requiring security checkpoints to screen people and bags at shopping center entrances. Even without security screening, however, the structure still could be protected to some degree against these smaller bombs by preventing them from being placed in direct contact with vulnerable points in the structure. This could be accomplished by hiding critical columns and beams in walls or spaces that are inaccessible to the public. Critical columns that must remain exposed could be protected by creating architectural barriers around them that are at least six inches away from the columns.

In a shopping center, these standoff distances could be created by placing columnar billboards around the columns. Critical structural columns may be present both in a center's interior and in exterior areas such as beneath overhangs or in underground parking structures. Movie theaters above parking lots or other easily accessible spaces are particularly vulnerable to bombs targeting columns.

Hardening Structures

Hardening the structure can be a useful mitigation strategy in some situations, particularly where it would be difficult to establish standoff zones for vehicles or where package bombs could be placed near critical structural elements. Extensive hardening would require radically different construction techniques and architecture than are used today. Shopping centers would end up looking more like concrete military bunkers and would be extremely expensive to build. Nevertheless, several steps short of building bunkers could be taken to strengthen the structure of a shopping center, particularly against progressive collapse.

The first of these is to harden specific elements of the structure, particularly those columns and beams that are critical to preventing progressive collapse. Several useful references provide a general overview of potential measures for new and existing structures.

According to these references, concrete columns in existing facilities can be retrofitted with protective wrappings of steel or composite materials that would hold the column in place even if the concrete inside had been turned to rubble. Steel columns can be wrapped with concrete to protect them from the force of the blast. In new structures, important columns can be built with spiral reinforcing, column spacing can be minimized, and floor slabs can be attached to columns so that they can withstand the upward pressures of an explosion. The degree to which an existing or new structure should be hardened and the best measures for achieving the desired level of protection would depend on an assessment of the likely threat and the effectiveness of the measures in reducing that threat. It would also require detailed analysis of the proposed protective measures by a structural engineer specializing in hardening against explosives.

Strategic Security Considerations Our analysis addresses security options implemented at the individual center level. Such tactical-level security, however, is only one component of the overall terrorism security strategy protecting a shopping center. Higher-level security efforts can also be important and should be included in any terrorism security strategy. An example of a potentially valuable mid-level security option that can be implemented company- or industry-wide is developing and sharing databases of suspicious persons and events (e.g., unexplained recurring visits to a particular center, visits to numerous centers). Most higher-level strategic components, such as intelligence gathering and analysis, border security, emergency response, and terrorism insurance, are generally outside the influence of a shopping center operator or the shopping center industry. However, by staying informed about initiatives and progress in these areas, shopping center operators may identify opportunities to express their interests and influence activities.

Special Operational Environments

The model does not consider the implications of special operational environments created by nonroutine events. Special events (e.g., concerts) have the potential to create unique situations that could have an impact on the likelihood or consequences of attacks and on the types and effectiveness of security options. A special event may increase the number and density of people (increasing the consequences) and might make an attack more desirable to terrorists (increasing the likelihood). In addition, these events generate deviations from routine activities, making it more difficult to notice unusual activities that could be indications of a terrorist attack (decreasing the effect of security measures). A special event transforms the venue from its originally designed purpose. Security measures taken to provide a permissive environment for shopping may not be optimal for special events.

Implications for Terrorism Security at Shopping Centers

We conclude with a discussion of some implications for terrorism security at commercial shopping centers raised by our analysis. These implications derive from the prioritization of terrorism security options at three centers that, in turn, is based on estimates of the relative risks of different types of terrorist attacks at shopping centers of how well different security options reduce these risks. It is important to reiterate that terrorism risk is uncertain, and the results of our analysis are contingent upon various assumptions about the likelihoods of different attack scenarios, the consequences of these scenarios, and the effectiveness and cost of security options.

We have examined the sensitivity of our results to several parameters and find that the results are generally robust over large variations in fundamental assumptions. In addition, we have attempted to be comprehensive when including scenarios and security options for consideration. Nonetheless, as discussed in Chapter Two, terrorism risk is evolving and it is unclear how well the future terrorism risk can be predicted from historical trends. This tenet applies not only to the likelihoods of different scenarios, but also to the lethality of attacks and the type and effectiveness of terrorism security strategies. Terrorism risk is dynamic, and assessments of terrorism security strategies must be updated frequently (e.g., Jackson et al., 2005a,

2005b). The implications discussed here apply to the current threat environment.

A strategy to reduce the risk of terrorism will be similar for most shopping centers. Our analysis indicates that the principal risk-reducing security options do not differ dramatically across the three types of centers examined in this report. Because the characteristics of the centers we examined are quite diverse, including large and small, indoor and outdoor, urban and suburban, this similarity is expected to hold for shopping centers in general. This means that many of the decisions regarding implementing terrorism security options can be managed centrally. Centralized management of a similar set of options at multiple centers would facilitate information sharing among centers, allowing pitfalls to be identified and avoided and best practices to be promoted. Given the fairly substantial operational impacts of some options, this could help minimize transition problems. Centralized security management can also create an economy of scale and increase efficiency

A similar set of options at most shopping centers may also help mitigate the confusion and anxiety among the public that could potentially arise if security efforts are increased. Especially if accompanied by a company- or industry-wide public relations effort, this could increase confidence that the increased security is safe and effective and is being well monitored.

Disaster preparedness plans and exercises that focus primarily on emergency response do little to reduce terrorism risk. The vast majority of terrorism risk derives from attacks using explosives, for which the effects are immediate and the hazard abates very quickly. As a result, little can be done to reduce consequences (casualties or property damage) of a terrorist attack once it has occurred. While security options may help mitigate consequences in some cases, the effects are small and generally apply to low-risk attack scenarios. As opposed to mitigating consequences, terrorism risk must be reduced by deterrence. This is the primary way in which most of the security options considered in this analysis are effective. Consequently, existing disaster preparedness plans and exercises, which focus primarily on the emergency response to a disaster, offer little toward reducing the risk of terrorism.

Such plans have great benefit for reducing the risks of threats such as fires and earthquakes and therefore represent an essential part of a shopping center's security strategy. However, shopping center operators should not assume that in having such a plan they have adequately addressed terrorism security. Terrorism security is very different from disaster preparedness. This means that terrorism security will involve separate planning, training, and exercising approaches that focus on concerns such as reporting suspicious packages and detecting weapons.

Centers that move to implement terrorism security options early may experience both challenges and advantages. Some of the high-priority security options identified in the analysis are expected to have negative collateral effects. Some options, primarily security checkpoints at parking and customer entrances, will impede access of shoppers into a center.

Some high-priority options may also elicit some amount of negative psychological reaction from customers. If these effects are great enough, they may cause some shoppers to choose to go to alternate shopping centers or to avoid shopping centers altogether. This effect would be a disadvantage to centers that implement terrorism security options. On the other hand, were the threat from terrorism to be perceived as increasing, the psychology may be reversed and customers may feel safer in centers with increased security. This would almost certainly be the case in the aftermath of an attack in the United States. One possible sequence is that a center that decides to implement terrorism security may at first suffer some decrease in customer traffic only to have it resume or increase as people become more accustomed to the new environment.

It would be instructive to examine the customer responses to increasing terrorism security. As noted earlier, some of the options highlighted in this analysis are being implemented at shopping centers currently, and customer responses could be tracked and evaluated. Case studies in regions with greater terrorist threats and greater security, such as Israel and the United Kingdom, could provide useful reference models and lessons that could assist decisionmaking and security implementation in shopping centers in the United States.

Tiered implementation may be the best strategy. One way to approach the problem of reducing the risk of terrorist attack is to implement a set of measures that is most appropriate for today's environment and develop plans today for further measures if the environment changes for the worse.

Those plans should address the issue of how best to deal with the longlead aspects of those measures, including precontracting for equipment or activities such as light construction or training staff to implement the measures in case they are needed. Efforts taken today to reduce the time it will take to implement future measures could reduce the disruptions to operations and revenue that could occur if the threat changes and customers are afraid to patronize shopping centers.

Ultimately, decisions about when to implement security options will be driven by assessments of the absolute risk of terrorism. Our analysis does not include any assumptions about the recurrence intervals of different attack scenarios or the likelihood of a terrorist attack compared with other security threats. Thus, though the analysis provides guidance about the relative priority of security options and how effective they are at reducing terrorism risk, it does not specify the absolute threat conditions necessary to warrant implementing any security options. In other words, the model indicates what to do once the initial decision has been made to implement terrorism security options, but it does not indicate how or when to make that initial decision.

Limiting terrorism security to temporary efforts such as is done currently may be entirely appropriate under the current conditions of generally low terrorism risk. Decisions to ramp up terrorism security would ideally be based on an understanding of the absolute terrorism risk, expressed in expected annual losses. Such estimates, however, are even more difficult to make and uncertain than the relative scenario likelihoods derived in this study. Some attempts to estimate absolute terrorism risk have been put forth in insurance industry models, but these attempts are restricted to catastrophic events (greater than 100 fatalities or $1 billion in losses).

In lieu of any reliable information about the absolute risk of terrorist attacks, decisions about when to implement security options are likely to be informed indirect indicators, such as government actions and guidance, political changes, media reporting, or industry trends.

Chapter

6

The Vulnerability of the UK's Nuclear Facilities to Terrorism

In addition to the threat of weapons of mass destruction — chemical, biological and nuclear — the risk that a Nuclear Power Plant (NPP) might be used as a radiological weapon has received much attention post-11 September 2001. While there is no danger of a nuclear-yield explosion if a NPP were attacked, a successful terrorist attack or sabotage attempt at a NPP containing a range of hazardous materials and facilities could cause the release of radioactive particles into the atmosphere. This would disperse radioactive contamination over a wide area. The contaminated area would thus become uninhabitable, with grave consequences for the environment, the economy and future generations. An attack on a NPP would at best cause the disruption to domestic and commercial energy supplies, at worst radioactive fallout, public hysteria and mass fatalities.

ATTACK ON A NUCLEAR POWER PLANT OR SPENT FUEL FACILITY

In 2002, the United Kingdom (UK) had in operation 31 nuclear reactors in 13 NPPs. Of these reactors, 30 are gas-cooled and graphite-modified types: 16 of these are the Magnox reactors operated by British Nuclear Fuels Limited (BNFL); while 14 are Advanced Gas-cooled Reactors (AGRs) owned by the private nuclear power generator British Energy. The last reactor to enter service was a Pressure Water Reactor (PWR) completed in 1995, owned by British

Energy. NPPs in most countries are protected by containment vessels several feet thick and are equipped with redundant safety systems. Armed guards and other security systems also protect them. In order to cause a core meltdown and disperse a substantial amount of the NPP's radioactive material into the atmosphere, attackers would have to defeat the plant's security systems and destroy or disable its multiple safety systems simultaneously. Yet NPPs are capable of withstanding a commando-style raid by only a small group of lightly armed insurgents. A heavily armed group might therefore be able to overwhelm a NPP's security systems, especially with insider knowledge of the security.

Besides a commando-style raid, other methods of attack exist. These might involve hijacked airplanes, a maritime vessel with crew-served weapons on-board (surface-to-surface missiles, for example), or a truck packed with explosives. In fact, a large truck bomb detonated outside the protected area of a NPP could cause sufficient damage to critical safety systems and lead to a core meltdown.[3] By far the most potentially devastating radiological release would come from sabotage to a NPP or spent fuel facility: both of these facilities contain huge concentrations of highly radioactive material and would generate the nuclear or chemical energy needed for wide dispersal of the radioactive material.

International security standards differ, however. The Three Mile Island NPP facility in the USA was designed to withstand the impact of a Boeing 707, although it might be vulnerable to a full speed, direct hit from larger commercial airliners, such as a 767. But the UK's NPPs were never constructed with such an attack in mind. The fact that 30 out of 31 of the UK's reactors are graphite-moderated types is also a cause for concern because when graphite is used as a moderator it burns easily. In 1986, the fire in the graphite-type Chernobyl reactor lasted for over a week and released radioactivity over 1,000 metres into the atmosphere, spreading it over a large area. If an airliner crashed into a UK graphite reactor, a similar long lasting fire with long-distance fallout is possible. Bellona recommends improved security at the UK's NPPs, including better containment for reactors to withstand the crash impact from an airliner or from a high-yield conventional explosive detonated offsite. Security improvements at the Magnox reactors could prove uneconomical, as they are due to close by 2010.

NPPs burn uranium fuel in their cores, which produce highly radioactive and physically hot spent fuel rods: rods are removed from the reactor and those from the Magnox and AGR stations are plunged into onsite cooling ponds for a short period of time before being transferred to containers (flasks) and sent to Sellafield for reprocessing – a method of handling spent nuclear fuel. Rods from the PWR station are initially stored in onsite water-filled storage pools. BNFL operates two reprocessing plants at Sellafield, Magnox B205 and Thermal Oxide Reprocessing Plant (THORP). B205 operates according to the Plutonium Uranium Extraction method and reprocesses fuel from British Magnox reactors. THORP was designed to separate plutonium for use in 'breeder' reactors, but now reprocesses spent nuclear fuel (SNF) from British AGRs as well as imported SNF.[4] Other than Sellafield, there are only two other major reprocessing plants in operation worldwide: Cap de la Hague in France and Mayak in Russia.

The Sellafield plant houses 21 steel tanks in above ground concrete cells that contain high level radioactive waste in the form of self heating, acidic liquid. This radioactive waste has to be constantly cooled and stirred to prevent a chain reaction, which is achieved by continuously being cooled and agitated to prevent the stored waste from boiling and causing a radiological release. The tanks contain 2,400kg of caesium-137, a radioactive material responsible for offsite radiation exposure from Chernobyl, although the amount released from Chernobyl was approximately 27kg. It is estimated that if an airliner crashed into one of the key structures at Sellafield, it would release into the atmosphere 44 times the radioactivity of the 1986 Chernobyl accident.

If the cooling system were sabotaged, or if terrorist attack on the facility were successful, it would release liquid waste into the Irish Sea, along with strontium-90, caesium-137 and technetium-99, which has a half-life of 213, 000 years. Such radioactive substances would contaminate fisheries and travel north from Cumbria, heavily contaminating fisheries in western Scotland. Anywhere downwind of Sellafield during the release would be rendered uninhabitable for generations, and people caught in the fallout would have a higher chance of contracting cancer. Depending on the wind direction, cities such as Dublin, Edinburgh, Leeds and Newcastle would be well within fallout range.

Indeed, in a report to the House of Commons Defence Committee on 9 January 2002, Dr Gordon Thompson, executive director of the Institute for Research and Security Studies in Cambridge, Massachusetts, suggested that an attack on the B205 facility could release 100 times the radioactivity produced by the Chernobyl accident, which would make the north of England uninhabitable for generations.

Moreover, a report by the Nuclear Installations Inspectorate on 2 July 2002 reported that two sets of tanks housing medium-level radioactive waste at Sellafield were so old and in such a dangerous condition that they pose an unacceptable risk. BNFL has been warned that neither the structural integrity of the tanks, nor the building containing them, could be guaranteed beyond ten years. While BNFL has already surrounded the tanks with a steel building and commissioned specialist machinery to empty the tanks, the condition of the tanks require the building of new tanks or another solution for processing the waste.

Bellona advocates the need for crash-proof tanks to contain the medium and high-level radioactive waste stored at Sellafield. The liquid waste should be immobilised as soon as possible and disposed of geologically.

ATTACK ON REPROCESSING OR STORAGE TRANSPORTS

In 1996, BNFL opened the Sellafield MOX Plant (SMP) for the production of mixed oxide (MOX) fuel, receiving its licence for production in October 2001. The only use for the plutonium that

THORP and B205 have produced is to mix it with uranium oxide and fabricate MOX fuel for use in light water reactors. While the UK has the facilities to produce MOX fuel, it does not use MOX fuel. And given the cost of conversion, British NPP operators have no plans to convert their plants to burn MOX fuel. BNFL, having already built a MOX fuel manufacturing plant, has been forced to look overseas for customers in countries including Germany, Switzerland and Japan.

The transportation of nuclear materials, such as fresh MOX fuel and SNF for reprocessing, means that there will be an ever increasing traffic in nuclear materials by air, land and sea. Shipments of SNF and fresh MOX fuel might be vulnerable to terrorist attack and could be used to create a radiological explosion or to gain the material to fabricate a radiological dispersal device such as a "dirty bomb".

No nuclear freight is allowed to travel through the Channel Tunnel. Previously, SNF for reprocessing sent to Sellafield was shipped into Dover Docks by train-ferry before travelling on by rail. The ferry has now been withdrawn from service and all flasks go by sea to Barrow-in-Furness, and then by train to Sellafield. Flasks are made of steel and are lead-lined in order to contain the intense heat and radioactivity of the spent fuel rods and are carried on special low-loading freight wagons. While the flasks are designed to meet International Atomic Energy Agency safety standards, a successful terrorist attack might cause either a high-speed derailment or collision, which could release the radioactive contents.

BNFL operates seven vessels for the transport of MOX fuel. Two of these vessels are armed with 30mm cannons. Armed officers from the UK Atomic Energy Authority (UKAEA) Constabulary, which provide security for civil nuclear sites and for the transport of nuclear material within the UK, are on guard against boarders. Should the Constabulary be overpowered, would-be attackers would than have to crack open the vessels' reinforced hatch covers and unload the rods without the aid of deck cranes. Yet BNFL's vessels only have a top speed of 13 knots and are not as maneuverable or well-defended as a military or coastguard escort vessel. *Jane's* maritime specialists suggest that the vessels are capable of repelling a light attack and should be protected by at least one well-armed frigate. And while MOX fuel flasks can resist temperatures of 800C for up to 30 minutes, fires on ships can burn for 24 hours at a temperature of 1,000C.

MOX fuel is plutonium and uranium blended and held in ceramic form, so it is possible to undertake the chemical separation of plutonium from fresh MOX fuel. While it is debatable whether or not this could be used to fabricate a crude nuclear device, the material could be used to make a dirty bomb capable of scattering plutonium dust in the wind: just one speck of plutonium breathed into the lungs is enough to cause cancer, so the population near any blast involving radioactive material would have to be evacuated immediately.

Given the security threats of transporting fresh and spent MOX fuel, including the risk of accidents at land and sea and nuclear material proliferation, as well as the additional costs of increasing security, Bellona calls for a ban to be placed on the international transport of MOX fuel.

REDUCING THE VULNERABILITY OF NUCLEAR FACILITIES

Since 11 September 2001, attention has been drawn to the physical protection of NPPs. By deploying point air-defence systems around Cap de la Hague, French defence officials have tightened security around Europe's largest nuclear processing plant. In the UK, the House of Commons defence committee stressed that attention should be focused on the vulnerability of nuclear installations. The UK Home Office, too, has underscored the need to protect the UK's key nuclear facilities through the government's Civil Contingencies Committee. The Royal Air Force Tornado F3 fighters based at Coningsby, Lincolnshire, are responsible for intercepting hijacked commercial aircraft deemed a threat to UK nuclear sites.

In July 2002, the British government published a White Paper entitled "Managing the Nuclear Legacy: A Strategy for Action" which proposed to transform the UKAEA Constabulary into a stand-alone force, the Civil Nuclear Constabulary (CNC). The new, armed force will be able to make arrests at non-nuclear locations such as sea ports, airports and railway stations. It will also be able to patrol and stop and search individuals and vehicles up to three miles from nuclear sites.

Bellona believes that these responses do not tackle the underlying vulnerability of NPPs, however. What is needed is a comprehensive upgrade of security systems including improved reactor containment. In fact, in the short term, security standards should be improved, and it would be prudent to enhance security systems. In the long term, however, Bellona advocates an end to commercial reprocessing and the vitrification and disposal of high-level radioactive waste preferably in a dry-storage geological repository. Nuclear energy provides 23% of Britain's total energy requirements, so reducing the need for nuclear power is feasible, especially on financial grounds.

In 2001, BNFL developed a £1.7bn "net asset deficit" in its accounts. To avoid prosecution under the 1985 Companies Act, BNFL managers called an extraordinary general meeting on 28 November 2001. Since then, the British government has set up a Liabilities Management Authority to take responsibility for and control the UK's nuclear waste including everything owned and run by the UK Atomic Energy Agency and BNFL. It appears that BNFL failed to set aside sufficient money to pay for cleaning up old nuclear power stations and has developed a £44bn deficit. The bill for dealing with nuclear waste alone exceeds £38bn, and the British taxpayer will now have to pay £1.5bn a year in liabilities.

APATHY AND INCOMPETENCE TRUMP TERRORISM IN CYBERSPACE

Today's threats to U.S. national security range from the bloody reality of terrorist suicide bombers who kill and maim individuals to weapons of mass destruction that potentially hold many thousands at risk. The U.S. information infrastructure is a vital element of U.S. national security, but the design and management of software render its terminals, nodes and networks demonstrably vulnerable to malicious manipulation.

Opinions vary as to the source, scope and severity of the cyberthreat; who should lead the defense or be held accountable when systems fail; and what role a privacy-fixated citizenry will yield to government in any of these matters. These are some of the issues said to be thwarting a coordinated action plan for shared public-private action in building a more resilient information infrastructure.

Insofar as the government's role, the Bill Clinton and George W. Bush administrations recognized their limited leverage over public/private systems and prudently opted to plead for partnerships in policing the information highway. And, both administrations pledged to lead by example by reducing vulnerabilities in federal information systems. However, the public sector has been reluctant to share data on cyberattacks, fearing that it would be mishandled to the detriment of business and privacy. Further, the goal of leadership has been undercut by the poor track records of federal agencies in reducing vulnerabilities—only five even bothered to take the first steps by inventorying their technical assets.

The U.S. Congress has tried to spur corrective actions, but it enacted laws that lack incentives for owners to self-police their networks, and it failed to demand accountability or provide sanctions when they did not. Rep. Adam H. Putnam (R-FL) wants to amend the Clinger-Cohen Act to specifically include security in software buying decisions.

News media coverage has added heat without light to the discussion. Articles titled "cyberterrorism" routinely garner front-page coverage, while those on worms, viruses, phishing, spyware and Trojan horses must duke it out for a few column inches in the financial section.

As for the public, an apathetic user community tolerates the cyberthreat as an expensive but insurable nuisance. The deciding vote on software security is being cast in the marketplace by buyers who readily acknowledge a growing dependence on efficient automated information systems and who rush to purchase software that features the coolest backward-compatible functionality. However, either they resist buying, or they do purchase but mismanage products that, however imperfect, do reduce system vulnerability.

Industry's role often is under fire. Federal policy is criticized because many believe that the software industry has manipulated the federal legislative and executive branches. Despite pleas of mea culpa from industry leaders and vows to reform, the software industry has deflected criticism of its faulty software by citing buyer preferences and by blaming security breaches on sloppy operating practices.

To date, the software industry has charted its own course opting for a strategy that favors maintenance of a competitive market position over product reliability and security. However, that policy now is being rethought. Reports from task forces of the National Cyber Security Partnership—a group of security technology experts, academics and business and government officials—call for improving security across the software development life cycle and propose that security be placed at the heart of the software design process.

Corporate indifference to the cyberthreat also is under fire. A Corporate Governance Task Force has challenged the user community to integrate information security governance into corporate governance, effectively making chief executive officers (CEOs)—rather than chief information officers (CIOs)—accountable for security.

Finally, a surprising blitz of ads from the organization Business Roundtable has demanded a balanced approach that reflects the shared responsibility of end users and suppliers.

A lack of agreement on threat sources and trends is yet another excuse for keeping cybersecurity fixes on the back burner. *Business Week* reported surveys showing that "for a third year in a row, attacks on computer networks have fallen." This is the lowest level of reported unauthorized use of systems since 1999, due, in the view of one commentator, to "organizations becoming savvier about security." Or, perhaps it is due to savvier reporting?

Don O'Neill of the Center for National Software Studies sees no lessening of cyberthreats. In an "Open Forum" column in the June 2004 issue of CrossTalk, he writes that both threat and vulnerability are increasing because of neglect by venders in "product trustworthiness and inadequate user commitment in security readiness."

O'Neill faults "unwise legislation, inadequate public-private collaboration, a patchwork of government regulatory infrastructure, and the lack of business incentive practices." He believes that the nation's software infrastructure is fragile, and when it is targeted by a competent determined attacker, it might collapse.

The U.S. Department of Homeland Security also sees no diminution in threat. An April 2004 report by its Office of Inspector General, titled *Progress and Challenges in Securing the Nation's Cyberspace*, finds that speed, virulence and maliciousness of cyberattacks and computer vulnerabilities have increased dramatically in recent years and that "industry experts agree that cyberterrorism ... is one of the nation's top five security threats and will likely remain so for years to come."

Adding strident voice to alarms of cyberterrorism is Robert Cook, CEO of Sigaba, who notes sophistication by terrorists in using Internet tools. He says, "It's not a stretch to believe the reports that al Qaida plans to use cyberterrorism as one of its tools."

That terrorists value the power of information systems in furthering their agenda is not at issue.

Daily they display skills in using Web sites, chat rooms and e-mail to transmit encrypted orders, transfer funds, recruit and train, plan and perform other vital management functions. But, beyond a suspicious pattern of probes on the Internet—which indeed could be a precursor of evil intent—a plausible rationale is yet to surface for terrorists intentionally damaging the very information infrastructure they depend on to command and control a dispersed and networked organization.

In fact, one commentator speculates that terrorist Web sites are so effective in exploiting the Internet for command and control of their cells and for reaching out to the hearts and minds of the Islam "street" that they now have become targets for U.S. military information operations.

The United States has been on heightened alert to a threat of cyberterrorism since September 11, 2001. This includes fears that attacks would cripple power systems, air traffic control, banking and communications. But, security expert Bruce Schneier writes in his June 2004 *Crypto-Gram*, "The impending cyberwar was a big dud … caused," he reasons, "by a misunderstanding of both the attackers and the attacks." Schneier acknowledges an information infrastructure filled with vulnerabilities, "but not generally the kind that cause catastrophic disruptions." Further, he argues that "attacks [on software based systems] are very difficult to execute" because that infrastructure is filled with interactions that we simply do not understand ourselves.

Schneier claims that less than 1 percent of all attacks on the Internet have originated from countries on the U.S. government's Cyber Terror Watch List, while 35 percent originated from inside the United States.

The insider threat is a significant cybersecurity menace. This recently was demonstrated by an employee theft of 92 million e-mail addresses from America Online. This prompted security expert Peter Neumann to comment on "this [insider] threat, which is largely ignored by the popular focus on hackers, spammers and others."

Writing in *The Washington Post* about industry attempts to curb the insider threat, Jonathan Krim says, "Computers are so pervasive that almost any employee is a potential threat." He adds that the extent of this threat is hard to measure because so much goes unreported and that "despite all of the new measures available, security experts say that companies remain woefully inattentive."

The term "insider" can mislead. Contracts for much software—and especially that used for U.S. military systems—are being outsourced offshore. Consequently, a foreign "outsider" easily can become an insider. A May 2004 report by the Government Accountability Office found that "Defense Department acquisition and software security policies do not fully address the risk of using foreign suppliers to develop weapon system software."

In his book *Beyond Fear*, Schneier says that people make security decisions based on perceived instead of actual risk. They underestimate risks they willingly take and overestimate risks in situations they cannot control. Schneier argues there is no single level of security applicable for all users. Instead, there is a condition to be determined by each consumer, based on that person's threat and risk assessments, and then only after application of tradeoffs to reach a comfort level. He suggests this approach to risk assessment:

- What assets are held so dear as to demand protection?
- How vulnerable are those assets and from what specific threat? Who is the feared attacker: an insider, journalist, vandal, competitor, criminal, hostile nation-state, nosy neighbor, curious adolescent? What is that attacker's specific objective and what protective steps might deter intrusion or reduce losses if protection fails?
- What tradeoffs are available to raise security to the user's comfort level? Tradeoffs could vary from the extremes of insuring or writing off losses to installing the most sophisticated detection, protection and restoration software. (However, not every cyberwayfarer has alternatives and tradeoffs. The U.S. armed forces, having opted to go light, mobile and wireless on a nonlinear battlefield, already have traded off mobilization and mass for overmatching power that depends, absolutely, on dominating the information domain.)

Some conclusions and supporting rationale can be sifted from this cacophony of dissonance and conflicting opinion:

- The cyberthreat is increasing because information about "things" has come to equal or exceed the worth of physical possession of things. As Wayne Crews of the Cato Institute writes, "technology puts us at even more risk if physical things become too dependent on [information] technology."
- Vulnerability will increase because digital technology creates subtle vulnerabilities that contain the seeds of catastrophic failures and because the user will either remain indifferent to the threat or prove incompetent in managing cascading system complexity.
- Emphasis on system interoperability and horizontal sharing of information through standards and open commercial technology, while necessary, inevitably will create what Schneier calls the growing risk of "class breaks"—that is because common systems share common vulnerabilities.
- While technology favors neither side, the defender always will be one step behind because he or she must defend all options while the adversary will be able to choose the time, target and tactic. However, having conceded this tactical advantage, the defender may find that growing system complexity also adds complication, uncertainty and the risk of unintended consequences to the plan of any adversary. How so? Because the weakest link now has become a moving target.
- The insider—including the privileged outsider—will remain the primary cyberthreat. As former Defense Department CIO Paul Strassmann cautioned more than a decade ago, "Don't blame hackers for problems that can best be explained by incompetence."
- Because the information infrastructure will remain fragile to determined attack and could collapse, emphasis also must be given to readiness, resilience, damage control and reconstitution.

- The case for cybersecurity is weakened when bonded to terrorists, to criminals, or even to potentially hostile rogue nations or nation-states. This coupling encourages preoccupation with "the evil them" whose identity is irrelevant to the erection of more effective defenses, rather than with "the inept us" where cooperation and collaboration can make a real difference in building a more secure information infrastructure.

Fortunately, consensus on threat is not a prerequisite for owners and operators to reduce vulnerabilities in their information systems. As Schneier reminds us, "the same countermeasures aimed at cyberterrorists will also prevent hackers and criminals. If organizations secure their computer networks for the wrong reasons, it will still be the right thing to do."

Chapter

7

Building Intelligence to Fight Terrorism

The Bush administration has begun to revise cold war rules governing national security information in order to counter terrorist threats to the United States. The president's homeland security plan calls for new intelligence efforts to protect the nation's borders, defend against threats within the United States, minimize infrastructure vulnerabilities, and improve emergency responses. Congress has given the new Department of Homeland Security responsibility for coordinating these strategies and assuring that accurate and complete information gets to those who need it.

BROOKINGS POLICY BRIEF SERIES

Policymakers must go further to build a new intelligence system to support transformed national security needs. Threats involving unknown perpetrators, methods, and targets cannot be countered with strategies designed for use by federal officials to combat more predictable adversaries.

Today, state and local law enforcement, public health, and emergency response personnel are on the front lines of detecting and responding to terrorist threats; corporate managers are responsible for securing key infrastructure such as energy supplies, chemical plants, and telecommunications; and workers and neighborhood residents may hold information that can help prevent attacks.

Cold war intelligence policies aimed to protect sources and methods and keep adversaries from gaining access to military secrets. To achieve these goals, defense and intelligence agencies compartmentalized acquisition, analysis, and dissemination of information, an approach that worked reasonably well as long as policymakers knew who the enemy was, what information to look for, where to look for it, and who needed to have it. Analysts became specialists and information was shared among carefully defined groups of federal officials and contractors who were specified in advance and who held appropriate security clearances based on lengthy, costly background investigations.

These policies are ill-suited to the challenge of counterterrorism. Their dual requirements of appropriate security clearance and "need to know" designation inhibit the free flow of information to and from today's diverse community of relevant federal, state, local, and private sector actors.

It is impossible to anticipate "need to know" in a world where enemies are little understood, means of attack are unpredictable, and potential targets are many, diverse, and changing. The need to cast a broad net—to gather information about threats and vulnerabilities from state and local governments and the private sector and return needed information to them—creates a heightened government responsibility to protect core values of openness and privacy.

Since September 11, 2001, the administration and Congress have adopted a number of incremental changes designed to improve the quality and integration of intelligence information. They have broadened government screening of airline passengers, foreign visitors, and imported goods, and added federal resources to state and local public health and emergency communication systems.

Incremental changes are not enough. Policymakers must build a new intelligence system to fight terrorism. The formal, hierarchical, and compartmentalized information strategies of the past need to be replaced with a new architecture featuring flexible, decentralized networks of public and private information providers, analysts, and users. Policymakers should establish procedures to assure access to critical information needed to address national security priorities while taking into account openness and privacy concerns. Public guidelines will ensure that new information strategies are consistent with these goals.

ANTI-TERRORISM INFORMATION STRATEGIES

Policymakers recognize that the intelligence system in place before September 11 failed to get the right information to the right people at the right time. As the joint House-Senate committee that investigated the 9/11 attacks observed: "Serious problems in information sharing... persisted, prior to September 11, between the Intelligence Community and relevant non-Intelligence Community agencies. This included other federal agencies as well as state and local authorities. This lack of communication and collaboration deprived those other entities, as well as the Intelligence Community, of access to potentially valuable information in the 'war' against Bin Ladin."

To date, administration and congressional efforts to reorganize national security intelligence have focused mainly on reducing barriers to sharing information among federal agencies, improving federal information technology capabilities, coordinating analysis of federal and local law enforcement and intelligence data, and supporting state and local emergency communication. At the borders, customs officials have enhanced cargo screening using radiation detectors and x-ray scanners and immigration authorities have upgraded checks on foreign visitors using improved databases. Around the country, newly expanded joint terrorism task forces bring together federal and local law enforcement officials. Terrorism investigators more easily combine law enforcement and intelligence data as permitted by the USA PATRIOT Act, which Congress passed one month after the terrorist attacks. Federal airport security officers conduct more rigorous screening of passengers under the terms of the Aviation and Transportation Security Act, enacted two months after the attacks. The new Department of Homeland Security, charged with coordinating domestic intelligence gathering and information sharing, has begun collecting data about vulnerabilities in the nation's critical infrastructure. A new Terrorist Threat Integration Center, under the supervision of the director of central intelligence, is charged with synthesizing counterterrorism intelligence from all sources.

Some of the changes have created serious concerns about potential conflicts between national security measures and principles of personal privacy and government openness. The Defense Advanced Projects Administration (DARPA), which sponsored research into data mining and pattern recognition technologies under its Terrorist Information Awareness (formally Total Information Awareness) program, was temporarily halted by Congress because the sponsors failed to address potential privacy concerns. Civil liberties advocates have challenged administration efforts to harness new information technology to screen airline passengers (the CAPPS II program) and proposals to share personal information about individuals gathered from a variety of sources authorized by the USA PATRIOT Act.

Similar concerns have arisen about conflicts with government openness, especially when secrecy has been expanded without public debate. Soon after September 11, federal agencies removed thousands of pages of public documents about the nation's infrastructure from their websites, including maps of pipeline and water supply locations and data about shipments of hazardous materials and security breaches at airports. In October 2001, Attorney General Ashcroft reversed a long-standing policy under the Freedom of Information Act (FOIA) that required agencies to disclose information unless disclosure would cause "foreseeable harm" and replaced it with one that allows agencies to keep government information secret if there is a "sound legal basis" for doing so. In March 2002, White House Chief of Staff Andrew Card ordered all agencies to adopt guidelines to prevent inappropriate disclosure of "sensitive but unclassified" information. Rejecting a bipartisan compromise, the administration supported a broad new exemption to FOIA in the Homeland Security Act for information voluntarily provided by businesses to the government about infrastructure vulnerabilities that might cause massive casualties or disruptions in a terrorist attack.

Many of these actions were couched as emergency measures—extraordinary steps to counter extraordinary threats. However, nearly two years after September 11, it is clear that they represent important building blocks for a new generation of intelligence policy. The president emphasized in his 2002 national homeland security strategy that "protecting the homeland from terrorist attack is a permanent mission."

More security issues that affect openness and privacy will be decided in the coming months. The administration will determine if additional rules are needed to shield "sensitive but unclassified" information from public view, which might include scientific research, law enforcement records, or infrastructure vulnerability reports. Policymakers have to define policies and procedures for the Terrorist Threat Integration Center as well as determine the future of the Terrorist Information Awareness and CAPPS II programs. Congress has promised to revisit the broad and controversial requirement in the Homeland Security Act that allows the government to withhold information about infrastructure vulnerabilities, and key components of the PATRIOT Act expire in 2005.

A New Intelligence Architecture

Defending against terrorism threats will require policymakers to replace the formal, hierarchical intelligence structure with a horizontal, cooperative, and fluid architecture that gets information from those who have it to those who need it through the development of virtual communities of information sources, analysts, and users. "Hard-wiring" intelligence relationships when actors, methods, and targets are uncertain impairs our ability to adapt to changing threats and vulnerabilities.

Advances in information technology can facilitate this transformation. Internet and teleconferencing technologies allow virtual communities to gather and share information in real time. Instead of focusing on central control, federal officials should spend more time setting priorities, coordinating communication, supplying technical assistance, and assuring data quality. Collecting more information from more sources will require more federal analytical capability to prevent information overload.

Assessing Information Needs

The first step in designing an intelligence system to fight terrorism while protecting openness and privacy is to understand what information is needed to support each homeland security challenge.

For example, to protect America's borders, we need more complete information about people and goods entering the country. To detect potential terrorist threats within the United States, we need to enhance traditional investigative techniques by cross-referencing databases such as airline reservation records, phone logs, and credit histories with government law enforcement, immigration, and intelligence information.

To protect critical infrastructure in areas such as agriculture, food, water, public health, emergency services, telecommunications, energy, transportation, banking, and finance, we need to map vulnerabilities against capabilities of potential terrorists, people who have access to those infrastructures, and the means available to carry out effective attacks. To respond to emergencies, we need two-way communication in real time between first responders and other officials about the extent and nature of the attack, the resources available to respond, and the risk of further terrorist action.

Guidelines for Protecting Openness and Privacy

The long-term acceptance by the American people of an enhanced intelligence effort will depend heavily on the adoption of clear, public guidelines governing the collection, retention, and dissemination of information, and the development of strong procedures for oversight and accountability. Modern information technology can play an important role in helping to implement and enforce these policies.

In principle, no one disputes that anti-terrorism measures should protect the values that anchor democratic processes and personal security in the United States. Introducing his homeland security strategy, President Bush called for protecting national security in ways that keep our fundamental values intact and cautioned that "[w]e should guard scrupulously against incursions on our freedoms, recognizing that liberty cannot exist in the absence of government restraint." He acknowledged that protecting such values might mean accepting a higher level of risk: "Because we must not permit the threat of terrorism to alter the American way of life, we have to accept some level of terrorist risk as a permanent condition."

In practice, however, policymakers must make difficult choices. Guidelines to promote security while furthering openness and privacy should be a matter of public debate and will need mid-course corrections as policymakers and analysts gain experience with new information practices and technologies. The recommendations that follow provide a framework for beginning such a deliberative process.

Emphasize information sharing. Openness can further security. Quickly identifying terrorist threats and infrastructure vulnerabilities calls for cooperative, fluid information networks. Reducing barriers to information-sharing rather than compartmentalizing secrets represents the greatest challenge in fostering such networks. State and local governments, the private sector, and the public have a central role to play in identifying suspicious activities and individuals and in finding and correcting security vulnerabilities. Sharing information about threats and infrastructure vulnerabilities enhances security by multiplying sources of information, empowering Americans to make their own choices about what risks they are prepared to accept, and creating market incentives and political pressures to reduce vulnerabilities.

On the other hand, security or commercial interests will sometimes override a presumption of openness. There may be little public benefit and considerable security risk in revealing floor plans of nuclear power plants or exact locations of military weapons or vaccine stockpiles, for example. In addition, trade secrets, which provide an underpinning for competitive enterprise, should continue to receive careful protection under federal laws.

An analogous situation occurs in the field of computer security, where software companies grapple with the question of whether to alert customers about vulnerabilities that hackers can exploit. Proponents of secrecy argue that revealing security weaknesses invites exploitation of those weaknesses. Proponents of openness argue that public knowledge helps spur solutions and provides users with information to guard against breaches. There is growing support for the idea of making programming code more accessible as a way to enhance overall security.

Maintain high hurdles for sharing personally identifiable information. Sharing personally identifiable information among commercial and government databases raises serious privacy concerns. In many cases the value of intelligence information does not depend on links to identified individuals. Sharing data about imported goods, suspected means of attack, likely targets, critical vulnerabilities, and emergency response plans raises few privacy issues. However, combining databases to screen individuals at border crossings, sharing law enforcement and intelligence information to identify suspects, "data-mining" to determine suspicious patterns of behavior, and employing commercial databases to screen airline passengers alters the patchwork of privacy protections that has been constructed over many years by private companies, Congress, and the courts. Requests to acquire and share such information should meet threshold tests:

- Intelligence architecture should be designed to minimize privacy intrusions and construct consistent technological barriers that limit users of personally identified information, restrict time periods for information-sharing, or remove personal identifiers altogether until a specified level of evidence is reached.
- Authorizations to access personal data should be subjected to rigorous substantive standards that balance the importance of national security needs against the seriousness of privacy intrusions.

- Access to data should require third party review. Depending on the seriousness of the privacy intrusion, approval could range from a signature by a high-ranking federal official to a court order.
- Data collection, analysis, and feedback should document how authorizations are used in practice, providing a basis for periodic adjustments based on experience.

Protect important secrets. While the emphasis of the new intelligence architecture needs to be on information sharing, important secrets must still be protected. In the cold war context, classifying data as top secret, secret, or confidential protected sources and methods of obtaining information and guarded military plans and capabilities.

In the homeland security context, such priorities remain important. But new areas of sensitive information—such as protecting the gene sequence of a lethal pathogen developed in a private lab—call for new approaches to limiting information access.

The traditional system of classification should be strengthened by congressional action to rationalize and update the system to reflect the new threat environment. Important as it is, the nation's protection of national security secrets remains a legal patchwork of mandates created by executive orders and presidential directives. Over time, the classification system has also suffered from overuse. More than two million individuals—mostly Defense Department officials and federal contractors—hold federal security clearances. According to the Information Security Oversight Office, an arm of the National Archives and Records Administration that oversees the classification system, federal agencies still create more than 260,000 official secrets each year and that number is increasing.

It is too early to predict the character and extent of new secrets that will be created by four agencies recently granted classification authority by President Bush (the Department of Health and Human Services, the Department of Homeland Security, the Environmental Protection Agency, and the Department of Agriculture).

Increasingly sophisticated tools can help protect sensitive information while assuring appropriate information sharing, such as "tear sheets" (unclassified versions of classified reports) and "metadata" (which can point individuals without security clearances to potentially relevant sources of information without revealing the sensitive information itself).

Conclusion

Even if policymakers are careful in defining a new structure for gathering, analyzing, and disseminating national security information, they cannot avoid difficult questions about how to improve security while furthering openness and protecting personal privacy. Vigorous public debate is essential to answering these questions. Clear guidelines, formulated in a deliberative process, can assure public confidence in new policies. Information technology can provide tools to minimize these conflicts, foster collaboration, and help assure that the right information gets to the right people at the right time. Nonetheless, missteps are inevitable. Procedures that provide accountability and oversight can assure that lessons from early experiences strengthen the nation's information strategies to fight terrorism.

Chapter

8

Reducing the Vulnerability of Public and Private Information Infrastructures

INTRODUCTION

Analysis of the effects of the terrorist attacks of September 11, 2001, suggests various "lessons learned" concerning public and private information infrastructures. What results are some insights to the range of challenges and opportunities facing policymakers as they seek to identify relevant technical solutions to homeland security concerns. This report considers these homeland security issues in the context of critical information infrastructure protection and continuity of operations (COOP) planning.

As part of the congressional and presidential efforts to develop and implement a comprehensive homeland security strategy and establish a Department of Homeland Security, the role of information technology (IT) has become an increasingly important focus. In Congress, bills have been introduced and are being actively considered in both the House of Representatives1 and the Senate2 regarding the establishment of a new department dedicated to homeland security issues.3 Although they differ on the details, the bills include provisions regarding the proposed department's organizational composition, administrative structure, and functional responsibilities. In July 2002, the President released the country's first *National Strategy for Homeland Security*, outlining the strategic objectives, critical mission areas, and initiatives in support of the Administration's proposed Department of Homeland Security. The strategic objectives include: prevent terrorist attacks within the United States; reduce America's vulnerability to terrorism; and minimize the damage and recover from attacks that do occur. Common to both the national strategy document and the proposed legislation is an emphasis on developing information sharing initiatives and fostering partnerships between and within the levels of government and the sectors of industry.

The heavy reliance upon information technology to carry out mission critical tasks and provide other citizen services highlights the need to ensure these assets are protected, backed up, and resilient to attack. Moreover, the growth of the use of electronic government (e-government) applications to conduct government-to-citizen interactions, as well as government-to-business and government-to-government transactions, has put additional pressure on the need to reconstitute systems quickly to minimize any disruptions and financial costs associated with a major infrastructure failure.5 In addition, renewed emphasis is being placed on reducing the vulnerability of the nation's critical information infrastructures while more fully integrating and utilizing public and private information technology assets.6 Taken together, these issues demonstrate the importance of ensuring the reliability and continuity of information technology systems, as part of the government's overall approach to homeland security. The accounts of successes and failures regarding how agencies and businesses responded to the September 11, 2001 attacks provide an unusual opportunity to examine options for further improving the nation's emergency preparedness.

RELEVANCE AND CONTEXT OF THE SEPTEMBER 11, 2001 ATTACKS

In addition to the destruction of buildings and the loss of life, the September 11, 2001 attacks on the World Trade Center (WTC) and the Pentagon inflicted heavy damage on elements of the country's information and communication infrastructure. This, in turn, affected how both public and private organizations were able to respond to the events of the day. First responders experienced difficulties communicating among themselves. Citizens and some governmental officials experienced problems communicating by telephone due to overloaded and destroyed circuits.

As described in the sections below, some agencies and businesses directly affected by the attacks had difficulties recovering and reestablishing data operations due to inadequate infrastructure and/ or the lack of backup systems. Faced with an overloaded telecommunications system, many turned to the Internet, which continued to function as designed, to send and receive e-mail messages regarding the safety of family, friends, and colleagues. However, even in areas not directly affected by the attacks, citizens and government employees sometimes found a dearth of information because some agencies shut down Web sites or did not use them to provide information regarding available resources and instructions on when and where to report for work.

For example, it was reported that as of nearly 48 hours after they occurred, neither the General Services Administration (GSA) or the Central Intelligence Agency (CIA) had posted any information regarding the terrorist attacks. It was also reported that of the Office of Personnel Management (OPM) shut down its Web site due to concerns related to cyberterrorism.

It is important to note that many of the technology-related problems that emerged from the September attacks have less to do with the capabilities of the technology itself than with how it was implemented.

For example, phone lines can be disrupted, so organizations with critical functions need to secure redundant, but separate, means to communicate. Data can be stored and sent nearly anywhere, but agencies need to establish protocols for regularly backing up important information to secure, remote centers. The mixed performance of information infrastructures suggests that both the public and private sectors need to reexamine their information planning and practices so that they can better weather and rebound from catastrophic events. The damage sustained by two important economic and military locations, combined with ongoing efforts to restore services and prepare contingency plans, also raise questions regarding the federal government's role and the private sector's ability to ensure the protection and continuity of the country's information infrastructure (e.g., telecommunications, computer networks, Internet, etc.) in the future.

Nearly a year after the attacks, many organizations are still evaluating the strengths and weaknesses of their information technology resources in the face of such unusual circumstances. It is likely that the full extent of the damage to information technology resources will not be made public due to concerns about national security and business continuity. Traditionally, both public and private sector organizations have been very reluctant to reveal publicly the extent to which their operations are affected by computer viruses and worms, hacker attacks, or similar security weaknesses. This reluctance to share information occurs for two primary reasons. The first is the interest in maintaining the confidence of customers/ constituents, and, by extension, in the case of publicly traded companies, maintaining market value.

The second reason is concern over being identified as a target for future attacks, and the possibility of revealing (unwittingly or not) other vulnerabilities. However, despite the validity of these concerns, the reluctance to share information with the appropriate actors can serve as an impediment to recovery and prevention planning by further embedding potential weaknesses into the information infrastructure the country has become increasingly dependent upon.

Despite the imperfect nature of the information available, a number of lessons learned can be identified and are discussed below. To place these lessons in context, the next section provides a brief synopsis of how the public and private information infrastructures performed and were affected in the wake of the initial destruction and the immediate reaction by individuals, businesses, and the federal government.

SUMMARY OF THE EVENTS AND IMPACT OF SEPTEMBER 11, 2001

Due to the evolving nature of available information, it is not possible to provide a comprehensive accounting of all the organizations affected by the terrorist attacks. However, a variety of examples are discussed in context to provide a sense of the range of issues facing the public and private sectors as they seek to implement new initiatives. One means to gain an overall sense of the immediate impact of the September 11, 2001 attacks is to consider how people and organizations communicated.

The attacks spurred a tremendous spike in telephone calls that overloaded the capacity of some networks. Verizon normally handles 115 million calls per day in New York City and 35 million in Washington, DC, for a normal daily total of 150 million calls. Following the attacks, the combined total jumped to 340 million calls. Similarly, Cingular Wireless said its call volume jumped 400%. Requests were made to international telecommunications carriers, such as France Telecom, to control the flow of calls to the United States in an effort to keep trans-Atlantic links open.9 Many people turned to cellphone-based text messaging, Internet-based instant messaging, and the use of two-way radio features of cellphones to get around the congested phone networks. AOL reported a 20% jump in instant messaging volume, handling 1.2 billion messages on September 11, 2001.

The National Communications System (NCS) activated the Government Emergency Telecommunications Service (GETS). Using a special phone number and a personal identification number, GETS calls receive priority handling before all other calls on phone lines operated by ATT, Sprint, and WorldCom. During the week following the attacks, 3,000 GETS calls were made in Washington. An additional 4,000 GETS calls to and from Manhattan were completed with a 95% success rate.

The General Services Administration (GSA) also provided mobile communications centers that supported several agencies, including the Federal Bureau of Investigation (FBI). In addition, the GSA Federal Technology Service (FTS) made 500 computers available to agencies within the first two days of the attacks. Many agencies used their Web sites to keep the public informed and provide information on how to help the victims. One of those was the Federal Emergency Management Agency (FEMA) Web site. FEMA was one of the first agencies to post information about the attacks on the morning of September 11, 2001. On September 12, the FEMA site had 3.4 million visitors, an all-time high for the agency. GSA used its site to notify people about the status of various governmental buildings. Many agencies, including the Department of Defense, used their sites to keep employees informed of changes. Some Members of Congress, including Senators Charles Schumer and Hillary Rodham Clinton of New York, and Senator George Allen of Virginia, also turned their congressional sites into information centers regarding the attacks.

FirstGov's Web staff, who were evacuated from their Washington, DC, offices, worked at home immediately following the attacks, collecting information, phone numbers, and URLs for relevant sites. They posted this information to the FirstGov site on September 12. Many commercial news sites and other government sites then posted links to the FirstGov site15, helping drive 448,552 unique visitors accounting for 1.75 million page hits during the week of September 9-15. FirstGov also changed its site update schedule from every two weeks to updating it every 12 hours.

NEW YORK - THE WORLD TRADE CENTER

At 8:45 AM, American Airlines Flight 11 crashed into the north tower of the World Trade Center. Eighteen minutes later, United Airlines Flight 175 crashed into the south tower. The eventual collapse of both towers inflicted heavy damage to the surrounding buildings and infrastructure, ultimately resulting in the collapse of other buildings on the site and the deaths of nearly 3,000 people. The attacks displaced large numbers of both public and private sector employees. The World Trade Center contained an estimated

430 tenants with 50,000 employees (not all present at the time of the attack), and typically received another 140,000 visitors on a daily basis.

According to the General Services Administration (GSA), more than 2,800 federal employees worked in offices leased by the GSA in Buildings 6 and 7 of the World Trade Center complex. Building 6 had over 2,000 federal employees from a variety of agencies, including the Customs Service, Bureau of Alcohol, Tobacco, and Firearms (ATF), the Occupational Safety and Health Administration (OSHA), the Export-Import Bank, the Foreign Commercial Service of the Department of Commerce, and the Pension and Welfare Benefits Administration of the Labor Department. Among the tenants of Building 7 were 760 federal employees from agencies including the Secret Service, the Equal Employment Opportunity Commission (EEOC), the Department of Defense, and the Internal Revenue Service (IRS). Another 25,000 federal employees were evacuated from four nearby buildings; 26 Federal Plaza, 290 Broadway, 40 Centre Street, and 500 Pearl Street.

The attacks also inflicted heavy damage on elements of the city's information and communication infrastructure, including both land lines and wireless services. One switching facility, which handled 40% of the lower Manhattan phone lines and 20% of the New York Stock Exchange's (NYSE) traffic, was damaged when steel beams from a collapsing building punctured the switching station, flooding it with water and debris. A second switching facility, which normally handles 80% of the NYSE's 15,000 phone and data lines, did not suffer direct damage, but was rendered inoperable by intermittent power outages.

In addition, several wireless cell sites were destroyed and others were rendered inactive by power outages. Communication between the New York Fire Department, the Emergency Medical Systems (EMS), and the New York Police Department were also cut off due to the loss of an antenna that had been on 1 World Trade Center.22 By January 2002, Verizon had restored service to 99% of the affected area. Local television stations were also affected. Nearly all of the broadcasters had their main antennas located on the roof of the north tower of the World Trade Center.

Two stations had backup antennas on the Empire State Building, allowing their signals to still be received by most citizens who were not wired for cable television. The other broadcasters had to utilize towers in more distant locations, such as Alpine, NJ, where they could only reach portions of the New York metropolitan area. As of late June 2002, broadcasters were continuing to work with lawmakers to try to identify a new site for a common tower that would be located within the 3.2 mile radius of the World Trade Center site, necessary to reach the local residents while not interfering with broadcasts in Philadelphia or Boston.

VIRGINIA - THE PENTAGON

At 9:38 AM, American Airlines Flight 77 crashed into the west face of the Pentagon, killing 64 passengers on board and 125 additional people on the ground. The crash and ensuing fire destroyed an estimated 10% of the Pentagon's office space, and reportedly disrupted one of the Pentagon's two major communications lines.25 The Navy lost 70% of its Pentagon offices, including a portion of the Navy's budget office, the Office of the Chief of Naval Operations, and its telecommunications operation center. The U.S. Army's Information Management Support Center also received significant damage, losing most of its desktop computers, its entire central help desk, and apparently was unable to access its backup tapes. In addition, the Defense Finance and Accounting Service was damaged. *Computerworld* magazine suggested that many of the Navy's top-secret network operations were probably damaged, although it was believed to be unlikely that this affected the Navy's ability to communicate sensitive information to Navy vessels.

The attack on the Pentagon caused the loss of knowledge assets, including hard copies and data on workstations and servers that were not duplicated or backed up and stored in a different physical location, according to media reports. It is not clear how much information may have been permanently lost or to what degree a lack of backed up information hampered efforts to continue the operations of the affected offices.

One office that was able to resume its functions quickly was the Defense Finance and Accounting Office, which maintains servers located in Ohio. Also, the Navy was able to utilize its recently signed Navy Marine Corp Intranet (NMCI) contract to assist its efforts to resume operations. Using the NMCI contract, the Navy relocated approximately 1,000 of its displaced personnel to temporary offices in Arlington, VA, and had 860 laptop computers, 335 desktop computers, and 30 servers, routers, and cabling delivered and installed in just over one week. The Navy's Budget Office, which was in the middle of preparing its budget that was due October 6 when the attacks occurred, lost part of its server farm. However, it had 50 computers and its server farm restored by Sunday, September 16. Efforts to reconstruct and repair the 400,000 square feet of damaged Pentagon offices, dubbed Project Phoenix, have progressed rapidly, with the first group of people moving back into their rebuilt offices on August 15, 2002.

Lessons Learned

In the months following September 11, 2001, there have been a number of accounts of successes, failures, and 'lessons learned' regarding continuity and disaster recovery planning. In many cases, these descriptions are specific to a particular organization or business activity. However, one can identify some observations and lessons learned that are widely applicable and that policymakers and business leaders may wish to consider as they develop and implement new homeland security initiatives.

Continuity of operations (COOP) and disaster recovery planning are not new concepts. However, surveys have shown that only about half of American businesses have disaster management plans in place. In many cases, past threats are often the motivating influences for organizations to make these plans. For example, Morgan Stanley, one of the tenants in the south tower of the World Trade Center, adopted thorough plans in response to bomb threats being made during the Persian Gulf War in 1991, and reinforced those plans following the 1993 bombing of the World Trade Center. The financial services firm's regular evacuation drills are credited as one of the reasons why nearly all of its approximately 3,500 employees were able to escape before the buildings collapsed.

In the case of information technology disaster recovery planning, preparation for the year 2000 transition (Y2k) has been cited by a number of private and public sector organizations as one of the main reasons they were able to respond and recover quickly from the September 11, 2001, attacks. Y2k planning began substantially in the 1990s, led primarily by the private sector and followed by federal and state government agencies. Y2k preparation spurred many organizations to operationalize strategies for backing up data, enabling remote working, and enhancing communication links between organizations, employees, customers, and vendors. Many tenants of the World Trade Center also cited the 1993 bombing of the building as their rationale for having developed extensive disaster recovery plans, which they, in turn, attributed to their success in evacuating employees and preserving vital data.

The amount of time and resources spent on information technology disaster planning can vary with the size and type of organization. According to the Gartner Group, a research and advisory firm, an average company allocates approximately three percent of its annual information technology budget to disaster recovery. In contrast, financial services companies, which have to meet requirements set by the Federal Reserve Board and/or the Securities and Exchange Commission (SEC), spend an average of seven to eight percent.

However, if it may seem costly to dedicate a significant portion of one's budget to planning for an event with a low chance of occurring, the financial consequences for being unprepared can be even higher. In the case of financial companies, many, if not most, had invested in data backup and disaster recovery facilities to one degree or another. While this allowed them to save a significant amount of customer and business-critical data, it is estimated that these firms will still spend $3-5 billion over the next two years to replace their destroyed information technology infrastructure.39 For example, Dow Jones Inc., a global financial news company and publisher of *The Wall Street Journal* and Barron's publications, was expected to spend $2 million to replace information technology hardware and office equipment.40 Although it had relatively few offices in or around the World Trade Center and a portion of the affected area of the Pentagon was not occupied, the federal government will also be spending a significant amount to replace lost and damaged information technology systems. Input, a Web-based information technology market research and marketing services firm, predicted that the federal government will spend $75 million, with the Customs Service alone expected to account for $15 million of that amount. While information technology disaster recovery planning is often compared to the preparations for Y2k, it is important to recognize that these scenarios are qualitatively different. Y2k had a finite time line with a clear indicator of success or failure. In contrast, the war on terrorism appears to be an open-ended and evolving process. As the examples below demonstrate, measures of success are relative, and the task of planning is never truly done. The lessons learned today can help prepare for tomorrow, but they do not represent the final word on information technology disaster recovery planning.

LESSONS REGARDING CONTINUITY AND RECOVERY PLANNING AND PRACTICES

The events of September 11, 2001, have brought a new urgency to continuity and recovery planning and practices. While attention has been growing over time, this multifaceted undertaking can often be a very challenging and frustrating process as planners try to coordinate disparate parts of their organizations while trying to strike a balance between how much they *cannot* afford to be unprepared and how much they can afford to spend on resources they may never use. Further complicating matters has been the tendency for organizations to "stovepipe" the different protections relevant to information technology disaster recovery planning. For example, information security has often been handled independently from physical security. Similarly, the compartmentalization of an organization's units and processes can contribute to a fractured planning process that can leave an organization vulnerable.

One reported example indicating the possible costs and consequences when an organization does not have a fully integrated plan is the May Davis Group. The privately held financial services company had its offices on the 87th floor of one of the World Trade Center towers. In addition to losing $100,000 of equipment, the firm apparently lost some regulatory documents and $1 million in revenue due to data loss and downtime.

A less severe example is the Secret Service field office, located in 7 World Trade Center, which did have a contingency plan, but had not fully implemented it at the time of the attack. The agency's field office was able to resume operations the following day at an alternative location. It reportedly lost some of the information it was collecting on criminal suspects.

Another example is Deloitte Consulting, whose primary telecommunications hub in New York City, located in the World Financial Center next to the World Trade Center towers, was put out of service, affecting an estimated one thousand employees in the area. As a consulting firm, Deloitte considers its ability to share information with clients to be its core business. During the weeks it took to rebuild its land line communication center, Deloitte's New York area employees used cell phones to stay in contact with customers and fellow employees.

Even organizations that have planned extensively can sometimes overlook small details that appear insignificant, but later prove to be important. One such example is American International Group (AIG) Inc. The financial services company has offices and information technology operations near the World Trade Center site. Using its backup business center in Parsippany, NJ, and a second previously contracted emergency facility in Livingston, NJ, AIG was able to use data from its automated backup system to be operational the day after the attacks. However, not all of its servers were part of the automated backup system, and the backup tapes for these servers reportedly were left behind when its building was evacuated.

Augment Disaster Recovery Plans

In many respects, the September 11, 2001, attacks established a new standard for disaster recovery plans – the complete destruction and loss of a building. Even among some of the most prepared organizations, their plans sometimes presumed the ability to eventually return to their offices, even if only to retrieve equipment and paper files. Modern fire safety and construction methods have largely made the possibility of a building collapse less likely, so many organizations developed plans that focused on the movement of data to be used temporarily at a backup facility. These same businesses and agencies must now consider whether to augment their disaster recovery plans to include the movement of people, the rapid acquisition of equipment and furniture, network connectivity, adequate workspace, and more.

Some organizations may need to be able to not just store, but also to run mission critical applications, at their backup sites, and staff may need to be trained to implement such a plan. The possible need for more sophisticated data backup facilities suggests organizations may consider establishing a 'hot site'. A hot site is a facility that has all of the data, equipment, software, connectivity, furniture, and office space assembled and ready to use so that an organization can continue its computer operations uninterrupted in the event of a disaster. In some cases, organizations will mirror their data directly to the hot site as an additional backup or in lieu of using backup tapes at the primary site. While hot sites provide the greatest amount of redundancy and readiness, the cost of establishing and maintaining such a site can cost millions of dollars, with additional yearly maintenance costs. This raises cost effectiveness issues. Some hot sites, however, might serve a dual purpose, such as a secondary data site or as part of a comprehensive backup system.

Organizations with more detailed recovery plans were often able to respond better to the events of September 11, 2001. In the case of the Occupational Safety and Health Administration (OSHA), the 21-member office had a contingency plan for its contingency plan. After evacuating, the OSHA employees discovered their first designated meeting site was inaccessible, so they regrouped at a nearby regional office. After this office was evacuated, they gathered at a third site to implement their plan to provide advice and technical assistance to businesses and agencies in an effort to protect workers from being exposed to hazardous substances and other safety risks at ground zero.

A second example is the New York Board of Trade (NYBOT), which handles trading for commodities such as coffee, sugar, and orange juice. NYBOT had invested in a hot site in Queens, NY, which included limited space for a reduced number of trading pits. According to one report, NYBOT had invested $1.75 million to establish the facility, which cost an additional $300,000 per year to maintain. However, while an extended outage would have resulted in the rapid loss of trading contracts to other exchanges in the United States and abroad, NYBOT's investment paid off, allowing it to resume modified trading operations one day after the attacks.

A corollary to this lesson learned is the need to assure that recovery procedures are well documented and safeguarded. Employees need to be well-informed and practiced for the responsibilities they are expected to carry out. Correspondingly, just as one would not keep the sole backup tapes of important information at the primary data center in which they were created, a prudent step would be to keep one or more copies of the recovery plans available at the appropriate off-site locations.

Backing Up Data *and* Backing Up Applications

A second lesson learned that is related to continuity and disaster planning and practices is the need to have a comprehensive backup system that captures more than just an organization's data files. As discussed above, most of the financial services firms in or near the World Trade Center had comprehensive data management and recovery systems in place. Some highly automated systems will begin backing up data to a remote center when a significant temperature change or power loss in the building is detected. Cantor Fitzgerald, one of the hardest hit financial services companies, losing 733 of its approximately 1,000 World Trade Center employees, including 150 information technology workers, lost none of its data due to a system that mirrored all of its software and data to its data center in Rochelle Park, NJ. In contrast, the U.S. Customs Service was not as well prepared. In addition to experiencing difficulties finding alternative office space for its 800 displaced employees, the office located in the World Trade Center complex did not have all of its files backed up to computers in its Washington, DC, headquarters. Several months after the attack, the Customs Service reportedly was still working to re-create some of its files from scratch while others are considered permanently lost.

In addition to backing up data, organizations also need to backup the data catalogs, directories, and software applications used with the data. Organizations that saved only their raw data had to spend a significant amount of time re-creating their applications, organizing the data, and reestablishing user permissions to access the data. One company that apparently experienced this problem was NYBOT.

Despite its extensive hot site contingency plan, NYBOT lost some financial records, applications, and e-mail files that were not backed up to the site. Some of this information was backed up to tapes, but the tapes were stored in a fireproof safe kept in their World Trade Center tower office.

In addition to taking a broader view of the digital tools and assets to backup and preserve, organizations – such as regulatory agencies and insurance companies – that still rely heavily on paper files may wish to consider digitizing some of their documents as they are received. Despite much touting of the so-called paperless office, the blizzard of paper that accompanied the dust and debris with the collapse of the towers suggests many organizations are still heavily dependent on their physical documents. However, the high cost of digital imaging requires companies and agencies to consider carefully which documents are most critical and often used. One company that did have a comprehensive digital imaging system in place before September 11, 2001, was Empire Blue Cross Blue Shield. Developed over the past ten years, starting with claims forms, the insurance carrier's optical storage system captures almost all of its paper documents. As a result, the company lost only about two days' worth of paper mail.

One company that decided to accelerate its plans to digitize and automate its paper-based information is Kemper Casualty Company, which had offices on the 35th and 36th floors of One World Trade Center. The Kemper data backup system had all but the previous day's and that morning's data backed up on tape at its headquarters. It was also able to re-create the lost transactions for the missing data. However, according to media reports, Kemper lost thousands of paper documents, including innumerable insurance policy applications. The company had to spend a significant amount of time and resources to re-create the information by going back to customers and Kemper agents.

The Securities and Exchange Commission, whose New York regional office was located in 7 World Trade Center, also did not digitize its paper records. While the regulatory agency did have a significant amount of its data and files backed up electronically, case files that took years to compile, informal notes written down from interviews and analysis, and other documents were lost. Some of these lost records reportedly were part of pending cases, including those related to investigations of insider trading and financial fraud. While the SEC can have parties submit new copies of documents previously provided, and it may be able to obtain some documents from agencies conducting parallel investigations, documents and other evidence from older cases and smaller companies that are not in operation any longer may be difficult to recover. The loss and reconstruction of the files may slow down the progress of some investigations and possibly result in others being discontinued.

A corollary to the lessons learned regarding comprehensive data storage plans is the need to fully and regularly test backup sites and media. Organizations that rely on 'cold sites' – backup sites that are not always in use and may require the organization to install hardware, software, or load data to become functional – in the event of a disaster, could experience further problems if they discover their tapes are corrupted or equipment does not work. One organization that regularly tested its backup systems and information was NYBOT. The exchange tested its backup site monthly and practiced its recovery plan every 60 days to assure its systems were working and its employees were familiar with the procedures.

Lessons Regarding Decentralization

A second major category of lessons learned concerns the decentralization of operations and the effectiveness of distributed communications. The rise of networked computing and the Internet has provided the opportunity to connect farflung locations around the country and the world. Many public and private sector organizations have used this technology to reach outward to new markets, deliver new services, and reduce communications costs. However, the lessons learned discussed below suggest there is also a need for organizations to turn this technology inward to reduce the vulnerabilities of internal operations and to strengthen communications links with internal, as well as external, constituencies.

Decentralize Operations

The maxim, 'don't put all of your eggs in one basket,' can be applied to a variety of situations: college applications, job searches, and investment portfolios. It can also be applied to the structure and location of an organization's operations. Although many of the tenants and neighbors of the World Trade Center had backup facilities, some of these facilities were located within a few blocks of their primary location, resulting in the loss, or at least the inaccessibility, of data at both sites when it was needed most. According to some industry experts, recovery sites should be located at least 20-50 miles way from the primary data center. In addition, some observers suggest that human resources should also be located in more than one spot to reduce the potential for losing a significant portion of one's workforce in a single event.

As was mentioned above, Cantor Fitzgerald lost 733 of its employees, including 150 of its information technology workers. However, despite this devastating loss, the firm was able to continue its operations in part by relying on employees in its other offices to assume some of the responsibilities of its World Trade Center office.63 Another company that benefitted from decentralization was Blackwood Trading LLC. The brokerage firm's offices were located six blocks from the World Trade Center, part of the area that lost power and communications service, but it mirrored all of its data at a remote site in Jersey City, NJ. It purposely chose a site physically distant from its offices to reduce the chance of a complete loss of data in the event of a terrorist attack or a natural disaster.64

Since September 11, 2001, several other firms have decided to heed the decentralization lesson. One of those organizations is Dow Jones. It had maintained offices at One World Financial Center, adjacent to the World Trade Center, which served as a hub for 800 employees and its data production center. While the damage to the building was not significant enough to prevent its eventual repair and reoccupation, the damage did render approximately 100 servers, 400 workstations, and an estimated "millions of dollars" of the company's networking equipment inoperable. As part of its new strategy to reduce its vulnerability, Dow Jones reportedly decided to permanently move the company's data center to its backup facilities in South Brunswick, NJ, and move only half of its employees back to its Manhattan location. The financial information company plans to rely on a network of news and data centers distributed around the country. It will also rely more heavily on remote offices, encourage telecommuting, and establish a new backup facility distant from its South Brunswick data center.

Empire Blue Cross Blue Shield, which benefitted significantly from its extensive backup system, has also decided to decentralize the 1,900 employees from its World Trade Center offices into three different facilities. In addition to spreading the risk, the insurance carrier also observed that it is easier to conduct a data recovery operation for a smaller portion of its operations as compared to the larger whole in the event of a disaster.

ENSURE THE ABILITY TO COMMUNICATE WITH INTERNAL AND EXTERNAL Constituencies

Another lesson learned related to decentralization is the need to ensure the ability to communicate with internal and external constituencies in the event of an emergency. The attacks of September 11, 2001, forced many companies to rely on ad hoc networks to communicate with employees. The overload of telecommunications networks, including cellular voice networks, left many people scrambling to find a way to get messages out. Some have suggested relying on wireless data backup systems as an alternative to voice networks in the case of an emergency. One such network that proved useful for many people is a data network, which is used to support the BlackBerry pager, a mobile e-mail and paging device.

In the weeks following the attacks, the Committee on House Administration supplied BlackBerry devices and monthly service to all 435 Members. Demand for BlackBerry pager devices by other federal agencies has jumped dramatically since September 11, 2001.

Most organizations are aware of the importance of communications with external constituencies: citizens and customers. In the case of government agencies, this function is becoming associated with electronic government. Many people searching for information and guidance during the uncertainty that followed the attacks turned to corporate and agency Web sites. However, the performance of these sites was mixed. Some sites immediately transformed themselves into centers for crisis information, while others were shut down altogether. The Office of Personnel Management (OPM) initially shut down its Web site citing cyber attack concerns. The site was brought back online late in the afternoon of September 11, 2001, with the announcement that agencies in Washington, DC would be open the next day. The Federal Aviation Administration's (FAA) Web site was also offline for a significant portion of the day.

The Department of Defense used its DefenseLink site to provide information and pictures about the attack on the Pentagon. DefenseLink, the Defense Department's main Web site, experienced a 243% increase in page hits the week following the attacks. In order to handle the increased traffic, DoD tripled the sites' bandwidth capacity. Other sites that experienced surges in Web traffic included the FBI, the Department of Justice, and FirstGov.

FEMA regularly updated its Web site with information. The number of visitors to the FEMA site demonstrates the expectations of citizens to be able to find information online. FEMA normally has 500,000 visitors to its site every day. On September 11, 2001, that number soared to 2.3 million. FirstGov was a bit slower in responding, but, by late in the day of September 12, had cobbled together a page providing links to information from a variety of federal, state, and local agencies, as well as non-governmental organizations helping with the crisis. The FBI established a special site to collect tips about the terrorists. Of the 80,000 tips reportedly received within the first five days of the attack, more than half, or 47,052, were received via the Web site. Following the anthrax incidents, the Centers for Disease Control Web site also experienced a notable increase in visitors.

LESSONS REGARDING REDUNDANCY AND PLANNING OF COMMUNICATIONS

The third category of lessons learned involves the institutionalization of redundancy in information infrastructures. Redundancy, as used here, includes having computer or network system components, including hardware, software, and telecommunications links, installed and ready to use as a backup in the event primary resources fail. A related aspect of redundancy is the ability to replace and/or reconstruct hardware and software quickly and easily when necessary to prevent extended periods of downtime.

Employment of Redundant Service Providers

Redundancy, or the lack thereof, proved to be critical to many agencies and businesses in lower Manhattan. As described earlier, most of the area's telecommunications lines were connected through two primary switching stations, one of which was destroyed and the other rendered useless due to a lack of electricity. Some organizations that thought they had redundant connections by contracting with two different service providers discovered that both providers used the same central switching office, leaving the organization without service. Approximately 40 of the competitive local exchange carriers in the area relied on Verizon's 140 West Street facility to provide their services.

One group of businesses that did not lose access to their data networks were the tenants of the New York Information Technology Center, an office building located at 55 Broad Street in Manhattan, six blocks from the World Trade Center. Among the services provided by the building's management company is a full telecommunications infrastructure served by 14 voice and data carriers. As a result, it was reported that none of the tenants lost access to their data networks, and the few tenants who did use Verizon's voice services were able to switch to another of the building's providers within 24 hours.

Two other companies that had redundant networks were Lehman Brothers and Empire Blue Cross Blue Shield. Lehman Brothers, which had offices both in and around the World Trade Center, had fully redundant networks in Manhattan and in Jersey City, NJ, along with duplicative wide-area links that kept all 45 of its branches connected. Empire Blue Cross Blue Shield, whose backup system was referred to earlier, also had multiple voice and data carriers that connected its World Trade Center offices to its redundant data centers outside of Manhattan, which allowed the insurance carrier to continue to serve its 4.5 million customers. Once its new building in Brooklyn is completed, the insurance carrier plans to install satellite receivers on the roof so it can transmit data between facilities worldwide. In addition to being a less expensive alternative to using several high speed land lines, the satellite receivers will also enable the company to continue to transmit data in the event that the city's land line infrastructure experiences a disruption.

Use of Generic Replaceable Technology

A related lesson that some organizations have cited as valuable to their ability to rebuild their systems quickly is the use of generic, replaceable technology. Agencies and financial firms faced with the need to rebuild their systems quickly — in some cases, in a matter of days — received a significant amount of support from many of the major technology vendors, including, but not limited to, Compaq, Dell, IBM, and Sun Microsystems. Drawing from their existing stock of equipment, and ramping up production, the vendors were able to supply large amounts of equipment on short notice. Several information technology companies donated equipment and services to federal agencies in Virginia and New York to assist with recovery efforts. Many vendors also provided discounts, sometimes as high as 80%, for their commercial clients.80 Vendor support also came in the form of emergency help desk support, cross-country equipment deliveries, and on-site technical support. For example, IBM helped Empire Blue Cross Blue Shield replace over 2,200 desktops and 413 laptops, while Compaq replaced the insurance carrier's 256 servers. Dell and Compaq also provided the American Red Cross with desktops, laptops, servers, and other equipment to assist with the relief efforts. Based on the experience of September 11, 2001, the ability to replace equipment quickly with easy-to-find products that do not require significant customization is likely to be one of the factors affecting organizations' future continuity and disaster recovery planning decisions.

Future Considerations

Although there are undoubtedly additional lessons learned from the September 11, 2001 attacks, the lessons highlighted in the previous pages provide a broad sense of the breadth and depth of the issues facing public and private sector organizations. While not all-inclusive, they emphasize three general approaches: the establishment and practice of comprehensive continuity and recovery plans, the decentralization of operations, and the development of system redundancies to eliminate single points of weakness. The lessons learned from September 11, 2001 build, in part, upon the lessons learned from the 1993 World Trade Center bombing and the preparation for the Y2k transition. However, as agencies and businesses move ahead with continuity planning and implementation, there are indicators that the character of this preparation is changing.

EMPHASIS ON BUSINESS CONTINUITY OVER DISASTER RECOVERY

One change is that the new lessons learned appear to represent the shift to a higher standard of continuity and disaster recovery planning. Comprehensive contingency plans, perhaps once viewed, at the least, as optional and, at the most, as a prudent measure, may now be seen as an integral part of developing and maintaining an organization's information technology infrastructure. Once considered a remote possibility, the permanent loss of a facility, while still unlikely, must now be taken more seriously. Consequently, an increasing number of organizations, including small and mid-sized companies who often have more limited resources, have begun to focus not just on disaster recovery, but on business continuity. In a networked economy, the costs of network downtime can be measured in tens of thousands of dollars per hour, and as high as one million dollars per hour for highly technology-dependent entities such as infrastructure services firms and energy companies. Other concerns, such as the loss of electricity, the increased frequency of computer viruses, and high-profile hacking attempts have also spurred many organizations to focus on comprehensive business continuity planning rather than disaster recovery alone. In addition to these higher standards, there is also greater recognition of the qualitative change in preparation. Whereas some organizations may have felt their Y2k readiness measures provided adequate protection, there is now a greater realization that continuity and disaster recovery planning is an open-ended and evolving process, requiring reinforced and redundant infrastructures, regular practice exercises, and testing of data backups and systems. For example, the Pentagon, which already had contingency plans in place, has since embarked on its Command Communications Survivability Project in an effort to redesign its information technology contingency plans.86 In Congress, Senator Ted Stevens introduced an amendment (SA 2450) to the Department of Defense Appropriations Act, 2002 (P.L. 107-117) on December 7, 2001 that would have required agencies to have "redundant and physically separate" telecommunications systems in an attempt to maintain the operability of communications of government offices in the event of an attack or catastrophe. The amendment passed on a voice vote in the Senate but did not pass in the House of Representatives.

INFORMATION SHARING AND COLLABORATION

Another change is the potential for increased information sharing between federal, state, and local government, as well as between the public and private sectors. While information sharing figures prominently in plans for law enforcement-related homeland security activities, it also may play an important role in continuity planning and critical information infrastructure protection. For example, the Chief Information Officers (CIO) Council, which serves as an interagency forum for the CIOs of thirty federal departments and agencies, decided to include a representative from the National Association of State Chief Information Officers (NASCIO) in its activities. In addition to collaborating on issues such as interoperability in wireless communications and electronic government initiatives, several state CIOs are working with the Office of Homeland Security on efforts to protect against terrorism.

Another example is Operation Dark Screen, initiated by Representative Ciro Rodriguez. The three-phase exercise will be conducted over several months during 2002 and 2003 as a partnership between federal, state, and local government, and the private sector. It is designed to test the partners' preparedness to protect critical infrastructures from cyberattacks. There are plans to conduct both a tabletop and a live exercise, as well as an opportunity to implement new protections based on the outcomes of the exercises. As activities such as Operation Dark Screen are carried out, and organizations continue to rebuild and reinforce their information technology assets, it is anticipated that further lessons learned will be added, providing a fuller assessment of our state of readiness, and guidance for the development of future homeland security initiatives.

Chapter

9

Counter-terrorism and the National Security of African States

Africa's recognition of the threat of terrorism to the continent has culminated in the galvanisation of national, regional and international efforts towards counter-terrorism. By addressing the safety of citizens, protection of territorial integrity and preservation of the primacy of states, these efforts converge with the classical demands of the national security of African states. However, certain practical fallouts from the implementation of these measures - such as human rights abuses - diverge from the overarching purpose of national security of states and undermine national cohesion and democratic principles. This article juxtaposes post-9/11 counter-terrorism efforts in Africa and the national security of African states arguing that more effective implementation strategies supporting counter-terrorism initiatives in Africa will not only help rid the continent of terrorist activities and associated threats but also help combat other criminal aspects of African society and security threats. However, if the drivers of Africa's counter-terrorism agenda do not steer initiatives clear of parochial politics and religion, the security of African states will be undermined by counter-terrorism.

INTRODUCTION

"African countries have long espoused the imperative need to combat and eradicate the phenomenon of terrorism .... In their collective resolve and determination to deal with a common threat, Member States of the Union have

adopted instruments and decisions creating a common framework for the prevention and combating of terrorism in Africa." – Alpha Oumar Konaré, Chairperson of the AU Commission.

"Internationally, we are seeing an increasing use of what I call the "T-word" – terrorism to demonize political opponents, to throttle freedom of speech and the press, and to delegitimize legitimate political grievances ..." - Former Secretary-General Kofi Annan.

Mindful of the threat terrorism poses to Africa, African states even before the 9/11 attacks had made commendable strides towards preventing and combating terrorism on the continent. This is starkly evidenced by the 1999 Algiers Convention which represents a common continental framework for the prevention and combating of terrorism in Africa. Notwithstanding the framework, post-9/11 security realities and the resultant demands of the United Nations (UN) Resolution 1373, revitalised the continent's efforts and harnessed international support for counter-terrorism initiatives on the continent.

The renewed African efforts and international support have culminated in the (1) designing of legal instruments to facilitate action against terrorism, and (2) the institution of operational measures to prevent, deter and combat terrorist activities on the continent. Countries such as Uganda, Tanzania, Mauritius, Gambia and South Africa have subsequently succeeded in enacting counter-terrorism legislation, whilst others such as Egypt, Tunisia, Libya, Algeria and Morocco have argued that their existing criminal codes can sufficiently deal with the situation.

In addition, operational measures aimed at reducing vulnerabilities and eliminating threats of terrorism through border surveillance and control, prevention of money laundering, and the prevention of falsification of travel documents have become mainstream elements of various national, regional and continental counter-terrorism approaches. In this direction many African countries including Algeria, Nigeria, Ghana, Ethiopia, Kenya, Senegal and South Africa have taken steps to standardise the application requirements and safety features of national identity documents such as passports, national identity cards as a way of preventing falsification and forgery.

In addition to these efforts, many internationally-supported programmes such as the Pan Sahel Initiative (PSI); Trans-Sahel Counterterrorism Initiative (TSCTI); the Joint Task Force-Horn of Africa (JTFHOA); the East Africa Counterterrorism Initiative (EACTI); and the African Union's (AU) terrorism prevention initiatives coordinated by its Terrorism Prevention Branch have all been implemented on the continent.

These initiatives, though diverse, fundamentally aim at denying terrorists of havens, eradicating sources of terrorist financing, reducing state vulnerability, and enhancing emergency preparedness and response capabilities with the ultimate goal of preserving the territorial integrity and sovereignty of the state, and ensuring the safety of citizens. In this pursuit, counter-terrorism initiatives glaringly converge with the broader goal of national security policy of African states. Nevertheless, practical fallouts in the execution of counter-terrorism in Africa give ample evidence of politicisation and 'religionisation' by parochial political entities for settling political scores. In many cases, this has resulted in wanton human right abuses under the guise of fighting terrorists and national saboteurs which are undoubtedly at variance with the overarching purpose of national security policy.

Against the background of these two sides to the counter-terrorism agenda in Africa, this paper juxtaposes counter-terrorism and the national security of states in Africa. The paper will also highlight the areas of convergence and divergence in order to underscore the importance of effective counter-terrorism initiatives in post-9/11 national security policy of African states. As a security threat, terrorism obviously falls within the domains of national security considerations. However, given its contemporary importance within global security discourse, this paper treats it as a stand alone conceptualisation in exploring its relationship with national security policy.

The paper argues that an appreciation of the relationship between counter-terrorism and national security has implications on (1) the allocation of national, regional and international resources towards the prevention and combating of terrorism and also (2) the stimulation of the idea of African ownership of counter-terrorism initiatives on the continent. Both points are important to the African counter-terrorism agenda which requires a shift in ownership and leadership from being principally Western-driven to a practically domesticated African-led agenda in attempts to sustain counter-terrorism efforts on the continent.

POINTS OF CONVERGENCE OF COUNTER-TERRORISM WITH NATIONAL SECURITY

Ongoing counter-terrorism efforts in Africa have two important points of convergence with the national security interests of states. First, the implementation of counter-terrorism initiatives inadvertently provides responses to other forms of criminality. Second, the emergence of cooperation as an indispensable philosophy underlying counter-terrorism efforts assists with the entrenchment of the collective security notion which is indispensable in efforts to combat contemporary threats to international peace and security. The ensuing sub-sections discuss these two points.

Counter-Terrorism - a magic bullet?

Many analysts have observed an increased level of sophistication of terrorist *modus operandi* resulting from their ability to exploit the benefits of information, finance, and ideas which flow via the internet and also from their extensive transnational criminal networks. Part of the emerging sophistication manifests in a symbiotic overlap of terrorist activities with transnational criminalities such as money laundering, human trafficking, resource exploitation and drug trafficking. Since 1994, this complexity has been a critical issue in the United Nations (UN) leading to the expression of apprehension by the global body about the growing and dangerous links between terrorist groups and drug traffickers and their paramilitary gangs.

This is particularly the case regarding the tendency of the connection between terrorism and the other crimes to lead to a mutual or symbiotic reinforcement of each other and most especially terrorism by:

- Providing financial resources;
- Aiding the ability of networks to thrive without state sponsorship and support thereby enhancing their ability to relocate;
- Access to specialist skills such as the forging of travel documents and money laundering; and,
- The emergence of wider and hardened terrorist recruits from existing transnational criminals.

Practical cases of the connection between terrorist networks and transnational crimes are rife in Africa. The al-Qaeda network, for example, is known to have been very active in the African diamond trade. In West Africa, it is alleged that the network took diamonds from the mines of eastern Sierra Leone and traded them for cash as a fungible alternative to bank accounts which could have easily been tracked and frozen. Currently in Nigeria, it is estimated that approximately $4 billion worth of oil is illegally siphoned from pipelines and shipped abroad by international smuggling gangs each year (about 60,000 to 100,000 barrels of oil a day). The profits are then used to finance the arms race between criminal gangs and tribal militia who exploit terror and kidnappings as tactics for registering their demands. The role of the international smuggling gangs thus goes a long way to inspire or fuel the violence and acts of terrorism in the Niger Delta region of Nigeria through their supply of weapons and funds required to plan and execute attacks.

Recent reports on West Africa indicate that the sub-region is increasingly becoming a drug trans-shipment zone for drug cartels. Drugs, particularly cocaine, are shipped to various countries along the Gulf of Guinea for subsequent deliveries to Europe. Similarly, active cross-border child-trafficking networks operate across at least thirteen West African countries and recruit thousands of children from their homes each year to other places to exploit them sexually and/or labour-wise.

Against the background that terrorism and these transnational criminalities thrive on the same vulnerabilities and utilize similar actors, effective counter-terrorism measures thus have the tendency of combating not only the threat of terrorism but also other transnational threats to national security. Appropriately crafted counter-terrorism measures which deal with fundamental vulnerabilities such as economic distress, ethnic and religious fault-lines, fragile governance, weak state structures and rampant human rights abuses effectively deprive terrorists of havens and recruiting grounds; strengthen the ability of the state to ensure the safety of its citizens and also preserve its territorial integrity and sovereignty. The strengthening of border security as a counter-terrorism measure in West Africa, for example, will thus serve to dissuade various forms of border-related crimes in the sub-region and their effects elsewhere. Similarly, the trial of terror suspects with existing anti-terrorism legislation will, apart from eliminating terrorists from states, also deter individuals who might attempt to exploit perceived weak national judiciary systems for criminal purposes.

In this regard, the successful implementation of appropriate counter-terrorism measures in African states – despite not being the 'magic bullet' to all the continent's security problems - has the tendency of cutting off the mutually-reinforcing and symbiotic relationships that exist or may emerge between terrorism and other transnational security threats in line with national security policy.

Giving Cooperation and Collective Security a jolt?

The 9/11 attacks highlighted the mutual vulnerability of both weak and strong states to the threat of terrorism. The realization has since highlighted the importance of all states in the global quest for security and accentuated the dependence of the counter-terrorism agenda on the ability of states to cooperate on a wide range of security issues such as tracking and blocking the finances and communication networks of terrorist organisations. According to

Lord Robertson, former NATO Secretary General: Outdated Cold War habits and capacities do us no good against 21st century threats unless we adapt them to meet these new challenges. We need a global, integrated response, with deep cooperation between states, international organizations, international financial institutions, the private sector, and non-governmental organizations - all working together, in new ways, to meet this new network of security threats.

Globally, this awareness has renewed emphasis on inter-state cooperation and has assisted states to pool resources towards the prevention and combating of terrorism. In Africa, inter-state cooperation has been fundamental to the effective realization of the counter-terrorism goals of the AU and is for that reason key among the underlying philosophies of the organisation's emerging counter-terrorism regime.

According to the AU Commission Chairperson, Alpha Oumar Konaré, African countries have adopted instruments and decisions towards creating a common framework for the prevention and combating of terrorism in their collective resolve and determination to deal with it as a common threat. The acceptance that all African states equally share the same vulnerabilities and are thus collectively threatened by terrorism and so are committed to acting collectively is an implicit reception of the collective security implications of the threat of terrorism. In other words, African states concede that the threat of terrorism to one state is a threat to all the remaining states on the continent, which is why members of the continental body, the AU, acceded to the provisions of the 1999 Algiers Convention as a guiding principle to their collective quest to prevent and combat terrorism.

By contributing to the projection of the ideals ,f collective security as a way of pursuing the realization of safety for citizens and the maintenance of territorial integrity of African states from the threat of terrorism, this article argues that counter-terrorism has contributed immensely to the classical demands of national security of African states in the 21st century.

Points of Departure from National Security

Many African countries have emerged from decades of autocratic and dictatorial regimes during which laws of the state were left at the behest of individuals with political influence. Some of these leaders criminalised politically dissenting views as part of efforts to protect the state from subversive entities and activities. This background - coupled with the lack of a common acceptable definition for terrorism and the absence of strong democratic principles, good governance, rule of law, and independent state structures in many African states - has increased the temptation of exploitation of the post-9/11 counter-terrorism agenda by some political leaders on the continent. Consequently, some political actors have found leeway to suppress political opponents and groups with politically and socially divergent views under the rubric of counter-terrorism. The counter-terrorism agenda is thus being exploited for the achievement of political goals, particularly the settling of political scores and the pursuit of motives which threaten democracy and the rule of law.

In Zimbabwe, for instance, President Robert Mugabe, has variously invoked the "war on terror" to justify his labelling of journalists as "agents of terrorism" or "terrorist sympathizers" and harassing them. Zimbabwe passed the Public Order and Security Act in 2002, and it has since been used on numerous occasions to detain journalists who criticize the government. Those who criticise the government have often been labelled "terrorists" and have been detained without any formal charges. In response to one of such situations involving the arrest of six journalists, a spokesman for President Mugabe insisted that it was an "open secret" that such journalists were assisting terrorists and declared categorically that, "as for the correspondents, we would like them to know that we agree with the United States' President Bush that anyone who in any way finances, harbours or defends terrorists is himself a terrorist. We [...] will not make any difference between terrorists and their friends and supporters."

In a similar situation, the Eritrean Ambassador to the US, Girma Asmerom, argued in favour of the September 18, 2001 arrest of journalists who protested the detention of former high-ranking government officials for publicly criticizing President Issayes Afewerki's leadership. In the Ambassador's argument, he cited the roundup of material witnesses and suspected aliens in America after the 9/11 attacks and concluded that the arrests of the journalists were justified.

While these events would have previously attracted stern criticism from states that have been known to champion the cause of freedom and human rights, these abuses have within post-9/11 realities gone uncondemned. This is explainable only within the context of the support such African countries provide to the war on terror, which is now the major pre-occupation of western powers. In Nigeria, for instance, an October 2001 massacre by the Nigerian army of at least 200 people in Benue State went uncondemned during President Obasanjo's visit to the US just a few weeks later to discuss the anti-terrorism campaign.

Pursuant to Kenya's introduction of the Suppression of Terrorism Bill in 2003, certain provisions - including those that sought to make it an offence for one to wear or use items associated with terrorists - was perceived as an attack on the Muslim community and their mode of dressing. Together with provisions that proposed to impose the duty to provide evidence to the contrary once the prosecution had established a certain threshold of evidence that tended to suggest the guilt of the person, many felt that the counter-terrorism agenda of the country sought to promote religious and ethnic prejudices or, at best, was based on religious and ethnic prejudices. This led to stiff opposition from certain elements in Kenya, among which was the Muslim community.

The State Security Investigations (SSI) of Egypt is noted for organising random 'sweeps' under the broader goal of counter-terrorism, which sometimes result in the detention of young men, who are then abusively interrogated and tortured into accepting fabricated charges levelled against them. In April 2006, for instance, Egypt's Interior Ministry announced the SSI's arrest of members of an extremist group alleged to have been plotting terrorist attacks on gas pipelines, tourist sites, and Muslim and Christian religious figures in and around Cairo. A year later, however, investigations by Human Rights Watch revealed scepticism about the charges levelled against the suspects, treatments given to them whilst in detention, and the legal grounds for the detention. A December 2007 Human Rights Watch report on the issue found that:

> Beyond coerced confessions, there appears to be no compelling evidence to support the government's dramatic claims. Indeed, it appears that SSI may have fabricated the allegations made against at least some and possibly all of them. The very name given to the group—"Victorious Sect"—may have been invented by SSI officers. Moreover, whether or not the original arrests were justified, it is clear that there are currently no legal grounds for the continued detention of the 10 men of the 22 who are believed to remain in custody.

According to some family members of the suspects and attorneys, the suspects may have been targeted because of their religious leanings and fears that they could be radicalised.

Given the tough actions by some African states and human rights abuses under the guise of fighting terrorism, scepticism has emerged towards African counter-terrorism measures and particularly about the extent to which western interests and conceptualisation is influencing and/or driving its direction and focus. For many, the counter-terrorism agenda has become another avenue where African governments are facing a dilemma in balancing donor agendas, legitimate national security interests, and domestic support for democracy and human rights.

This perception - coupled with exacerbating poverty levels, and populations over high levels of corruption amongst political leaders who are often also the exploiters of the counter-terrorism agenda - the counter-terrorism agenda is rather becoming a threat to state stability. In the case of the SSI detentions in Egypt, for instance, the efforts are objective rather counter-productive. This is because rather than contribute to the grand goal of reducing violence from terrorism in the country, the arrests and detentions are rather contributing to the emergence of a culture of retaliation owing to the radicalisation of detainees who upon release then find a reason to revenge torture carried out on them whilst in detention. In this context, counter-terrorism initiatives are contributing to the creation of volatile security situations that can escalate into political, religious or politico-religious violence resulting from polarisation in many weak African democracies and fragile states.

Against this background, this paper argues that even though counter-terrorism should ideally serve a national security purpose, at the practical level, it is practically providing a context for human rights abuse, the suppression of political opponents and the deprivation of the rights and freedoms of citizens in some African states – outcomes which are practically divergent from the polemical demands of national security policy.

On the other hand, it could be argued that an effective counter-terrorism initiative has the potential of helping to contain other forms of criminalities such as money laundering, human trafficking, resource exploitation and drug trafficking. It can also inspire the African commitment to the notion of fighting a common vulnerability or threat – a conception which is necessary in upholding the centrality of cooperation and collective security in the quest for peace and security on the continent. However, an ineffective implementation of counter-terrorism initiatives on the continent may undermine the cohesion of states and accentuate ethnic, religious, political and politico-religious fault-lines in some states thus providing the basis for instability and insecurity.

Given the fact that the latter case is parallel to the ultimate aim of national security, it is important for African states to be circumspect in their ownership of national security prioritisation on the continent. With the prevailing over-dependence on western-driven initiatives, it may be difficult for many states to fully prioritise their national security needs in a vacuum and without considering external influences. It is thus necessary for the continent to wean itself off western-driven and western-funded approaches for national security to enable states to prioritise national security strategies based on the actual needs of African states devoid of any donor-driven approach.

A purely African approach to prioritizing security should also inform regional and continental approaches to prioritizing all threats to national, regional and continental threats, including terrorism. In doing this, however, caution has to be taken to craft national security policy responses according to a range of individual threats (including counter-terrorism responses) but within national realities in a way that they do not undermine the tenets of national security or other national security policy responses. By following a more top-down continentally-driven approach, more specific security policies which flow from national security priorities may achieve better coherence with overarching national security priorities, and not be left to the crafting and influence of the donor community.

It is widely recognized and accepted that many African states emerging from conflict and suffering from state fragility must – in some respects – leave themselves open to external influence at the programmatic level of assistance. However, as more democratic political reforms become introduced, a locally-driven strategic analysis in support of national security must encourage the mergence of the strategic and programme level activities in the medium term. This is important in order to avoid the growth of programme level dependencies which are not in line with basic national security interests and objectives. Failure to undertake the strategic level approach will result in programme-level activities exerting undue influence over the strategic national security agenda. In the post-9/11 era, there is ample evidence of where this has happened with externally-initiated or externally-influenced counter-terrorist programmes across African states.

Addressing this dilemma will be difficult due to the pursuit of foreign policy interests by strong western states with the ability to sustain their pursuit. At the same time, many African states will lack the capacity and skill-sets to move with the political reforms in shaping strategic level priorities and responses, according to – as one author phrases it - "...the world *they* live in." Perhaps the time is ripe to stop under-estimating the levels of knowledge within these states but encourage the promotion of 'skill-sets' required to influence strategic national security processes. Success in this area will bode well for the shaping of programmes such as counter-terrorism according to what is best for the country in question.

CONCLUSION

The counter-terrorism agenda in Africa after 9/11 converges with the classical demands of national security policy in the provision of safety for citizens, the preservation of territorial wholesomeness and sovereignty. Notwithstanding this fact, improper implementation and exploitation of counter-terrorism initiatives has resulted in the over-securitisation and politicisation of issues, and the abuse of counter-terrorism for suppression, personal vendettas, prosecution of innocent citizens and the persecution of religious groups. This has manifested in human right abuses and tough actions by states, a situation which practically diverges from the primary demands of national security policy by contributing to insecurity.

To avoid occurrences in which counter-terrorism efforts will counter-productively add to insecurity through the polarisation of society and lead to the escalation of violence, it is incumbent on national, regional and international actors to prosecute and/or oversee the counter-terrorism agenda responsibly as a central part of national security policy. In doing so, and in recognising that strong western donors will continue the strong pursuit of their own foreign policy interests, prioritisation should be given to the development of strategic planning capacity for national security across the African continent.

Chapter

10

How to Deal with Terrorism

After the attacks of 9/11, the American president declared a "Crusade" against terrorists. This "Crusade" was, after some think-ing, changed into a "War Against Terrorism." This war on terrorism is totally based on deterrence and preemptive strikes. Ac-tual and prospective terrorists must be wiped out by killing or at least capturing them, hold-ing them prisoner, or (perhaps) putting them on trial and sentencing them to imprisonment for long periods or indefinitely. Such treatment is expected to make the penalty for the crime so harsh that no individual will engage in ter-rorist activities in the future.

INEFFECTIVENESS OF DETERRENCE

History and recent experience suggest, however, that deterrence is ineffective and may even be counterproductive in dealing with terrorism. Moreover, the extent of terrorist acts may well increase rather than decrease. A poli-cy based on deterrence has a second disadvan-tage—It threatens civil and human rights in the countries engaged in fighting terrorism. Deter-rence thus tends to undermine exactly those values it claims to protect.

Many people share this concern but see no alternative to deterrence. I want to show that such alternatives do exist and are viable. Three strategies are proposed:

(1) Reduce vulnerability by decentralizing society;

(2) Strengthen positive incentives to leave the terrorist camp;

(3) Divert media attention from terrorist groups.

DECENTRALIZATION REDUCES VULNERABILITY TO TERRORIST ATTACKS

Any system with many different centers is more stable due to the ability of the vari-ous centers to substitute for each other. When one part of the system is negatively affected, another part or parts can take over. This ba-sic insight also applies to terrorism. A target's vulnerability is lower in a decentralized society more so than in a centralized society. The more centers of power there are in a country, the less Economists' Voice www.bepress.com/ev August, 2006

Terrorists are able to hurt it. In a decentralized system, terrorists do not know where to strike because they are aware that each part can sub-stitute for the other so that a strike will not achieve much. In contrast, in a centralized sys-tem most decision-making takes place in one location. This power center is an ideal target for terrorists and therefore is in great danger of being attacked.

As a means of reducing vulnerability, decentralization can be achieved in various ways:

- Decentralize the *economy* by relying on the market as the major form of resource allocation.
- Decentralize the *polity* by resorting to the classical division of power between the government, the parliament and the courts. Decentralization over space is achieved by a federalist structure with decision-making power attributed to lower levels of the polity (states, provinces, regions and communes).
- Decentralize the *society* by allowing for many different actors such as churches, nongovernmental organizations, clubs and the family.

POSITIVE INCENTIVES TO ACTUAL AND PROSPECTIVE TERRORISTS NOT TO ENGAGE IN VIOLENT ACTS

Positive sanctions consist in providing people with previously nonexistent or unattainable opportunities increasing their utility. The *oppor-tunity costs of remaining or becoming a terrorist* are raised because other valued possibilities are now available. Various approaches are possible.

Terrorists can be reintegrated. One of the most fundamental human motivations is the need to belong, and this also applies to terrorists. The isolation from other social entities gives strength to the terrorist group because it has become the only place where a sense of belonging is nurtured. An effective way to overcome terrorism is to break up this isolation. The (potential) terrorists must experience that there are other social bodies able to care for their need to belong. Interaction between groups tends to reduce extremist views, which are more likely to flourish in isolated groups of like-minded people. Segregation reinforces extremism and vice versa. Therefore, breaking up this vicious circle of segregation and extremism should lower terrorists' inclination to participate in violent activities.

There are various methods of motivating terrorists to interact more closely with other members of society, thus overcoming their isolation. The terrorists can be involved in a *discussion process*, which takes their goals and grievances seriously. Moreover, terrorists can be granted *access* to the normal *political process*. This lowers the costs of pursuing the political goal by legal means and hence raises the opportunity costs of terrorism.

The same principle of anti-terrorist policy can be applied to nations supporting or harboring terrorists. If such countries are internationally isolated and identified as "rogue states," they tend to become more extreme and ideological. A more fruitful strategy is to help them to re-enter the international community and to adopt its rules.

Repentants can be welcomed. Persons engaged in terrorist movements can be offered incentives, most importantly reduced punishment and a secure future life if they are prepared to leave the organization they are involved with and are prepared to talk about it and its projects. Terrorists who credibly show that they wish to renounce terrorist activities should be supported and not penalized (Principal Witness Programs).

A member's opportunity costs of remaining a terrorist are therewith increased.

Valued opportunities can be offered. Persons inclined to follow terrorist ideas and undertake terrorist actions can be invited to visit foreign countries. Universities and research institutes, for example, can offer such persons the opportunity of discussing their ideology with academics and other intellectuals. Liberalism is based on the conviction that the atmosphere of discourse existing in such places of learning tends to mellow terrorist inclinations. If prospective terrorists do not change their views, the situation is not worse than before. The very least to be achieved is that the (potential) terrorists have access to new and radically different ideas, compared to the situation in which they live within a closed circle of other extremists.

Providing terrorists positive incentives to no longer engage in violent actions represents a completely different approach from the conventional anti-terrorist policy of deterrence based on coercion. An effort is made to break the organizational and mental dependence of persons on the terrorist organizations by offering them more favorable alternatives.

ATTENTION TO BE DIVERTED FROM THE TERRORIST GROUPS

The relationship between terrorists and the media can be described as "symbiotic." The interests of the terrorists are similar or even identical to those of the media: Both want to make news, and both want the terrorist act to remain in the news as long and as prominently as possible.

Terrorists have become very skilled in using the media to achieve a maximum effect. They have learned to exploit the media to propagate their political demands to millions and even billions of people. Terrorists have fully adjusted their tactics in order to accommodate media needs.

Terrorists can be prevented from committing violent acts by reducing the utility gained from such behavior. A specific way for terrorists to derive lower benefits from terrorism consists in the government ascertaining that a particular terrorist act is *not attributed to a particular terrorist group.*

This prevents terrorists from receiving credit for the act and from gaining the public's attention associated with committing the act. The government must see to it that a particular terrorist group does not monopolize media attention.

This does *not* mean that the government should suppress information. This is not possible in an open society. The government can divert attention from terrorist organizations and their goals by supplying *more* information to the public than desired by the terrorist group responsible for a particular violent act.

It must be made known that *several* terrorist groups *could* be responsible for a particular terrorist act. Experience shows indeed that in the case of most terrorist attacks *several* groups of terrorists have claimed to be responsible. The authorities have to reveal that they never know with certainty which terrorist group may have committed a violent act. Rather the government must publicly discuss various reasonable hypotheses.

The strategy of refusing to attribute a terrorist attack to one particular group systematically affects the behavior of terrorists. The benefits derived from having committed a terrorist act decreases for the group having undertaken it because the group does not reap the public attention hoped for.

The political goals it wants to publicize are not propagated as much as desired. This reduction in publicity makes the terrorist act (to a certain degree) senseless, as modern terrorism essentially depends on publicity. Terrorists who are ready to take a high risk, even the risk of death, in order to put forth their political beliefs, feel deeply dissatisfied. Their frustration is intensified by the feeling that other, not equally as "brave" political groups, are given a free publicity ride. This frustration is often intense because terrorist groups tend to be in a state of strong competition even when they have similar political beliefs.

CONCLUSIONS

The proposed anti-terrorist policy based on a *positive approach* has two important ad-vantages over a coercive policy:

- The whole interaction between terrorists and the government takes the character of a *positive sum game*: All sides benefit. The effort of the government is no longer directed solely towards destruction. Rather, the government makes an effort to raise the utility of those terrorists who choose to enter the programs offered. It provides alternatives to persons considering becoming terrorists. In contrast, deterrence policy by necessity produces a worse position for both sides. The terrorists are punished (incarcerated, killed, or mutilated), while the deterrence strategy is very costly in terms of resources and civil rights.
- The strategy *undermines the cohesiveness of the terrorist organization*. The incentive to leave is a strong threat to the organization. The terrorist leaders no longer know whom to trust because, after all, most persons can succumb to temptation. An effort to counteract these temptations by prohibiting members from taking up the attractive offers leads to conflicts between the leaders and the rank and file. With good outside offers available to the members of a terrorist group, its leaders tend to lose control. The terrorist organization's effectiveness is thereby reduced.

The application of the economic approach to terrorism offers a range of superior anti-terrorism policies to deterrence. They are effective in dissuading potential terrorists from attacking. All of these policies are based on the notion that a positive approach is preferable to one based on the use of force.

The policies are "positive" as they do not seek to harm or kill potential and actual terrorists, but to reduce terrorist activities. The policies are not retributive but anti-terrorist. The positive approach here championed is not the only effective strategy and it does not work in every case; but, compared to the now dominant deterrence and preemption policy, the favorable features by far prevail. There is no need to restrict policies to deterrence; the positive approaches presented are in many respects superior alternatives.

A crucial question is why deterrence policy is so often undertaken though it is far from successful, and why the positive policies are disregarded. The reason is that government politicians derive additional private benefits from using force. The same holds for the military, the police and the secret service. In contrast, the proponents of positive anti-terrorist policies are weak, at least in the short run. However, the outcome of the political struggle can be influenced by political persuasion, giving the positive approach a better chance.

Chapter

11

The Challenge of Protecting Critical Infrastructure

In protecting critical infrastructure, the responsibility for setting goals rests primarily with the government, but the implementation of steps to reduce the vulnerability of privately owned and corporate assets depends primarily on private-sector knowledge and action. Although private firms uniquely understand their operations and the hazards they entail, it is clear that they currently do not have adequate commercial incentive to fund vulnerability reduction. For many, the cost of reducing vulnerabilities outweighs the benefit of reduced risk from terrorist attacks as well as from natural and other disasters.

The National Strategy for Homeland Security, released on July 16, 2002, reflects conventional notions of market failure that are rapidly becoming obsolete: "The government should only address those activities that the market does not adequately provide—for example, national defense or border security. For other aspects of homeland security, sufficient incentives exist in the private market to supply protection. In these cases we should rely on the private sector." The Interim National Infrastructure Protection Plan (NIPP), released by the Department of Homeland Security (DHS) in February 2005, takes a similar position.

Although some 85% of the critical infrastructure in the United States is privately owned, the reality is that market forces alone are, as a rule, insufficient to induce needed investments in protection. Companies have been slow to recognize that the border is now interior. National defense means not only sending destroyers but also protecting transformers. In addition, risks to critical infrastructure industries are becoming more and more interdependent as the economic, technological, and social processes of globalization intensify. Just as a previous generation of policymakers adapted to the emergence of environmental externalities, policymakers today must adapt to a world in which "security externalities" are suddenly ubiquitous.

The case of CSX Railroad and the District of Columbia illustrates the tensions that have emerged over the competing needs for corporate efficiency and reduced public vulnerability to terrorist acts. Less than a month after a January 2004 train crash in South Carolina resulted in the release of deadly chlorine gas that killed 9 people and hospitalized 58 others, the District's City Council passed an act banning the transportation of hazardous materials within a 2.2-mile radius of the U. S. Capitol without a permit. The act cited the failure of the federal government "to prevent the terrorist threat." Subsequently, CSX petitioned the U.S. Surface Transportation Board (USSTP) to invalidate the legislation, claiming that it would "add hundreds of miles and days of transit time to hazardous materials shipments" and adversely affect rail service around the country. USSTP ruled in CSX's favor in March 2005, putting an end to the District's efforts.

Shortly after the decision, Richard Falkenrath, President Bush's former deputy homeland security advisor, highlighted in congressional testimony the severity of the threat that the act was intended to address: "Of all the various remaining civilian vulnerabilities in America today, one stands alone as uniquely deadly, pervasive, and susceptible to terrorist attack: toxic-inhalation hazard (TIH) of industrial chemicals, such as chlorine, ammonia, phosgene, methylbromide, hydrochloric and various other acids."

If industry itself is not motivated to invest in protection against attack and the federal government does not take the initiative, who will take responsibility for protecting chemical plants, rail lines, and other critical infrastructure? Who will make it harder for terrorists to magnify the damage of an attack by first attacking the infrastructure on which effective response depends? Who will ensure that these and other elements of the infrastructure are not used as weapons to kill or maim thousands of people in our cities? Is there, then, an adequate combination of private organizational strategies and public policies that will ensure reliable and resilient service provision in the long term? As the CSX case illustrates, consensus on how best to protect critical infrastructure has not emerged, despite the urgency created by terrorist threats, as well as the ongoing challenges of dealing with natural disasters.

An infrastructure is "critical" when the services it provides are vital to national security. The list of infrastructures officially considered critical is growing. In addition to the chemical sector, they are transportation, the defense industrial base, information and telecommunications, banking and finance, agriculture, food, water, public heath, government services, emergency services, and postal and shipping. The threat of catastrophic terrorism has created a new relationship between national security and routine business decisions in private firms providing infrastructure services.

Managers of these firms, like business managers elsewhere, are highly motivated to seek efficiency increases. The never-ending race for economy of scale and of scope and justin- time processes that guarantee better results also leads to reduced redundancy, concentrated assets, and centralized control points. The new double-deck Airbus A380, the largest aircraft ever built, is designed to carry as many as 550 passengers in the quest for a decrease in the cost per passenger seat. More than half of the chickens destined for our supermarket shelves are processed by a handful of firms in Arkansas. Transformers used in primary power distribution have become so large that installations contain only one of them. The Internet is increasingly relied on for critical communications in the event of attack or disaster, not withstanding its well-known vulnerabilities to a variety of disruptions.

Before 9/11 and particularly since, much work has been directed at identifying vulnerabilities at the scale of individual firms, of industries, and more recently, of geographical regions. Many sound engineering-based proposals exist for reducing vulnerability. Large apartments and office towers can employ ventilation systems that detect and trap poisonous gases. Power distribution plants can better protect their largest transformers and store replacement units in safe places. Local governments can install LED traffic lights with trickle-charged batteries that will not fail during a blackout. Trains carrying toxic and explosive materials can be routed around cities. A 2002 National Academies study, Making the Nation Safer: The Role of Science and Technology in Countering Terrorism, contains other proposals to reduce vulnerabilities through the use of technology; subsequent work has added to the list. However, neither vulnerability assessments nor studies based on principles of engineering design address the competitive pressures and other incentives that have led private firms to build infrastructures in their current forms.

Comprehensive public policy for critical infrastructure protection must begin with an understanding that "protection" per se should not be the goal. As a means of reducing vulnerability to attack at the regional or countrywide scale, it is minimally effective. In an open society, higher fences and thicker walls do little to reduce aggregate vulnerabilities. In many instances, protection simply shifts the focus of terrorists to other, less heavily fortified targets.

Even if one accepts the word "protection," what is being protected is not the infrastructure itself but the services it provides. With regard to terrorist threats, the policy goal should be to build capabilities for prevention of attacks that interrupt such services and for effective response and rapid recovery when such attacks do occur. Sustainable policy must account for both the potential tradeoffs that exist at the firm level between efficiency and vulnerability and for the institutions and the incentives potentially affecting that tradeoff. Ultimately, policy must

- structure incentive systems for investment that enhance prevention of, response to, and recovery from the most likely and damaging attacks;

- ensure adequately robust internal operations of private firms, including greater system reliability for their services;
- limit imposed costs on firms to guarantee the competitiveness of our economy; and
- do all of the above in a manner that can be sustained by a complacent public with a short memory that may tire of the high costs and consumer inconvenience that government policies aimed at making critical industries less vulnerable may entail.

Although efficiency and vulnerability are produced jointly, they are not assessed together. A market economy routinely accounts for improved efficiency, because shareholders are always looking for the best return on investment in the short term. However, vulnerability may be assessed only after it has been exposed by active study or system failure.

Organizations are most likely to account for vulnerabilities that are linked to their own core activities. They will ignore equally serious consequences of attacks on, or attacks that employ, an infrastructure service that is assumed to be reliably available. Airlines, for example, have an inherent incentive to become intimately familiar with the factors that determine the risk of a crash. Beginning in the 1970s, airline managers were also compelled to systematically address hijacking threats. However, before 9/11, none were truly prepared for the possibility that passenger jets would be used as weapons of large-scale destruction.

Accountability for and accounting of vulnerabilities distant from core business activities are relatively uncommon, particularly when the perceived probabilities of occurrence are very low. Although economic incentives drive the accounting of core-business vulnerabilities, legal, organizational, and political dynamics drive the response to vulnerabilities that lie outside the core business concerns of any single firm or industry. Traditional tools of risk assessment and risk management have become very sophisticated in recent years as a result of environmental, health, and safety regulations.

Nonetheless, such tools remain largely inadequate in coping with high-impact, lowlikelihood events. For many large technological network systems, the challenge of ensuring reliable operations has increased because operations both within and among firms have become increasingly interdependent. Elements of infrastructures in particular have become so interdependent that the destabilization of one is likely to have severe consequences for others.

As the scale and reach of these large technological systems have increased, the potential economic and social damage of failures has increased as well. The sources of such major disruptions lie in technical and managerial failures as well as natural disasters or terrorist attacks, as illustrated in the Northeast Blackout of August 2003. Economic and social activities are becoming more and more interdependent as well, so that the actions taken by one organization will affect others.

In this context, the incentives for any single organization to invest in prevention, response, and recovery are blunted. Without a global approach to understanding interdependencies and security externalities, determining the source of disruptions and quantifying the risk of such disruptions are difficult. Private decisionmakers will have neither adequate information nor adequate motivation to undertake investments that are more than justifiable from the standpoint of the system as a whole.

As terrorist attacks have emerged as potential threats to infrastructure, privatesector executives and policymakers must grapple with far greater uncertainties than ever before. This is particularly challenging because terrorists can engage in "adaptive predation," in which they purposefully adapt their strategies to take advantage of weaknesses in prevention efforts. In contrast, actions can be taken to reduce damage from future natural disasters with the knowledge that the probability associated with the hazard will not be affected by the adoption of these protective measures. The likelihood of an earthquake of a given intensity in Los Angeles will not change if property owners design more quake-resistant structures. The likelihood and consequences of a terrorist attack are determined by a mix of strategies and counterstrategies developed by a range of stakeholders and changing over time. This dynamic uncertainty makes the likelihood of future terrorist events extremely difficult (if not impossible) to estimate and increases the difficulty of measuring the economic efficiency of public policies and private strategies.

In that context, although private-sector actors can reduce system vulnerability by reducing dependence on vulnerable external services, decentralizing critical assets, decentralizing core operational functions, and adopting organization practices to improve resiliency, these organizations may face sanctions from markets for taking such actions if they reduce efficiency, raise costs, or reduce profits. Indeed, markets rarely reward investments that reduce vulnerability to events so rare that there is no statistical basis for quantitative risk assessment.

Steering between market approaches that tend to remove system slack (increasing vulnerability to catastrophic system failure) and the redesign of private infrastructures to ensure more reliable functioning (though at higher cost to consumers), the federal government has generally opted for policies of partnerships between private-sector operators and government agencies. The Interim NIPP emphasizes the role of sectorspecific agencies in coordinating private actors. The federal government also has overseen the development of a number of reliability regimes that involve combinations of government oversight and private-sector enforcement.

In both public/private and private/private partnerships, the tension between organizational autonomy and the independence of the constituent units of the large-scale system makes communication and coordination critical. When managers are not fully informed (or worse, are misinformed) regarding the actions and status of remote units, effective decisionmaking is not possible. Actions in one unit can have unintended and perhaps serious consequences elsewhere. Providing sufficient slack, encouraging constant and clear communications, and creating a consistent belief structure and safetyembracing culture help reduce this problem. Large-scale systems need to be flexible in adapting to rapidly changing situations.

Extraordinary levels of coordination of many organizations, public and private, will be required to secure any improved level of prevention, response, and recovery. Continuous but expensive organizational learning will be essential to producing an auto-adaptive response capability that will enable infrastructure service providers to deal more effectively with adaptive predators and dynamic uncertainty.

Yet such imperatives are unlikely to be tolerated by most private-sector organizations operating under normal business conditions, where bottom lines matter, where threats are difficult to discern, and where attacks are extremely infrequent. Sustaining watchfulness and the ability to deal with low-probability, high-impact events is the single most difficult policy issue facing critical infrastructure providers and homeland security agencies today. Critical infrastructure protection needs to be understood as not only deploying a tougher exoskeleton, but also developing organizational antibodies of reliability that enable society and its constituent parts to be more resilient and robust in the face of new, dynamic, and uncertain threats.

Even though technological and managerial procedures may be in place to limit the occurrence of a devastating event and reduce its effects through resilient infrastructure, the possibility of suffering a large loss must still be seriously considered. Should that happen, the question of who should pay for the economic consequences is likely to take center stage. In the 2002 National Strategy, the White House considered recovery as a fundamental element of homeland security. In most developed countries, insurance is one of the principal mechanisms used by individuals and organizations for managing risk. Indeed, insurance is a key mechanism not only for aiding in recovery after an attack but also in inducing investments to make an attack less likely.

A well-functioning insurance market plays a critical role in ensuring social and economic continuity when large-scale disaster occurs. Private insurers paid about 90% of the $23 billion in insured losses that resulted from the four hurricanes that hit Florida in 2004. Two-thirds of the $33 billion in insured losses from the 9/11 attacks were paid by reinsurance companies (mostly European) that operate at a larger level worldwide. Because of the huge payouts, however, these companies either substantially increased their prices or stopped offering terrorism coverage altogether.

The collapse of the market for terrorism insurance after 9/11 motivated the passage of the Terrorism Risk Insurance Act of 2002 (TRIA). TRIA established a three-year risksharing partnership between the insurance industry and the federal government for covering commercial enterprises against terrorism for losses of up to $100 billion. Under TRIA, insurers are required to offer terrorism coverage to all of their commercial policyholders, who can in turn accept it or refuse to buy it. About 50% of firms nationwide purchased terrorism insurance in 2004. In case of an attack by foreign interests, the federal government would pay 90% of the insured losses above an insurer's deductible, providing free upfront reinsurance to insurers. The government can recoup ex post part of its payment against all commercial policyholders, whether or not they bought terrorism insurance. The statute creating TRIA ends December 31, 2005, and it is not clear whether Congress will renew it in its current form, modify it, or let it go.

The TRIA and Beyond report, a detailed 10-month study by the Wharton School's Center for Risk Management in collaboration with a broad spectrum of public and private organizations, was released in August 2005. It concludes that TRIA "has provided an important and necessary temporary solution to the problem of how terrorism insurance can be provided to commercial firms," but does not constitute "an equitable and efficient long-term program and should be modified."

Routine government involvement in most catastrophic risk coverage programs (floods, hurricanes, earthquakes, and terrorism) is an implicit recognition of the necessity for the public sector to protect insurance infrastructure. Yet the respective roles and responsibilities of public and private actors in providing adequate protection to victims of terrorist attacks remain unclear. The creation by Congress or the White House of a national commission on terrorism risk coverage before permanent legislation is enacted, as urged by the Wharton team, would certainly help create a more efficient and equitable long-term solution that includes a necessary safety net for ensuring that insurance can play its traditional role in the recovery from major disasters or attacks involving critical infrastructure.

In addition to its prime role in recovery, insurance can be a powerful tool in inducing critical infrastructure investments that enhance prevention and response. As a third party between government and private firms, the insurance industry would play a key role in this domain. A firm or an individual investing in security and mitigation measures should be eligible to receive lower insurance rates. On the surface, the analogy to homeowner's insurance and hurricane and flood insurance, where this policy is prevalent, seems compelling. But a closer look reveals that the potential role of insurance in inducing private investments in prevention and response is more red herring than silver bullet.

First, it is possible that having insurance will induce a manager to engage in riskier behavior than would have otherwise been the case—the moral hazard problem in insurance. Second, the link between the price of insurance and security/mitigation measures in the context of terrorism threats is tenuous at best. The current evidence is that almost none of the insurers providing coverage for terrorism in the United States have thus far linked in any way the price of coverage to the security measures in place. Why is this the case? The significant decrease in the price of terrorism insurance four years after 9/11, combined with the relatively high price for reinsurance (when available), does not provide a large window for price reduction. Perhaps more important, the dynamic uncertainty due to adaptive predation by terrorists makes it extremely difficult to measure and to price the efficiency of any security measure. Without a price, there cannot be a market.

Enhancing capabilities in the United States for prevention, recovery, and response relating to attacks on critical infrastructure will not be easy. In the long term, responding to this challenge will not only require changes in the technologies and structures adopted by threatened firms. It will also require improving the effectiveness of private strategies and public policies, reflecting an emerging balance of public and private roles and responsibilities.

Institutional capabilities to identify, negotiate, and implement such policies are at least partly in place. The union of 22 federal bodies under the umbrella of the new DHS, along with the current reform of the intelligence services, is the most significant federal reorganization of the past half-century, although DHS has yet to give priority to addressing the vulnerability of critical infrastructures.

The transformations induced by the corporate trust crisis and the new Sarbanes-Oxley era are also changing how most firms operate, but it is unclear that the changes taking place will add anything to counterterrorism capability in private industry. Finally, for the general public, an important issue will be willingness to sacrifice for security, whether through higher prices and taxes or through loss of freedom and privacy.

Beyond infrastructure vulnerability assessments, continuity of operations planning, and deliberate investment in a small set of obviously cost-effective technologies, the following structural, organizational, and financial strategies should be considered to improve the capacity of the critical infrastructure service providers and public authorities to perform their functions:

- strike a balance between strategies that emphasize anticipation (reducing the likelihood of attack) and those that emphasize resilience (reducing the damage resulting from attack);
- recognize and support high-reliability organizations and reliability professionals;
- enhance the capabilities of autoadaptive response systems of various types;

- reward information-sharing about technological and organizational changes and encourage organizations to emphasize safety;
- promote dialogue among citizens and stakeholders to define priorities and explore options for action; and
- develop incentive programs to induce private investment in security by relying on market forces to the extent possible.

Strategies to protect critical infrastructure are not viable unless they are politically and economically sustainable. Sustainability may be enhanced by a deliberate policy of seeking win-win options that promise public and private benefits beyond vulnerability reduction. Public relations, reputation, and the possibility of tort liability may motivate some firms to invest even without additional government pressure. Understanding the motives, constraints, and capabilities of potential attackers may inform decisions regarding investments in prevention, response, and recovery.

The challenge of critical infrastructure protection is a multifaceted one requiring a variety of responses. Market mechanisms and engineering design both have roles, but neither is sufficient. As national security increasingly finds its way into the boardrooms of U.S. corporations, rigid and limited public/private partnerships must give way to flexible, more deeply rooted collaborations between public and private actors in which trust is developed and information is shared. By directly addressing at an operational level the potential tradeoffs between private efficiency and public vulnerability, such collaborations will lead to better, if not definitive, solutions.

SUMMARY OF SELECTED COUNTER-TERRORISM INITIATIVES

The National Academies responded to the terrorist attacks of September 11th in multiple ways. Following a meeting of leaders from the science, technology and health care communities with leading former government officials, a number of initiatives were undertaken by the end of September, supported by the Presidents from Academy funds. Other activities, some of which pre-dated September 11th, emanated from many of the 80 boards within the National Research Council. An analysis of the combined activities, below, leads to the conclusion that the Academy activities relating to counter-terrorism span all segments of the "public health model" of prevention, detection, response, recovery and attribution and also cover the several domains of potential terrorist threat, including. biological, chemical, nuclear and radiological, information technology, transportation, energy facilities, cities and fixed infrastructure. A better understanding of the roots of terrorism in order to lessen the fertile ground in which terrorism can recruit its perpetrators or build popular support is being addressed in several initiatives involving the social and behavioral sciences and in international activities.

S&T AGENDA FOR COUNTERING TERRORISM

This project is aimed at helping the federal government, and more specifically the Executive Office of the President, to use effectively the nation's and the world's scientific and technical community in a timely response to the threat of catastrophic terrorism. A committee of distinguished scientists and engineers with supporting panels will help to develop an integrated science and technology program plan and research strategy.

Phase 1 of the project will by June prepare a framework for the application of science and technology for combating terrorism and using additional experts serving on panels will prepare research agendas in eight key domains (biological; chemical; nuclear and radiological; information technology; transportation; energy facilities, cities, and fixed infrastructure; behavioral, social and institutional issues; and systems analysis and systems engineering).

The committee will also examine a series of cross-cutting and multidisciplir.ary issues, including interdependent vulnerabilities, and implementation obstacles. At the discretion of the government, phase 2 will review key government research programs and provide recommendations for building improved interagency capabilities and coordination. A final report for phase 1 will be produced by

June 2002. A phase 2 report would be produced by September 11, 2002.

NEAR-TERM ASSISTANCE FOR THE U.S. GOVERNMENT

On urgent topics where the government needs immediate assistance, the Academies are inviting scientific experts to meet with government representatives in one-day meetings. Although no written reports are produced and no formal Academy advice is provided, the dialogue is very beneficial to federal agencies, including the inter-agency Technical Support Working Group (TSWG) on counter-terrorism.

Recent examples include a meeting for the U.S. Postal Service on sanitizing the mail (11/14/01); a meeting for the Dept. of Justice on how to analyze the anthrax-infected letter to Senator Leahy (12/7/01); a meeting on human factors for the FAA's sky marshall program (12/5-6); a meeting on biological and chemical *forensics* for TSWG (12/11); a meeting on biological and chemical *decontamination* for TSWG (12/14); and a meeting on through structure imaging (2/8/02). A meeting on explosives detection is planned for March.

Combating Terrorism: Prioritizing Vulnerabilities and Developing Mitigation Strategies

The National Academy of Engineering has begun a 12-month project to identify, assess, and prioritize vulnerabilities to the nation's vital infrastructures posed by global terrorism, and outline strategies (technologies, policies) to mitigate priority vulnerabilities in a manner consistent with a free, open, and prosperous society.

Using various fact-finding, forecasting, consensus-building, and risk analysis techniques, the project committee is seeking to integrate expert knowledge of the nature of modern terrorism (motives, capabilities, sociology, psychology), terrorist weapons and delivery systems, and the vulnerabilities of vital infrastructures to measure and rank order the myriad terrorist threats to the nation.

International Collaborative Activities with Foreign Counterparts to Reduce Near-Term Threats and Long-term Root Causes of Terrorism

Priority activities include:

- Cooperation on Preventing Terrorists from Obtaining Nuclear Materials in Russia, which will include two projects. The first will be a joint effort with the Russian Academy of Sciences to produce a "white paper" assessing the steps that can be taken immediately by the two governments to reduce the risks that nuclear weapons or materials could fall into the hands of terrorists. Working together, the two academies will also identify an agenda for longer-term U.S.-Russian cooperation, including continuing inter-academy attention to problems that may arise and how they might be overcome. The second project, to be carried out in cooperation with Russian specialists, will be directed to increasing Russian capabilities for ensuring adequate protection of plutonium and highly enriched uranium. It will take into account the economic difficulties faced by the institutions responsible for such protection. The project will draw on the experience from the cooperative programs and other relevant experience in addressing practical steps that can be taken at the Federal and institutional levels to require and encourage appropriate measures to prevent theft or diversion.
- Continuation of the U.S.-Russian InterAcademy Project on conflicts in multiethnic societies with special attention to areas of the former Soviet Union with large Muslim populations.
- InterAcademy meetings and activities (on both a bilateral basis and on a multilateral basis through the InterAcademy Panel) with scientists and science organizations from the Middle East and predominantly Moslem nations, such as Iran, Pakistan, Afghanistan, Indonesia, and Turkey.

Planning meeting for a study on building the capability of foreign affairs and development agencies to help in reducing the risk of terrorism, a study that would complement the NRC report on "The Pervasive Role of Science, Technology, and Health in Foreign Policy: Imperatives for the State Department."

- Continuation of the US-Russian InterAcademy Project on counter-terrorism, with particular emphasis on the potential use of advanced technologies by terrorist groups.

Peer Review of Cooperative Research Proposals from Institutes that Participated in the Former Soviet Biological Defense Program. This project involves the review of proposals prepared for the Department of Defense, the evaluation of projects underway, and the identification of future cooperative research activities. It also provides for two two-week familiarization visits by American scientists interested in establishing research collaboration with Russian colleagues on dangerous pathogens.

Public Health Initiatives

The Institute of Medicine will conduct new activities as well as capitalizing on work currently in progress to develop and communicate anti-terrorism strategies based on public health principles. The goal is to provide guidance on specific issues of national, local and individual concern within the framework of a comprehensive strategy to assure the health of the public in the 21st century. Priority (near term) activities include:

- A series of workshops under the Forum on Emerging Infections. The first was held on November 27-28, 2001 and addressed Biological Threats and Terrorism: Assessing Science and Response Capabilities. The second, on February 6-7, 2002, focused upon Issues of Resistance: Microbes, Vectors and the Host with implications for counter-terrorism responses.
- A comprehensive study of the safety and efficacy of anthrax vaccines will be released in March. Completion of this

Department of Defense funded study was accelerated in response to the current need to make decisions regarding manufacture and use of anthrax vaccine.

- On November 5th, the IOM Council issued a Statement on Vaccine Development, assessing the country's capacity to develop, produce and store vaccines. The recommendations include creation of a National Vaccine Authority. This statement was introduced as part of the testimony by Dr. Richard Klausner before the Senate Commerce Committee on February 5, 2002.
- The 1992 IOM report on Emerging Infectious Diseases is being updated and expanded. The committee will include an extensive discussion of issues related to bioterrorism. The report will be issued in early 2003.
- A committee report providing a vision for assuring public health in the 21st century will be issued in the Spring of 2002. It will provide a framework for integrating investments and activities related to counter-terrorism into the overall public and private sector infrastructure to assure public health.

Issues Affecting Universities Arising out of Terrorism Events: Workshop on Implications for Research, Scientific Communication, and Foreign Students

A workshop was held on December 13-14, 2001. Issues such as visa and foreign student tracking policies were discussed by representatives of major research universities. Also discussed were protections that can be achieved to avoid the diversion of biological agents from research facilities. The implications of possible restrictions on biomedical research, scientific communication, and on graduate student participation were also examined. A report was provided to the Presidents in February 2002, outlining topics and recommendations for studies by various units of the National Academies. An all-staff meeting will be held in February and briefings of interested constituencies will be held in coming months. Follow-up work will be undertaken by, among others, GUIRR, COSEPUP, the Openness and Security Roundtable, and the Science, Technology and Law Program.

Preliminary Evaluation of US Industrial Vulnerabilities and Near-term Protective Measures

Evaluations by the appropriate NRC boards have been undertaken in cooperation with volunteers to identify vulnerabilities in key industries, e.g. chemical and energy industries, and measures that might lessen this vulnerability or reduce the consequences of strikes to key infrastructure. The Board on Chemical Sciences and Technology met with chemical industry representatives on this topic on 12/9/01 and with federal agencies on 12/10/01. The Board on Life Sciences and the Board on Agriculture and Natural Resources have held similar meetings. Other boards will meet with relevant industries in the weeks ahead.

Communicating to Local Governments and Private Citizens about Preparedness for Terrorism Events

A meeting requested by Dr. Marburger will be held in the spring of 2002 to plan how better to link federal and state governments on S&T policy, including for combating terrorism. Science representatives of each of the states will attend.

ADDITIONAL SPECIFIC BOARD-BASED ACTIVITIES

An Assessment of Naval Forces' Defense Capabilities Against Chemical and Biological Warfare Threats

At the request of the Chief of Naval Operations, the Naval Studies Board is conducting a study to:

(1) examine existing and potential chemical and biological warfare threats to naval force operations in littoral regions and deep ocean regions of the world;

(2) examine and project chemical and biological defense technologies, tactics, and procedures;

(3) evaluate R&D and identify priorities for providing naval forces with needed capabilities; and

(4) examine testing and evaluation procedures (in conjunction with training procedures) for ensuring adequate defensive capabilities. It is anticipated that a published report will be available by July 2002.

Improving Cybersecurity Research in the United States

A study by the Computer Science and Telecommunications Board will be conducted to determine the extent and nature of current federal research in cybersecurity and to identify areas of research that are not adequately supported.

Information and Security: Enhancing Information Management and Data Mining Capabilities for Combating Terrorism while Protecting Civil Liberties

A planning meeting for a study is being organized by the Computer Science and Technology Board (CSTB). The study will consider research opportunities in data mining as well as ways to minimize the privacy and civil liberties implications of anticipated increased collection and integration of personally identifiable information.

Improving Research Standards and Practices to Prevent Misuse of Biotechnology Research

A study will review and assess the current rules, regulations, and institutional arrangements and processes in the United States that provide oversight of research on dangerous biological pathogens, including within government laboratories, universities and other research institutions, and industry. The review will focus on how choices are made about which research is and is not .ppropriate, and how information about relevant ongoing research is collected and shared. It will consider, but not be limited to, the "biosafety" practices that govern the conduct of research and the handling and transport of materials. The study will recommend changes to improve

U.S. capacity to prevent the destructive application of dangerous biological pathogens while still enabling the conduct of legitimate research.

Agricultural Bioterrorism

The Board on Agriculture and Natural Resources is conducting a study to evaluate the ability of the U.S., to deter, prevent, detect, thwart, respond to and recover from an intentional biological attack against the nation's food and fiber supply. The report is expected in summer 2002.

What Terrorists Value

The Division of Behavioral, Social Sciences, and Education will conduct a study on the social, cultural, organizational, and psychological context of the terrorism now directed at the U.S., and the implications for new approaches to deter terrorism.

Assessment of Technologies Deployed to Improve Aviation Security

This study by the National Materials Advisory Board (NMAB) sponsored by the Federal Aviation Administration, is assessing the operational performance of passenger screening, explosives detection systems and hardened cargo containers in airports and compare that performance to their performance in laboratory testing, with a focus on ways to deploy these systems more effectively to improve aviation security. The Committee will complete and issue a second status report by March 2002.

Assessment of Practicality of Pulsed Fast Neutron Analysis for Aviation Security

This National Materials Advisory Board study, sponsored by the Federal Aviation Administration, is assessing the practicality of pulsed fast neutron analysis (PFNA) for detecting explosives and other contraband in cargo and passenger baggage in an airport. The capabilities of PFNA are compared with the capabilities of explosives-detection equipment currently available for deployment and with the expected future development of current equipment. The Committee plans publication of their findings in mid 2002.

Advanced Energetic Materials and Manufacturing Technologies

This study by the Board on Manufacturing and Engineering Design is investigating and assessing the manufacturing technologies required to scale up and produce bulk quantities of advanced energetics and suggest opportunities and strategies for government investment. Although these new materials are more difficult to manufacture when compared to standard explosives, they are equally difficult to detect using current systems. The study, sponsored by the Department of Defense, is underway.

Materials and Manufacturing Processes for Advanced Sensors

This study by the Board on Manufacturing and Engineering Design is examining potential technologies for detect-to-warn systems for biological agents. Their charge is to review the DTRA-specified requirements for these systems and identify those requirements that will especially drive the detection concepts and architectures - e.g., less than one minute detection times, continuous operations with attendant implications for consumables and their costs - and understand to what extent, if any, these, or related, parameters (e.g. detection sensitivities), may be relaxed. The committee is also considering examples of representative operational scenarios or architectures (to be provided by the sponsor), which will be invaluable in putting these system requirements and tradeoffs in context.

TRANSPORTATION INITIATIVES

Support for Transportation Security Research (TRB)

The Transportation Research Board administers two cooperative research programs, one for state departments of transportation and one for the public transportation industry. In October 2001, $2 million was allocated from the Transit Cooperative Research Program and $1.25 million from the National Cooperative Highway Research Program to provide flexible, on-going rapid response research on transportation issues related to emergency incident prevention, preparedness, response, and recovery, paying particular attention to potential terrorist threats. Consultants have been selected and work will get underway in February and March 2002. The National Cooperative Highway Research Program is currently supporting the development of manuals for vulnerability assessments and emergency response planning.

Standing Technical Committee on Critical Infrastructure Protection (TRB)

TRB maintains approximately 200 standing technical committee that support information dissemination activities in transportation. The Committee on Critical Infrastructure Protection, which was established two years ago, facilitates the dissemination of state-of-the practice and state-of-the-art information on infrastructure security and protection and encourages research in this field. It sponsors TRB's website on security and organized security sessions at TRB's Annual Meeting in January 2002.

Survey on Vulnerability Assessment (TRB)

TRB is conducting, in cooperation with the American Association of State Highway and Transportation Officials, a survey of states to determine whether and to what extent they have addressed infrastructure planning and security in their planning efforts. All states responded to the survey, whose results were summarized at several TRB Annual Meeting sessions in January 2002.

TRB Annual Meeting (TRB)

TRB's Annual Meeting is one of the largest gatherings of transportation professionals in the world. The January 2002 meeting included over 30 security and recovery related sessions. An overview session will involve the DOT modal administrators, the new head of the Transportation Security Agency, and the Deputy Secretary covered topics such as port and waterway security, airline passenger screening, and protecting public transportation facilities.

Transportation Associations—Information Sharing (TRB)

TRB organized a meeting of a number of transportation associations to share information about the security issues they are confronting and the activities under way. The group will meet again in April 2002.

Redundancies in Transportation Systems (TRB)

A planning meeting will be held to examine multi-modal transportation infrastructure redundancy to enhance defense against terrorist disruption.

Emergency Evacuation in Metropolitan Areas: Barriers and Opportunities (TRB)

A planning meeting will be held to discuss technical and institutional barriers to improved metropolitan-wide evacuation and emergency response.

Vulnerability of the Electric Power Transmission and Distribution System to Terrorism (BEES)

A planning meeting will be held to discuss reducing the impact of terrorist attacks on the electric transmission and distribution system.

Safety of Our Nation's Water Supplies (WSTB)

A series of activities will be held to discuss safety of the short term security and longer term research initiatives relevant to water supply safety from terrorist attacks.

Forum on How Natural Disaster Research Can Inform the Response to Terrorism (NDR)

The Natural Disasters Roundtable (NDR) will conduct a two-day workshop to develop thoughts on how responses to natural disasters might be applied to threats provided by terrorism. Topics to be considered include engineering design, promoting public awareness and understanding, evacuation planning, recovery planning, utilization of technology to detect and monitor public health risks, public health system needs, and mental health consequences.

Interdependent Vulnerabilities for Critical Infrastructure Protection (BICE)

A one-day workshop was held on October 31st to help develop methodologies to analyze interdependent vulnerabilities. The Board on Infrastructure and the Constructed Environment is developing a workshop series to address these problems.

Chemical Stockpile Activities (BAST)

The Board on Army Science and Technology has conducted a fast-trackreview of proposed process changes for the *expedited* disposal of the chemical weapons stockpile inventory. Letter reports were provided to the Army in January 2002.

A second BAST activity is an examination of the state of the stockpile as delivered to disposal facilities and the effects of stockpile condition on processing, handling, monitoring and stakeholder reaction. A third activity is an evaluation of process changes for alternative technology at the Aberdeen Bulk-Only Chemical Agent Disposal Facility.

Homeland Defense (BAST)

To help determine areas of emphasis for science and technology employed by the U.S. Army in support of counter-terrorism/ antiterrorism initiatives, the National Research Council Committee on Homeland Defense will review, assess, and offer recommendations relative to homeland defense in the areas of indications and warnings, denial and survivability, recovery and consequence management, and attribution and retaliation technologies.

Roundtable on Terrorism (Committee on Law and Justice) (DBASSE)

As part of the Academies' investment in 'root-cause' analysis of terrorism, the Forum will discuss relevant social science tools to summarize the knowledge base on terrorism. The objective would be to improve understanding of the current situation, giving rise to terrorism both in the United States and in the Muslim world. A series of workshops and commissioned papers will examine such topics as:

- Understanding International Terrorism with emphasis upon research from political science and sociology
- A more specific contextual examination of terrorism in the Middle East
- Organizational analysis and terrorism
- A profile of terrorists
- Recent uses of profiling and their application to combating terrorism
- Money laundering
- Collective behavior of populations under the threat of danger

General Education of the Media and Public on Terrorism Vulnerabilities and Responses

On 12/6/01, the Academies and the Foundation for American Communications (FACS) co-sponsored a Conference for News Executives ["Terror and Homeland Defense: Bringing the Stories Home"] at the Reserve Officers Association. Approximately 50 media representatives attended.

Cybersecurity and Authentication Technologies (CSTB)

The Computer Science and Telecommunications Board has issued a letter report synthesizing a decade of work on cybersecurity, focusing on issue identification and practical guidance. CSTB's Committee to Study Authentication Technologies and Their Implications for Privacy has undertaken to develop a brief, interim report addressing issues associated with the concept of national identification systems. The resulting pamphlet will be ready in the winter.

Chemistry and National Security (BCST)

The Board on Chemical Sciences and Technology held a workshop in January on "chemistry and national security."

Mathematics and Homeland Security (BMS)

The Board on Mathematical Sciences is holding a workshop in April on mathematical topics relevant for homeland security, including pattern recognition and data mining, epidemiological modeling, voice and image recognition.

Chapter

12

Reducing the Threat of Nuclear Terrorism

Paradoxically, with the end of the Cold War – a time in history where large parts of the Northern Hemisphere could have been be annihilated in a less-than-an-hour nuclear exchange – today's nuclear security picture is as unclear as ever. Well-established nuclear weapon states still hold sizeable nuclear arsenals, juvenile nuclear weapon possessors are boosting their stockpiles, and a new set of states have revealed disturbing nuclear ambitions and a strong appetite for nuclear weapons. Prospects of renewed horizontal – and possibly vertical – state nuclear-weapon proliferation are real. And, as this wasn't enough, some sub-national groups have revealed a definitive interest in nuclear explosives.

The topic of this paper is the most novel and undefined, and probably least understood, of all contemporary nuclear dangers: the threat of nuclear terrorism. While the effects of such a scenario would be quite limited compared with an all-out nuclear exchange, the intentional use of even a single nuclear weapon in a densely populated area would leave in its wake a massive, unprecedented public health and environmental catastrophe.

Assessing and understanding the risk seems essential. However, the (fortunate) lack of empirical data, limitations in terrorist trend analysis, and the inherent complexities surrounding of the issue of nuclear terrorism render any probabilistic assessments a daring endeavour. Temptations to try to identify the probability of future acts of nuclear terrorism in accurate and absolute terms should thus probably be avoided.

Through a simple stepwise risk assessment methodology, where risk is viewed as a product of probability and consequence, this paper attempts to qualitatively assess the technical aspects of the nuclear terrorism threat, and how this risk best can be reduced. The work of Bunn et al. (2003, 26) on the successive steps towards a successful act of nuclear terrorism will be used as a framework for the analysis. It will be shown that the most efficient way to reduce– and in fact even eliminate – the risk of nuclear terrorism is to initially deny terrorists access to fissile material through optimal protection, control and accounting practices. Not only seem any other countermeasures further down the line to be more costly. The effects tend to be more arbitrary and with less secure outcomes.

Throughout the paper, no attempt will be given to assess the motivational side of nuclear terrorism, to discuss possible nuclear terrorism scenarios beyond the use of crude nuclear explosive devices,2 or to criticize any of and the current hard-driving political rhetoric surrounding the phenomenon of nuclear terror.

NUCLEAR TERRORISM RISK ASSESSMENTS

As nuclear weapons are of limited or no use for the overwhelming majority of terrorist groups (Rapoport 2001), the probability (P) of nuclear terrorism may generally be regarded as low. At the same time, however, any successfully performed acts of nuclear terrorism would leave devastating consequences (C) in its wake. Nuclear terrorism may therefore be seen as a low-probability/ high consequence event. As such, the risk is not zero, and cannot – and should not – be neglected:

R= P x C, = > R “‘ 0

Accordingly, it has been argued that governments should institute measures to make nuclear terrorist threats less likely to emerge, and should create operational capabilities that can give them a reasonable chance of detecting, defeating and minimizing the consequences of the nuclear terrorist threat (Falkenrath 1998, 58). From a medical point of view, however, the ability of health personnel to provide post-attack prophylaxis is limited. Risk elimination and prevention of nuclear terrorism thus seem key.

Any terrorist with nuclear ambitions will have to follow a specific stepwise path to accomplish the goal of nuclear havoc. The steps will be of both a motivational and a capability-building character. To maximize the chances of preventing a nuclear terrorist attack, each of these successive steps should be systematically assessed.

Step Action

S1 Form a highly capable group with extreme objectives S2 Decide to escalate to the nuclear level of violence S3 Steal nuclear weapons material S4 Acquire nuclear weapons material S5 Smuggle material to safe haven S6 Construct nuclear explosive device S7 Smuggle nuclear explosive device into target country S8 Transport nuclear explosive device to target location S9 Detonate nuclear explosive device.

Each of the steps has to be performed in the order indicated, as each rests upon the previous one. The probability for a successful nuclear terrorist attack may thus be expressed as the product of the probability of all single steps S1,S2, ..., S9:

P = P(S1) x P(S2) x..... P(S9) = _ P(S i) i = 1, 9

Steps S1 and S2 are both of a motivational or intentional character, and fall therefore outside the core scope of this paper. Steps S3–S9, however, will all be the subject of further analysis. Each of these (technical) steps are a prerequisite for nuclear terrorist havoc – and each and every one of them depends upon the preceding step. The total probability P may thus be severely limited – even reduced to zero – if one or more of the partial probabilities P(Si) become minuscule or zero.

This is an essential point: The risk of nuclear terrorism could be (drastically) reduced – even eliminated – by installing proper barriers at critical points along the nuclear terrorist pathway. This allows, moreover, for a comparative "cost–benefit" analysis to determine where in the "nuclear terrorism chain" investments are likely to yield the highest gains (in terms of reduced probability of nuclear terrorism). The different steps and associated countermeasures – will be discussed in the following.

Stealing Nuclear Weapons Material (S3)

The initial step towards a technical nuclear capability is to get hold of sufficient quantities and qualities of fissile material. While most of the fissile material worldwide is duly protected and accounted for, the huge amounts produced during the Cold War could make proper control challenging. As the quantity of weapons-useable material increases, so does the proliferation risk of the material (Dreicer and Rutherford 1996, 30). There have been multiple documented cases of theft of kilogram quantities of weapons-useable material, especially in countries of the former Soviet Union. In February 2002, US intelligence confirmed to Congress that weapons-grade and weapons-useable nuclear materials have been stolen from some institutes in Russia (Collina and Wolfsthal 2002).

During the past decade, unprecedented co-operative work between the USA and Russia has been carried out to secure fissile material. However, much of the challenges remain. Hundreds of metric tons of nuclear material lack improved security systems. As of March 2003 – after a decade of cooperation – the US Department of Energy (DOE) had assisted Russia in protecting about 228 metric tons, or some 38%, of its weapons-useable nuclear material (United States General Accounting Office 2003, 25).

Insider thefts have turned out to be a particular problem. Soviet-era physical security systems were built on a philosophy of "guards, guns and Gulag" (Bunn et al. 2002, 35). Morale in the nuclearweapon complex then was high, and insiders were not really a threat, as personal surveillance was tight and potential buyers of stolen fissile material absent. Post-Soviet experiences have proven otherwise (Koupriyanova 1999).

Acquiring Stolen Nuclear Weapons Material (S4)

Fresh fissile material is only mildly radioactive, with a limited level of toxicity in solid form. The material can be held safely in bare hands. It becomes hazardous only if finely divided, dispersed and ingested into the lungs. Due to the extreme density of the material, critical masses of weapons-grade uranium and plutonium occupy only small volumes – about a grapefruit size for uranium and a golfball size for plutonium (Harris 2001, 82). These small volumes and low toxicities could make handling of near-critical amounts of fissile material relatively uncomplicated.

However, no final buyer – only sellers and middlemen – has yet been identified in what seems to be a fairly persistent black market for fissile material. According to the IAEA's Illicit Trafficking Database,5 about 600 illicit trafficking incidents have taken place since 1 January 1993. Of these, some 400 incidents have been confirmed by states. A little less than half of the confirmed cases (175) involve nuclear material, including 18 cases with highly enriched uranium or plutonium (Anzelon 2001). None of the quantities of seized nuclear material was in itself enough to produce a workable nuclear explosive. On the other hand, one successful transfer of high-quality nuclear material could be one too many, and the seizures produce a disturbing picture. The extent to which undetected illicit trafficking has occurred remains unknown.

Smuggling Nuclear Material to a Safe Haven (S5)

If the country of origin of the fissile material is different than the planned country of destination for the nuclear explosive device, the material may have to be transferred across several international borders. To customs and other law-enforcement officers this represents an opportunity for intercepting the material. Unfortunately, the low radiation signatures complicate such seizures, as do the need for specialized training and equipment, the number of legitimate border crossings, and – of course, limited opportunities and customs resources to control all travellers and goods.

Every day, more than 15 million cargo containers are moving around at sea or land, or await delivery. Inspectors examine only two percent of the containers, and often only after these have travelled long distances (Economist 2002). Despite comprehensive efforts and extensive international co-operation, only a fraction of the drugs smuggled is stopped, and it seems unlikely that this fraction should be any higher for fissile material. Experiences with the interdiction of drugs and other trafficking suggest that seizures represent as little as 10% – and a maximum of 40% of the gods actually being smuggled (Williams and Woessner 1995, 2).

Constructing Nuclear Explosive Device (S6)

After arriving in their safe haven or point of destination with the nuclear material, the terrorists need to assemble the various weapons components. To construct a workable nuclear explosive device any actor – a state or a sub-state group – must follow a series of technical steps (Carnegie Analysis 2001):

(1) develop a design for its nuclear device or obtain such a design from a nuclear weapon state,

(2) produce the fissile material for the core of the device or obtain it from an external source and then shape the fissile material into appropriate nuclear parts,

(3) fabricate, or obtain from outside, the non-nuclear parts of the device, including the high-explosive elements and triggering components that will detonate the nuclear core,

(4) verify the reliability of these various elements individually and as a system, and, finally, assemble all of these elements into a deliverable nuclear armament, commonly referred to as "weaponization".

None of these steps are straightforward. Constructing even a crude nuclear explosive device could thus be a daunting task for terrorists. However, a modest (terrorist) program aiming simply at producing crude nuclear weapons could probably circumvent the need for extensive domestic know-how and resources, and the rapid spread of technological knowledge may boost terrorists' weaponization attempts. The design and production of nuclear weapons today is a far simpler process than it was during the Manhattan Project (Military Critical Technologies 1999). Not only is much of the basic technical information needed to construct a workable nuclear device readily available in the open literature (see e.g. Serber 1992, Barnaby 1996). States and terrorists would have highly differing requirements to their weapons (Bremer Maerli et al. 2003, 731–732). This could make weapons designed to meet the "terrorist nuclear weapon standards" less technically challenging than traditional state nuclear weapons.

Firstly, a state would be at least as concerned with the nuclear device not going off during storage and transportation, as with optimising the yield and detonation of the weapon. While safety requirements are strong for states, such concerns could be given less consideration by terrorists, especially groups with strong affection to martyrdom. Secondly, the reliability concerns may be equivalently low amongst terrorists. While an ignition failure or a fizzle yield would be unfortunate from the viewpoint of terrorists, states must have some assurances that their weapons do function if they are supposed to do – e.g. during a nuclear exchange.

As such, reliable nuclear weapons could be a matter of survivability for a state. Again, this will raise performance requirements and complicate production. Thirdly, any explosion in the lower kiloton range represents an unprecedented terrorist yield, and even failed plutonium explosives may serve as radiological dispersion devices. States on the other hand, want fairly accurate and known yields to predict damages and the number of weapons needed. Similarly should the security of their nuclear devices be an issue for states, and probably not for terrorists.

Fourthly, nuclear weapons for military uses are normally required in fairly large numbers, and they must be delivered by conventional military means (missiles, mortars etc.). This requires large-scale industrial structures, with a (invariable) stock of competent workers.

It could, moreover, require indigenous fissile material production capacities, as dependence on (potentially perfidious) external suppliers could negatively impact the future nuclear capacity of the state. To terrorist group, a single supply of high-quality fissile material may be adequate for their (limited) nuclear ambitions.

Smuggling Nuclear Explosive Device into Target Country (S7)

After a workable nuclear device has been constructed, it will have to be transferred to the location of planned detonation, a process which could also involve border crossings. Blocking such nuclear smuggling has inter alia been a major part of the US Homeland security measures to better control US borders. In the wake of rumours about Al-Qaeda's alleged progress toward obtaining a nuclear or radiological weapon in Afghanistan, hundreds of new and sophisticated radiation detection sensors were deployed to US borders, overseas facilities and points around Washington DC. The sheer size and weight of the explosive devices could render clandestine transport difficult. The ability of the sensors to detect the devices and the nuclear materials, however, may be limited. After assembly radiation signatures from the fissile material are likely better masked due to the metal casing of the explosive device – making border detection harder and handling easier.

Transporting Nuclear Explosive Device to Location (S8)

One of the most important constraining factors for state nuclear weapons is delivery. The weight capacity of delivery vehicle and the space available must be large enough to carry a military nuclear warhead. Development of reliable delivery systems and slender nuclear explosives are technically challenging and expensive, sometimes leaving nuclear bomb planes the only alternative for states. Crude terrorist nuclear weapons, however, will easily fit into a van – and perhaps even an automobile. Other non-military means of delivery could involve trucks, hot-air balloons, or ships. The terrorist means of delivery into or against a country is thus essentially infinite. Clearly, this level of relative mobility and limited size coupled with weak gamma ray radiation (discussed above) could make detection of a crude nuclear device in a busy urban environment extremely challenging (Harris 2001, 83). To avoid transportation altogether, possible perpetrators could assemble the nuclear explosive device in an out-of-the-way downtown residence (Boutwell et al. 2002). If the device is detonated by a timer and remote control, this could provide ample time for getaway.

Detonating Nuclear Explosive Device (S9)

The final step will be to detonate the nuclear device – releasing the devastating blasts, heat and radiation. Of course, the device may fail or fizzle – producing a limited yield. Once potential terrorists have the needed material, however, the actual construction of the ignition for the nuclear explosive device may be comparatively easier (Schaper 2002, 19). The ease of which this should happen depends upon the technical sophistication of the weapon, hereunder for instance the use of neutron triggers (Serber 1992, 51).

Compared to having a stolen intact nuclear warhead at hand, terrorists who construct their own crude devices would probably have an easier task detonating the device – knowing the device from scratch and avoiding (potential) difficulties associated with any permissive action links (PALs) to prevent unauthorised use etc. Uranium-based, crude gun-type devices could be an item of particular concern due to the low neutron-background. According to Luis W. Alvarez, a Nobel Laureate in Physics and a prominent nuclear weapon scientist in the Manhattan Project, gravity itself may suffice to set of a nuclear explosion with highly enriched uranium.

ASSESSING THE STEPS AND POSSIBLE COUNTERMEASURES

The number of steps terrorist have to perform on their way towards nuclear havoc offer governments opportunities to install a range of different countermeasures. Initial measures will focus on risk prevention through boosted security at facilities containing fissile material. Later countermeasures emphasises risk responses, e.g. through surveillance and detection of fissile material and/or of potential perpetrators.

Each and one of the steps towards nuclear terrorist havoc will challenge possible perpetrators. The risk of nuclear terrorism would for instance be drastically reduced if the perpetrators had a hard time smuggling the nuclear explosive into the target country (S7). The probability of successfully transferring a crude nuclear device a cross a border would depend highly on the level and sophistication of the (technical) border control and terrorists' own skills. In reality, however, efforts to detect and interdict nuclear smugglers are extremely unlikely to reduce the likelihood anywhere close to zero (Allison 1995, 69).

The detection of fissile material is anything but easy. Assuming – probably far too generously – that customs and others are indeed able to seize 60 to 70% of the nuclear gods, this could still leave one third of the illicit nuclear material outside the hands of law enforcement officials. Experiences from drug trafficking, moreover, suggests that when law enforcement is increased along one route, this tends not to result in less trafficking, but rather a re-routing along new routes that involves less risks for the perpetrators (Williams and Woessner 1995, 3). Since 1994, reported illicit trafficking incidents in Europe have declined. Simultaneously, however, since 1999 there has been a revival in such incidents in the Caucasus, Central Asia, and Turkey (Zaitseva 2002).

Similar considerations could be made for detection of a readily assembled nuclear explosive device inside a country or a city. The radiation emitted from the device is limited and possible hideouts numerous. For any hopes of a successful detection, rescuers need to be fairly close to the object. The possibility of higher neutron backgrounds due to lower enrichment levels and the relatively higher amounts needed for more fissile material in crude nuclear devices than intact nuclear warheads, could increase radiation levels, and thus ease detectability. However, for a hidden crude nuclear explosive device, the shape, material composition, and shielding is unknown – further complicating detection.

Nuclear terrorist risk assessments need, moreover, to take into consideration the differing standards between possible terrorist nuclear explosive devices and state nuclear weapons. While military nuclear weapons must meet an array of requirements before fielded, terrorists' obstacles to constructing a nuclear explosive device may be lower than anticipated. While responsive countermeasures like border-control, intelligence, sting operations, etc. clearly have a role to play in fighting nuclear terrorism, law-enforcement officers and others may thus fight in vain – and against the clock – the closer the potential nuclear terrorist perpetrators are to succeeding. A key factor that, moreover, should affect decisions about nuclear terrorism threat reduction activities is that the nature of the terrorist threat and the targets, weapons, and means of delivery will change over time, often in response to successful countermeasures (Committee on Science and Technology for Countering Terrorism 2002, 36). Terrorists will adapt to the defences in place and seek the weakest known spots. Reducing vulnerability by protecting particular targets may therefore be neither prudent nor desirable.

Anther option would be detection of suspects and possible perpetrators. This may call for rigours countermeasures including extensive public surveillance. Such surveillance could, however, be at odds with fundamental civil liberties and should be used with care.

Conclusion From an assessment of the various steps on the nuclear terrorism pathway, it seems clear that that the most effective countermeasures are those focusing on the early steps – and in particular those that can prevent fissile material from being stolen in the first place. Highly enriched uranium and plutonium are the essential ingredients of any nuclear device. Possession of a sufficient amount of fissile material establishes a critical step and the primary impediment towards accomplishing a functioning device (Arbman et al. 2002). Denying terrorists access to these materials would thus effectively reduce the risk of nuclear terrorist havoc to zero, independent of other technical capabilities and competence (associated with subsequent steps) that the terrorists might have. As such, it represents the nuclear terrorism chokepoint and probably the most cost-effective way to avoid nuclear terrorism. Denying terrorists fissile material could thus be the be-all and end-all of efforts to prevent nuclear terrorism. Technical barriers should by itself no longer be regarded sufficient to avoid large-scale nuclear havoc.

In sum, only preventive, and not responsive, countermeasures are likely to provide the long-term and sustainable nuclear security solutions that everyone is looking for. Averting acts of nuclear terrorism are likely to be much more cost-efficient than dealing with its consequences. Therefore, the stocks of highly enriched uranium and plutonium should be duly protected – and drastically and urgently reduced.

Chapter

13

Due Diligence: Estimating Vulnerability

FUNDAMENTAL CHANGES

Vulnerability assessment methodologies developed by DoD and other federal agencies are currently the best available resources for terrorism risk assessment. In order for these resources to be feasible and relevant in commercial buildings, they must be significantly simplified and civilianized. Bringing government experience and expertise regarding terrorism risk and building security to the commercial sector will involve two fundamental changes in the way buildings are designed, managed, and operated, and in the way that due diligence is used to evaluate existing buildings for acquisition or refinancing. First, businesses will need to carefully evaluate functional aspects of their operations in order to prioritize security requirements. Second, tradeoffs will be required in the level of security provided to ensure continued viability of business operations. Reducing vulnerability to terrorist threat will involve both physical measures to modify a facility and operational changes. Mitigation will consist mainly of measures to thwart tactics that terrorists might use in attacking organizations and facilities.

DUE DILIGENCE ASSESSMENT OF VULNERABILITY TO TERRORIST ATTACK

Due diligence procedures are employed to assess valuations for property acquisition or financing and to identify risks related to the deal. Such procedures may also be used as part of insurance underwriting. Due diligence often includes both detailed property inspection and rigorous audits of available financial and construction documentation. At the same time, due diligence is a highly specialized field requiring both expertise and extensive prior experience to render sound judgments and recommendations to decision makers.

A Property Condition Assessment (PCA) is used (at levels of detail and rigor appropriate to the investment being considered) as part of due diligence to help make prudent investment decisions. The assessment consists of analysis and assessment of physical conditions of a property by an on-site inspection and review of available construction and operations documentation.

Investigators use professional judgment to identify items needing further expert investigation and those that can be readily evaluated by inspection. Vulnerability to terrorist attack should become a distinct element of due diligence condition assessments in the future. Professionals conducting property condition assessments of vulnerability to terrorist attack must have competency in building systems, operations, and security disciplines.

For terrorism risk and security concerns, a due diligence assessment should also include a property condition assessment investigation of operational procedures and the vulnerability of those procedures to terrorist attack.

MITIGATION OF VULNERABILITY

Strategies for reducing exposure to terrorism risk may be in the form of operational actions or construction projects (either new or existing building renovation). They could include reorganization of land uses, reorientation of roadways, security improvements to site entries, and improvements to the facility, including the existing structure and surrounding site area. For some strategies, the process may include the identification of multiple scenarios, or alternatives, for achieving the desired goal.

PROCESS MODEL FOR TERRORISM RISK REDUCTION USED IN FEDERAL FACILITIES

United States military services and government agencies have long been involved in assessing vulnerabilities and protecting facilities, especially for off-shore installations. Terrorism and terrorist attack have been a part of the assessment of threat and vulnerability of government facilities for several decades. While each government agency has used its own procedures, the general approach has been elaborated and presented in FEMA 426, *Reference Manual to Mitigate Potential Terrorist Attacks Against Buildings.*

The terrorism risk reduction process starts with establishment of protection priorities and proceeds to assessment of threats, both providing information to a vulnerability assessment. The vulnerability assessment in turn leads to identification of mitigation options and risk management decisions based on a comparative evaluation of risk, liabilities, and mitigation costs and benefits.

PROTECTION PRIORITY

The first step of the process to assess risk to terrorist attack is to identify the relative importance of the people, business activities, goods, and facilities involved in order to prioritize security actions. This applies to both new and existing facilities. Three actions are recommended in accordance with FEMA 426:

- Define and understand the core functions and processes of the business or institutional entity.
- Identify critical business infrastructure:
  - Critical components (people, functions, and facilities)
  - Critical information systems and data
  - Life safety systems and safe haven areas
  - Security systems
- Assign a relative protection priority, as simple as high, medium, or low, to the occupants, business functions, or physical components of the facility (note that FEMA 426 describes

a 9-step scale of values for describing asset values; the 3-step variation presented here is a simplified process):

High Priority. Loss or damage of the facility would have grave consequences, such as loss of life, severe injuries, loss of primary services, or major loss of core processes and functions for an extended period of time.

Medium Priority. Loss or damage of the facility would have moderate to serious consequences, such as injuries, or impairment of core functions and processes.

Low Priority. Loss or damage of the facility would have minor consequences or impact, such as a slight impact on core functions and processes for a short period of time.

THREAT ASSESSMENT

Military experience indicates that the terrorist threat is from people with the intent to do harm, who are known to exist, have the capability for hostile action, and have expressed the intent to take hostile action. Threat assessment is a continual process of compiling and examining information concerning potential threats. Information should be gathered from all reliable sources. The assessment process consists of:

- Defining threats
- Identifying likely threat event profiles and tactics

Defining Threats

Defining threats involves analysis of information regarding terrorist existence, capability, history, intention, and targeting:

- Existence is the assessment of who is hostile to the organization, or community of concern.
- Capability is the assessment of what weapons have been used in carrying out past attacks.
- History is the assessment of what the potential terrorist has done in the past and how many times.

- Intention is the assessment of what the potential terrorist hopes to achieve.
- Targeting is the assessment of the likelihood a terrorist (the specific one may not be known) is performing surveillance on the particular facility, nearby facilities, or facilities that have much in common with the particular organization. The Homeland Security Advisory System is a color-coded hierarchy of threat conditions. The threat level for a specific business facility could be similarly developed in coordination with local law enforcement, intelligence, and civil authorities.

Identifying Likely Threat Event Profiles and Tactics

Identifying the likelihood of specific threats and tactics involves evaluation of attack intentions, hazard event profiles, and the expected effects of an attack on the facility and organization. The profiles describe the mode, duration, and extent of the effects of an attack, as well as mitigating and exacerbating conditions that may exist. These and more specific descriptions can be used to identify threats of concern to individual organizations.

Assigning a Threat Rating

The ultimate product of a threat assessment is the assignment of a *threat rating* to each hazard of concern to a particular organization. The threat rating, like *protection priority*, is based on expert judgment and may be as simple as high, medium, or low.

- High Threat. Known terrorists or hazards, capable of causing loss of or damage to a facility exist. One or more vulnerabilities are present and the terrorists are known or reasonably suspected of having intent to attack the facility.
- Medium Threat. Known terrorists or hazards that may be capable of causing loss of or damage to a facility exist. One or more vulnerabilities may be present. However, the terrorists are not believed to have intent to attack the facility.
- Low Threat. Few or no terrorists or hazards exist. Their capability of causing damage to a particular facility is doubtful

An organization may reasonably be concerned only with high threat ratings in the near term, but may want to consider addressing medium threats over time.

Alternative: Assigning a Level of Protection Against Threat

In the absence of experience, assessing terrorist threat is the most difficult aspect of planning to resist terrorist attack. An effective alternative approach may be to select a level of desired protection for a business operation based on management decision- making, and then proceed to a vulnerability assessment. The Department of Defense correlates *levels of protection* with potential damage and expected injuries. The GSA and Interagency Security Committee (ISC) also use the level of protection concept, though the definitions differ slightly. The following levels are based on DoD definitions:

- High Protection. Facility superficially damaged; no permanent deformation of primary and secondary structural members or non-structural elements. Only superficial injuries are likely.
- Medium Protection. Damaged, but repairable. Minor deformations of non-structural elements and secondary structural members and no permanent deformation in primary structural members. Some minor injuries, but fatalities are unlikely.
- Very Low Protection. Heavily damaged, onset of structural collapse. Major deformation of primary and secondary structural members, but progressive collapse is unlikely. Collapse of non-structural elements. Majority of personnel suffer serious injuries. There are likely to be a limited number (10 percent to 25 percent) of fatalities.

Note that the 'very low' level is not the same as doing nothing. No action could result in catastrophic building failure and high loss of life.

VULNERABILITY ASSESSMENT

A terrorism vulnerability assessment evaluates any weaknesses that can be exploited by a terrorist. It evaluates the vulnerability of facilities across a broad range of identified threats/hazards and provides a basis for determining physical and operational mitigation measures for their protection. It applies both to new building programming and design and to existing building management and renovation over the service life of a structure. The useful product of a vulnerability assessment is the assignment of a *vulnerability rating* of all appropriate aspects of building operations and systems to the defined threats for the particular facility. As with protection priority and threat ratings, vulnerability can be cast as high, medium, or low.

- High Vulnerability. One or more significant weaknesses have been identified that make the facility highly susceptible to a terrorist or hazard.
- Medium Vulnerability. A weakness has been identified that makes the facility somewhat susceptible to a terrorist or hazard.
- Low Vulnerability. A minor weakness has been identified that slightly increases the susceptibility of the facility to a terrorist or hazard.

The Building Vulnerability Assessment Checklist, presented in abbreviated form in Appendix B, compiles a comprehensive list of questions to be addressed in assessing the vulnerability of facilities to terrorist attack. A subset of the checklist, discussed in the following section, is particularly useful in the initial screening of existing facilities to identify and prioritize terrorism risk reduction needs. Such an assessment can be integrated into a due diligence assessment associated with acquisition, refinancing, or insurance underwriting.

INITIAL VULNERABILITY ESTIMATE

Because of the uncertainty of the threat, many insurers, lenders, and owners need a quick, qualitative assessment of the vulnerability of existing buildings to terrorist attack. As experience is gained and more robust vulnerability assessment tools are developed, the rigor of data collection and analysis will increase. For now, the estimate of vulnerability to a simple qualitative scale (high, medium, or low as defined by the vulnerability ratings described above) may provide useful information. Answering even basic questions concerning vulnerability to terrorist attack may involve three means of data collection:

- Visual inspection
- Document review
- Organization and management procedures review

Visual Inspection

A property condition assessment of vulnerability to terrorist attack includes an onsite visual inspection encompassing evaluation of the site and all facility systems including architectural, structural, building envelope, utility, mechanical, plumbing and gas, electrical, fire alarm, communications and information technology systems. Equipment operations and maintenance procedures and records and security systems, planning, and procedures should also be scrutinized. The investigation may need to go beyond the site to vulnerability of utility and other infrastructure systems.

The on-site inspection team should work with the property owner to obtain plans, specifications and related construction documents as necessary. Equipment operation and maintenance procedures and records as well as security procedures should also be scrutinized. All documents should be reviewed assessing concerns related to terrorism vulnerability.

Organization and Management Procedures Review

Because of the transitory nature of the terrorist threat and its uncertain duration, the most effective approaches to terrorism risk reduction in facilities may emphasize reorganization of operational functions and procedures rather than modification of physical systems. The vulnerability assessment team must scrutinize business and operational practices to identify opportunities to reduce exposure to attack. This will involve scrutinizing both owner and tenant operations at the building site.

Assessment of Vulnerability to Expected Methods and Means of Attack

Each building system and business procedure should be assessed on its vulnerability to a range of terrorist attack methods and means.

Based on military experience, common terrorist tactics include the use of moving or stationary vehicles, covert entry, and/or disguise in mail or shipping materials to deliver destructive weapons.

At present, terrorist attacks might include blast effects, airborne contamination, waterborne contamination, or some combination of attack mechanisms. For additional information, see FEMA 426 and FEMA 427, *Primer for Design of Commercial Buildings to Mitigate Terrorist Attacks.*

Chapter

14

Biological Warfare and Terrorism

INTRODUCTION

Other articles in the CBRNE section discuss the specific clinical management issues involved with treatment of patients exposed to potential bioterrorism pathogens and toxins. This article focuses on the larger logistic and emergency management issues of such an event. The complex relationships among various medical disciplines and with the rest of the response community cannot be overemphasized. Medical support falls within the realms of public health, emergency medical services, and traditional fixed site health care. Appreciating that a bioterrorist event is a hybrid disaster, with similarities to a public health emergency and a traditional disaster, is important.

Assumptions

The following assumptions must be made concerning a bioterrorist event to effectively and realistically plan for response:

- With or without advanced warning, the actual time and location of the release of a biological agent most likely will be covert.
- Terrorists desiring maximum effect will opt for aerosolized release of the pathogen.
- Exposed individuals will have minimal physical and immunologic protection.

- Signs and symptoms of illness will be delayed from hours to weeks and initially may mimic minor nonspecific illnesses or naturally produced disease syndromes.
- Arrival of assistance from state or federal agencies will be delayed from 24-72 hours after request and may take longer for full operation.

PRE-EVENT PROCEDURES

Threat Awareness and Pre-event Surveillance

Successful treatment of patients exposed to many of the biological agents is exquisitely time dependent. Morbidity and mortality increase significantly with any delay. Barring discovery by law enforcement or intelligence communities or terrorist announcement of an impending release, the determination that a bioterrorism event has occurred most likely falls to the medical community. The determination of a bioterrorism event by the medical community is through the following:

- Presumptive diagnoses by astute clinicians
- During an autopsy or as the result of specific diagnostic tests ordered based on a patient's clinical condition
- Result of epidemiologic investigations

Pre-event Communication with Law Enforcement

Communication between the medical and law enforcement communities has been rare in the past. Physicians are reluctant to breach patient confidentiality. Law enforcement personnel do not wish to compromise ongoing investigations or unduly alarm the public, especially when evidence or information is not explicit enough to validate suspicions. Nonetheless, information sharing between these disciplines should be explored. Terrorist activities, thefts from biological laboratories, or information received from police agencies may impart forewarning if provided in a timely, discrete manner to appropriate offices of the local health care network. Conversely, if a diagnosis associated with pathogen production is made, passing this information on to the appropriate authorities for further investigation may be prudent. Since entry into the health care system is often through emergency departments and primary care clinics, open dialogue between these providers and law enforcement personnel is advisable and encouraged.

EVENT DISCOVERY

Event Discovery by Clinical Providers

Frontline clinicians may be singularly positioned to first identify a possible bioterrorism attack. However, sole reliance on this method of discovery is fraught with problems. Many pathogens produce early symptoms that mimic naturally occurring diseases. Some findings are so ubiquitous that a rare provider orders further laboratory or radiographic tests early in the course of the disease, unless significant physiologic derangements are present or the index of suspicion is raised due to prior intelligence information. Most physicians have not evaluated or treated patients with many of the diseases produced by these agents. Since a delay occurs between exposure and symptoms, patients present at various times, to various care providers, rather than simultaneously to one location.

Event Discovery by Diagnostic Tests or at Autopsy

Most diagnostic studies performed early are nonspecific, and few laboratories are equipped to provide the sophisticated testing required to identify the specific pathogens used in a bioterrorist attack. A patient presenting with findings consistent with early Venezuelan equine encephalitis looks remarkably similar to any other patient with aseptic meningitis, and routine testing of cerebrospinal fluid does not alter this picture. This exact problem occurred during the initial outbreak of West Nile virus encephalitis in New York City in the summer of 1999. Findings and initial tests were consistent with St. Louis encephalitis, and several months passed before the causative agent was determined to be West Nile virus.

Laboratory workers attempting to isolate certain pathogens without the proper equipment or safeguards are at risk. In general, smallpox and the various viral hemorrhagic fever viruses should be isolated only in laboratories with Biosafety Level IV capabilities. Currently only 2 facilities in the United States have such capabilities: the Centers for Disease Control and Prevention (CDC) and the US Army Medical Research Institute of Infectious Diseases (USAMRIID). Other organisms, such as *Yersinia pestis,* require Biosafety Level III capabilities for appropriate safety.

Many viral pathogens require sophisticated testing, such as enzyme-linked immunosorbent assay or polymerase chain reaction, that is not widely available.

Finally, definitive diagnosis of those pathogens not requiring sophisticated testing or extreme safety precautions requires time for culture growth. Still, certain pathogens can be identified in local laboratories, at least to the degree to justify empiric treatment and health care network alert.

Y pestis is a bipolar gram-negative rod that can be identified through Gram stain. The identification of *Brucella* species in conjunction with a suggestive clinical picture may trigger expedient actions based on a presumptive diagnosis only.

Only anthrax produces nearly pathognomic radiographic findings; suspect anthrax in any previously healthy patient with rapidly progressive sepsis and an unexplained widened mediastinum on routine chest film.

Unless accompanied by acral or digital necrosis due to small vessel thrombosis or by hemoptysis and gram-negative rods in the sputum of large numbers of previously healthy patients, the lobar pneumonia of inhalational plague may be misdiagnosed in the clinical setting.

In fact, pathologists may be the first clinicians to consider bioterrorism. Unfortunately, many pathogens produce n arly identical gross and microscopic findings at necropsy, and further tests are required. However, very few pathogens produce the extensive necrotizing hemorrhagic mediastinitis found in a patient who has succumbed to inhalational anthrax.

Discovery through Population-based Surveillance

Two distinct subsets of evaluations may assist in accelerating the discovery of a bioterrorist release of a pathogen: syndromic surveillance and analysis of mined data.

In syndromic surveillance, data are collected from likely portals of entry into the health care system on patients who present with specific, prospectively identified clinical syndromes. If an unexpected variation in the incidence of these syndromes appears, a more intense but expedient epidemiologic investigation may be warranted.

Problems with this method include the requirement for cooperation by caregivers in providing this information in a timely fashion and balancing the sensitivity and specificity of the analytic method. Data collection and reporting can be labor intensive for a relatively low yield, and few incentives exist for a health care system already strapped for resources.

Data mining is a method only now being evaluated fully as a possible investigative tool. Since many of these pathogens produce symptoms or discomfort in victims before specific diagnoses are entertained, affected persons may exhibit predictable behavioral patterns that, if identified, can trigger full-scale investigations.

Statistical analysis may identify trends earlier than traditional methods by capturing information such as school or work absenteeism; use of specific over-the-counter medications; use of emergency departments, emergency medical services, or primary care clinics for nontraumatic complaints; raw incidence of animal illnesses; poison center data; and nontrauma deaths.

Should either of these methods identify a significant trend, expedient epidemiologic investigations may be warranted. These investigations require establishing a case definition, identifying those patients who meet established criteria, and determining that the incidence of the particular disease is out of the ordinary. Influenza is a disease of the winter months, and finding it during the winter is expected. Plague, although rare, still is found episodically in certain western states. The finding of even one patient with plague in the

Northeast United States, particularly the inhalational form, should trigger, at a minimum, enhanced epidemiologic surveillance.

Epidemiologic investigation is resource intensive, and, barring significant augmentation of staff to collect and analyze data, this method alone may not be responsive enough to serve as the primary means of determining that an event has occurred. Epidemiologic investigation does have great value as the disaster unfolds, as is discussed later.

BIOTERRORIST EVENT

Indicators of a Possible Bioterrorist Event

High index of suspicion on the part of clinical providers and an epidemiologic surveillance system that is rapidly responsive, sensitive, and specific are important to early recognition of an event. If a communications network exists that allows free exchange of information, a variety of clues may promote such early recognition.

These clues include the following:

- Large numbers of patients with similar symptoms of disease
- Large numbers of patients with unexplained symptoms, diseases, or deaths
- Higher than expected morbidity and mortality associated with a common disease and/or failure to respond to traditional therapy
- A single case of a disease caused by an uncommon agent
- Multiple unusual or unexplained clinical syndromes in the same patient
- Disease with an unusual geographic or seasonal distribution
- Unusual typical patient distribution
- Unusual disease presentation
- Similar genetic type among pathogens from temporally or spatially distinct sources
- Unusual, atypical, genetically engineered, or antiquated strains of pathogens

- Endemic disease with a sudden unexplained increase in incidence
- Simultaneous clusters of similar illness in noncontiguous areas
- Pathogens or toxins transmitted through aerosol, food, or water contamination, suggestive of sabotage
- Ill persons presenting at nearly the same time from a point source (eg, a tight cluster of patients meeting case definition), with a compressed epidemiologic curve (the rate of change of new cases is significantly higher than predicted based on historical or modelling data)
- No illness in persons not exposed to common ventilation systems when illness is observed in those in proximity to those systems
- Death or illness among animals that may be unexplained or attributed to an agent of bioterrorism that precedes or accompanies illness or death in humans

Diagnosis

Exact diagnosis of diseases caused by biological warfare or terrorism is important for a number of reasons, beyond treating an individual patient. These reasons include the ability to predict the spread of the disease, generate prognoses, and attribute responsibility. Without explicit criteria for identifying cases, these efforts are undermined. The concept of case definitions, used by public health departments and the CDC, is very important in this effort. Some syndromes do not have confirmatory laboratory tests, although laboratory evidence may be a component of the case definition. Other diseases have such characteristic presentations that diagnosis may be based on these findings alone. Some are diagnosed on the basis of epidemiologic data. For many, substantial amounts of information must be collected before a final case classification is possible. Finally, for forensic purposes, the identification of as many of the specific characteristics of the pathogen as possible is important.

Gathering the necessary information and diagnostic testing for classic case definition requires time, especially if sophisticated laboratory tests are required. In the case of a rapidly progressive virulent outbreak, a delay in instituting treatment until definitive diagnosis has been made results in increased morbidity and mortality. Therefore, "diagnosis to treat" becomes a viable and necessary option. This option is most valuable once occurrence of an attack has been determined, but it is also valuable for postprophylactic treatment of the population at risk. Standardized diagnosis to treat criteria have not been developed, but clinicians should work with emergency planners and public health officials to prospectively identify those criteria necessary to commence treatment of large segments of the population prior to definitive diagnosis.

Emergency Response to a Bioterrorist Event

The demand placed on the health care system (e.g., public hospitals, for-profit hospitals, community health centers, emergency medical services) following a bioterrorism attack will be unprecedented. Indeed, most disasters in US history have been marked by relatively little loss of life in comparison to infrastructure destruction; only 6 disasters in US history have resulted in more than 1000 fatalities.

Due to public health initiatives, the concept of major epidemics likewise has been modified. The available model that is closest to an overwhelming, rapidly progressive, infectious disease epidemic is the Spanish influenza epidemic of 1918, in which an estimated 650,000 Americans died and approximately 40% of the population was affected. Community health care systems must plan ahead to cooperate and expeditiously expand personnel, resources, and facilities to handle the additional demand for services that such an event would cause.

All states and local areas have emergency response plans that are geared toward natural disasters. A bioterrorism event poses a series of unique challenges. Unlike the typical focal disaster, an epidemic due to a bioterrorism attack will be unpredicted, progressive, and widespread. The following will overwhelm local health services very quickly:

- Shortfalls of ICU beds, ventilators, and other critical care needs
- Shortages of chemotherapeutic agents
- Needs for ancillary or nontraditional treatment centers
- High demand for mortuary and/or funeral services
- High demand for social and counseling services
- Shortages of health care workers due to absenteeism

Demands on medical care may last weeks to months after the initial onslaught. Essential community servants (e.g., medical care personnel, police, firefighters, ambulance drivers, other first responders) may be affected. Elderly and other high-risk populations may be fearful of leaving their homes and seeking proper medical attention for chronic medical conditions and may require home visits for health care. Once an event has been discovered, medical management of the ensuing disaster will be focused on alerting the appropriate officials, containing the epidemic, providing postexposure prophylaxis to the population at risk, treating ill patients, handling deceased individuals, and addressing the psychological needs of the community. Because of the criminal nature of such an attack, forensic and law enforcement issues also have to be addressed.

Both medical and public health disaster response activities are coordinated through one organizational structure, the Incident Command System (ICS). Many different organizations participate in the response to a disaster. The ICS provides a common organizational structure and language that allows different kinds of agencies and/or multiple jurisdictions of similar agencies to work together effectively in response to a disaster.

ICS Structure and Hierarchy

The organizational structure of ICS is built around 5 major management activities. Note: Not all activities are used for every disaster.

- Incident command
- Operations
- Planning
- Logistics
- Financial/administrative

Functional requirements, not titles, determine ICS hierarchy.

Important Principles

- An important part of disaster planning is the identification of the incident commander and other key positions before a disaster occurs.
- ICS must be started early, before an incident gets out of control.
- Medical and public health responders, often used to working independently, must adhere to the structure of the ICS in order to avoid potentially negative consequences, including the following:
    - o Death of personnel due to lack of training
    - o Lack of adequate supplies to provide care
    - o Staff working beyond their training or certification
- The structure of ICS is the same regardless of the nature of the disaster. The only difference is in the particular experience of key personnel and the extent of the ICS utilized in a particular disaster.

Alerting and Notification

During planning sessions well before an event, address the timing of release of information to the public, the content of information provided, and the methods of release. Many natural disasters (e.g., hurricanes, flooding) allow sufficient forewarning that area evacuation may be possible. For others, such as tornadoes, evacuation may not be possible, but additional precautions and shelter-in-place actions may be taken to lessen the impact of the event. Terrorists are unlikely to afford a community that luxury, and equally doubtful is that local governments will order evacuation based on even a credible threat, given the increasing frequency of biological terrorism hoaxes that have plagued communities across the country in recent years.

Containment

In all probability, the realization that a major epidemic is at hand will precede the exact identification of the pathogen involved. Nonetheless, identification is of utmost importance, since the transmissibility of infection must be known to contain the spread of the disease. Diseases that are transmissible through casual contact, by nonhuman vectors, or by respiratory droplets, such as smallpox or pneumonic plague, carry high rates of secondary infections, whereas other diseases pose little risk to those not initially infected.

Barring identification of the time and location of release and the amount and virulence of the pathogen, determination of the area of exposure and population at risk is very difficult and requires the expeditious and concerted efforts of local public health investigators and epidemiologists supported by state and federal agencies. Agent characteristics may be helpful, since certain pathogens are exquisitely fragile outside a host, regardless of meteorologic conditions. Analysis of activities of initial victims during the prodromal or incubation period is necessary to estimate time and location of release. As more epidemiologic information becomes available, these determinations may be refined.

Once estimates of the area of exposure and population at risk are determined, forced or voluntary isolation and quarantine may reduce the spread to secondary contacts. Isolation is the process of separating infectious persons from others. As a practical point, isolation primarily occurs within the confines of hospitals. Quarantine, originally applied to the maritime industries, is the limitation on freedom of movement to prevent the spread of a disease. Animal and vector control also may be important determinants in containing the spread of certain diseases. Disease transmission through tainted water supplies is highly unlikely, since routine water purification systems effectively kill most pathogens, and those that survive are not in concentrations sufficient to cause disease. However, one or two notable exceptions exist, such as *Cryptosporidium parvum.* This organism is quite resistant to chlorine, and very small swallowed doses can cause infection. Recently, several widespread outbreaks involving municipal water supplies and public swimming pools have occurred.

Mass Prophylaxis

Postexposure prophylaxis serves 2 purposes: to prevent secondary infections in the case of transmissible diseases and to improve community morbidity and mortality. The prognosis in patients with active disease caused by the common pathogens of warfare or terrorism is uniformly poor, with mortality rates approaching 100% if treatment is delayed until patients become symptomatic. Additionally, very little treatment beyond supportive care is available for many of these patients. The importance of postexposure prophylaxis is obvious and cost effective.

Most hospitals and pharmacies have gone to "just in time" pharmaceutical procurement, and stockpiles to handle surge demand are meager at best at most locations. As part of the federal initiative to address deficiencies in the capability to respond to a bioterrorism attack, the Office of Emergency Preparedness of the Department of Health and Human Services established 4 National Medical Response Teams, and the CDC instituted the National Pharmaceutical Stockpile (NPS) program.

Three National Medical Response Teams, in North Carolina, Colorado, and California, are capable of providing medical treatment after a chemical or biological terrorist event. The response teams are fully deployable within 6 hours to incident sites anywhere in the country with a cache of specialized pharmaceuticals to treat as many as 1000 patients. A fourth team is dedicated to the National Capital Area.

The Strategic National Stockpile (SNS) program consists of a 2-tier response. The first tier consists of eight 12-hour "push packages" of pharmaceuticals and supplies that can be delivered to the scene within 12 hours of the federal decision to deploy the assets. These packages allow for the treatment or prophylaxis of disease caused by a variety of threat agents, including anthrax, tularemia, plague, smallpox, and botulism preparedness. The second tier is the Vendor-Managed Inventory, which arrives at the scene 24-36 hours after activation. The Vendor-Managed Inventory packages consist of additional pharmaceuticals and supplies, tailored to a specific agent, and are sent if needed.

Logistics of mass prophylaxis are magnified by the difficulties in determining the population at risk, and initial estimates are likely to be high. Community emergency planners must have an accurate inventory of pharmaceuticals and medical supplies on hand. They also must have detailed plans and procedures for safeguarding, distributing, and dispensing community stores; for patient screening and tracking; and for receiving, distributing, dispensing, and providing security for arriving SNS supplies. Ambulatory, home-ridden, and homeless patients require provisions. Establish sufficient dispensing locations to prevent an additional burden on hospitals and to ensure delivery of these medications in a timely fashion. The difficult ethical issue of prioritizing who receives critical medications, especially if shortages are anticipated, should be resolved prior to an event.

MASS PATIENT CARE

Another Herculean task is addressing the needs of patients requiring treatment or requesting evaluation for possible treatment. Anticipate a large number of individuals requesting evaluation and treatment who have little or no risk of exposure and who are completely asymptomatic. These latter patients, referred to frequently as the "worried well," result in a significant additional burden, possibly 5-10 times as great as the number of actual ill or injured.

Primary components of mass patient care include the following: (1) personnel and material resource protection, (2) decontamination, (3) triage, (4) treatment, and (5) disposition.

Facility and/or Medical Personnel Protection

Although frequently omitted as first responders in most documents concerning weapons of mass destruction, the true first responders in a covert bioterrorism attack are the health care providers and ancillary staff at hospitals, clinics, and private physician offices. Consider both collective and personal protection.

Collective protection includes positive pressure ventilation systems and high-efficiency particulate air filtration. Both require major modifications in existing facilities and are cost prohibitive. Unless the health care facility is directly downwind from the release site, virtually no risk of major contamination of the facility by airborne spread is present. However, these systems may be considered for new construction. Expedient collective protection may include shutting off ventilation systems and closing and sealing all exterior doors and windows. Since a bioterrorism attack is most likely to occur at some time prior to discovery, these actions may have little effect on facility personnel protection. Personal protection includes vaccinations and postexposure chemoprophylaxis, personal protective equipment, and augmented standard infectious disease protocols. Provide chemoprophylaxis to all health care personnel as soon as a diagnosis is known. Although many ultimately do not need this treatment, staff shortages at a time of greatly increased demand translate into a further degradation of health care response and increased community morbidity.

Controversy continues to exist about the level of personal protective equipment required for hospital personnel. With the exception of the T-2 mycotoxins, intact skin provides an adequate barrier to infection. Re-aerosolization has not been well studied and was considered to be negligible in the past. However, as was demonstrated in the anthrax attacks that occurred in 2001, reaerosolization may occur in certain situations. Unless a patient presents immediately after a release, little risk exists to health care providers from exposure to residual weaponized pathogens. However, some agents are highly contagious through respiratory droplets; add these precautions to standard precautions until the exact diagnosis is made. Personnel involved with decontamination of a suspected bioagent should wear respiratory and splash protection, at a minimum (ie, Occupational Safety and Health Administration Level C).

Decontamination

Most patients who have been infected with a pathogen by a bioterrorism attack do not develop symptoms until 1 day to several weeks after the attack. The exceptions to this are patients exposed to biological toxins, who may develop symptoms several hours after exposure. At present, most biological agents do not survive for long periods outside a host. Even the relatively hardy spore of anthrax is degraded by direct exposure to UV light; consequently, decontamination is not necessary unless the attack is overt and recent. Several cidal and static decontamination solutions are under investigation, but for mass decontaminations, copious amounts of soap and water are probably sufficient. The issue of capture of effluent from decontamination is more significant with chemical than with biological agents, since these pathogens and toxins are denatured through water treatment facilities.

Triage

Traditional triage from a mass casualty event involving trauma primarily is based on physiologic parameters, anatomic sites of injury, and attempts to separate patients requiring minimal effort to stabilize from those who require immediate surgery or further life-saving interventions. Patients with physical injuries or vital signs incompatible with life without extensive use of resources are identified as expectant. Triage in the wake of a bioterrorism attack may require triage based on prognosis alone. In the case of anthrax or pneumonic plague, a patient with any symptoms has a very poor prognosis, despite vigorous treatment, and, in the presence of an overwhelming number of patients, these minimally ill patients may need to be triaged to the expectant category based on their poor prognosis. As with postexposure prophylaxis, give some consideration to these potentially difficult decisions prior to the crisis.

Treatment

Local health care systems have little time to prepare for a bioterrorism event after the fact. These organizations also may suffer significant staff shortages due to absenteeism or illness among medical personnel. All health care systems must modify operations significantly to reduce routine demand while increasing the supply of health care. Health care systems must have prospectively developed plans for a graduated expansion of available health care. Methods may include the following:

- Diversion of patients with minor complaints or health problems to other sites of care
- Public service announcements: Announcements requesting telephone triage may prove beneficial and may protect individuals not affected by the bioterrorist pathogen.
- Cancellation of elective appointments, procedures, and surgery: In addition to freeing up space, hospital gurneys, and beds, this method makes available staff who may be used to augment other departments and services.
- Early discharge of unexposed but hospitalized patients to skilled nursing facilities, home health care, or remote health care facilities: Patient's families may be able to provide initial posthospitalization care under the direction of visiting nurses or through telephonic direction from hospital care providers.
- Doubling up of single or even shared hospital rooms
- Using open wards in auditoriums, cafeterias, or other locations within the confines of the health care facilities or establishing expansion facilities near existing hospitals
    - o Although certain aspects of patient privacy and comfort are sacrificed, this method of expansion of facilities was used effectively during the influenza epidemic of 1918.
    - o Its purpose primarily is to extend nursing services to more patients than can be accomplished on wards with private rooms.
- Temporary doubling of shifts for staff

- Recruitment of volunteers, retired health care workers, or students from medical, nursing, dental, lab tech, and other allied health care schools from the community: Whether or not volunteers will come in the case of a bioattack cannot be predicted, but volunteers from these sources may serve to expand the pool of available health care providers for the expected surge of patients. Expeditious credentialing mechanisms will need to be developed. Many functions in hospitals do not require allied health care providers, and volunteers may be of great value in freeing up more skilled personnel.
- Evacuation of affected patients (may prove problematic)
  - The National Disaster Medical System claims to have nearly 100,000 beds available nationwide.
  - The wisdom of evacuating patients who may transmit the disease to new communities must be balanced with the need to contain the spread of the disease and the desires of family members to remain close to their relatives. This decision ultimately may have to be made by elected state or federal officials in the interest of national security.

MASS FATALITY MANAGEMENT

A bioterrorist event is likely to produce significant numbers of fatalities, especially during the early phases of response. Local medical examiners, morgues, and funeral homes most likely will not be able to absorb the surge. Once activated and mobilized, the National Disaster Medical System includes a number of deployable Disaster Mortuary Operations Response Teams. At least one of these teams has additional training in handling contaminated or infected remains. Issues involved with fatality management include the following:

- Infection control
  - Enforce the same precautions required for live victims while handling deceased patients, during autopsy, and during disposal or disposition of the remains.

- Survivability of all potential pathogens in corpses has not been studied.

- Victim identification and tracking
  - Even in a massive catastrophe, legal, moral, ethical, psychological, and religious reasons exist to identify the dead.
  - Release or cremation of remains will be delayed unless positive identification occurs or, at a minimum, enough evidence is collected (eg, dental radiographs, fingerprints, photographs, potentially DNA samples) for determination later.
- Establishment of temporary morgues
  - In the event of mass fatalities, the ability of hospitals and medical examiners to maintain all remains is doubtful.
  - Without safeguards and training, local funeral homes may be resistant to accepting contaminated bodies. Processes must be in place prospectively to augment the existing system through the use of temporary morgues.
  - These sites require temperature and biohazard control, adequate water, lighting, rest facilities for staff, and viewing areas and should be in communication with patient tracking sites (probably the American Red Cross) and the emergency operations center.
  - Security also may be an issue.
- Disposal or release of remains
  - Many moral, cultural, and religious issues are involved with disposal of the deceased. Although under a declared disaster, the governor and the President have extraordinary powers, at some point a decision must be made concerning the release of remains to families for interment or cremation or to the state for chemical cremation or incineration.
  - Develop appropriate plans and decision algorithms in advance.

AFTERMATH

Psychological Issues

In any disaster, the tendency is to underplay the importance of addressing the psychological needs of the community—the victims and their families, survivors, and response personnel. Failure to address this important aspect of response and recovery impedes effective response during disaster operations and may have important long-term effects on the community well after recovery operations have been completed.

The loss of property or family members and friends under traumatic conditions is difficult at best, and disasters are no exception. When an entire community is affected by a disaster of any nature, the entire community may suffer short-term psychological effects, and a significant percentage of these individuals may develop posttraumatic stress disorder. Short-term mass crisis counseling may improve overall function and reduce the incidence of posttraumatic stress disorder among the population.

First responders and health care workers tend to deny their feelings and not deal with their own psychological trauma, especially during the actual crisis. Critical incident stress debriefing and interventional counseling for these personnel are required to reduce the incidence of long-term sequelae.

Legal and Forensic Issues

Superimposed on the ensuing disaster that a bioterrorist event creates are the myriad diverse legal and forensic issues that are involved in community response to the event. Many of these have not been resolved yet, at either the state or federal level, and, because of different state and local statutes, no standardized templates address them all.

During the planning process, address the major law enforcement and forensic issues that may affect health care operations, including the following:

- Declaration and enforcement of quarantine

- Legal requirements for community immunization or forced postexposure prophylaxis
- Security at health care facilities, temporary morgues, neighborhood treatment centers, and antibiotic dispensing stations
- Evidence collection (both physical and testimonial)
- Patient privacy
- Interstate licensing of providers and liability

Recovery from the Event

In most disaster planning processes, the tendency is to focus on disaster response to the exclusion of recovery. A biological event does not cause physical destruction, and the community material resources remain intact. The 2 primary issues facing community governments and the local health care systems are environmental surety and long-term community mental health.

Most biological pathogens cited in bioterrorism research have very short life spans outside a host. Plague may become endemic among the rodent population of an area, posing a continued threat to the community. Anthrax spores have maintained viability under extreme environmental conditions for decades. Although not cited as a typical bioterrorist pathogen, the virus that causes animal foot-and-mouth disease is one of the hardiest known. Depending upon the pathogen released, ensuring that areas of high concentration are safe for use is necessary. Schools, auditoriums, or other sites used as inpatient expansion facilities require confirmation of contamination removal, if for no reasons other than legal liability and peace of mind of the community. This also may apply to traditional fixed site treatment facilities.

Should a major event occur, psychological problems would remain an issue for the community and possibly for the entire United States. An interesting anecdote from the Spanish influenza epidemic of 1918 is the paucity of literature or coverage of this disaster, both after the event and in historical documentation. A variety of reasons for this have been postulated, but estimates state that as much as one third of the population had a close friend or relative die from this epidemic. Apply the lessons learned in recent hurricanes, in which whole communities were displaced, to any community that suffers a bioterrorist attack.

SUMMARY

A terrorist event presents unique challenges and obstacles to the health care system, well beyond those typically observed in US disasters. Bioterrorism represents the most extreme example. Material and human resource deficiencies at a time of greatly increased demand require unique and innovative solutions if death, disability, and major psychological impairment are to be ameliorated. Only through cooperative, comprehensive planning, across communities and vertically through all levels of government, is this able to be accomplished.

Chapter

15

Terrorism and Biological Warfare

HISTORY OF BIOLOGICAL WARFARE

Biological weapons include any organism (such as bacteria, viruses, or fungi) or toxin found in nature that can be used to kill or injure people. (Toxins are poisonous compounds produced by organisms.)

The act of bioterrorism can range from a simple hoax to the actual use of these biological weapons, also referred to as agents. A number of nations have or are seeking to acquire biological warfare agents, and there are concerns that terrorist groups or individuals may acquire the technologies and expertise to use these destructive agents. Biological agents may be used for an isolated assassination, as well as to cause incapacitation or death to thousands. If the environment is contaminated, a long-term threat to the population could be created.

History: The use of biological agents is not a new concept, and history is filled with examples of their use. Attempts to use biological warfare agents date back to antiquity. Scythian archers infected their arrows by dipping them in decomposing bodies or in blood mixed with manure as far back as 400 BC. Persian, Greek, and Roman literature from 300 BC quotes examples of dead animals used to contaminate wells and other sources of water. In the Battle of Eurymedon in 190 BC, Hannibal won a naval victory over King Eumenes II of Pergamon by firing earthen vessels full of venomous snakes into the enemy ships. During the battle of Tortona in the 12th century AD, Barbarossa used the bodies of dead and decomposing soldiers to poison wells. During the siege of Kaffa in the 14th century AD, the attacking Tatar forces hurled plague-infected corpses into the city in an attempt to cause an epidemic within enemy forces. This was repeated in 1710, when the Russians besieging Swedish forces at Reval in Estonia catapulted bodies of people who had died from plague.

During the French and Indian War in the 18th century AD, British forces under the direction of Sir Jeffrey Amherst gave blankets that had been used by smallpox victims to the Native Americans in a plan to spread the disease.

Allegations were made during the American Civil War by both sides, but especially against the Confederate Army, of the attempted use of smallpox to cause disease among enemy forces.

Modern Times: Biological warfare reached sophistication during the 1900s.

During World War I, the German Army developed anthrax, glanders, cholera, and a wheat fungus specifically for use as biological weapons. They allegedly spread plague in St. Petersburg, Russia, infected mules with glanders in Mesopotamia, and attempted to do the same with the horses of the French Cavalry.

The Geneva Protocol of 1925 was signed by 108 nations. This was the first multilateral agreement that extended prohibition of chemical agents to biological agents. Unfortunately, no method for verification of compliance was addressed.

During World War II, Japanese forces operated a secret biological warfare research facility (Unit 731) in Manchuria that carried out human experiments on prisoners. They exposed more than 3000 victims to plague, anthrax, syphilis, and other agents in an attempt to develop and observe the disease. Some victims were executed or died from their infections. Autopsies were also performed for greater understanding of the effects on the human body. In 1942, the United States formed the War Research Service. Anthrax and botulinum toxin initially were investigated for use as weapons. Sufficient quantities of botulinum toxin and anthrax were stockpiled by June 1944 to allow unlimited retaliation if the German forces first used biological agents. The British also tested anthrax bombs on Gruinard Island off the northwest coast of Scotland in 1942 and 1943 and then prepared and stockpiled anthrax-laced cattle cakes for the same reason.

The United States continued research on various offensive biological weapons during the 1950s and 1960s. From 1951-1954, harmless organisms were released off both coasts of the United States to demonstrate the vulnerability of American cities to biological attacks. This weakness was tested again in 1966 when a test substance was released in the New York City subway system.

During the Vietnam War, Viet Cong guerrillas used needle-sharp punji sticks dipped in feces to cause severe infections after an enemy soldier had been stabbed.

In 1979, an accidental release of anthrax from a weapons facility in Sverdlovsk, USSR, killed at least 66 people. The Russian government claimed these deaths were due to infected meat, and maintained this position until 1992, when Russian President Boris Yeltsin finally admitted to the accident.

Bioterrorism and biowarfare today: A number of countries have continued offensive biological weapons research and use. Additionally, since the 1980s, terrorist organizations have become users of biological agents. Usually, these cases amount only to hoaxes. However, the following exceptions have been noted:

In 1985, Iraq began an offensive biological weapons program producing anthrax, botulinum toxin, and aflatoxin. During Operation Desert Storm, the coalition of allied forces faced the threat of chemical and biological agents. Following the Persian Gulf War, Iraq disclosed that it had bombs, Scud missiles, 122-mm rockets, and artillery shells armed with botulinum toxin, anthrax, and aflatoxin. They also had spray tanks fitted to aircraft that could distribute agents over a specific target.

In September and October of 1984, 751 people were intentionally infected with Salmonella, an agent that causes food poisoning, when followers of the Bhagwan Shree Rajneesh contaminated restaurant salad bars in Oregon.

In 1994, a Japanese sect of the Aum Shinrikyo cult attempted an aerosolized (sprayed into the air) release of anthrax from the tops of buildings in Tokyo.

In 1995, 2 members of a Minnesota militia group were convicted of possession of ricin, which they had produced themselves for use in retaliation against local government officials.

In 1996, an Ohio man attempted to obtain bubonic plague cultures through the mail.

In 2001, anthrax was delivered by mail to US media and government offices. There were 4 deaths.

In December 2002, 6 terrorist suspects were arrested in Manchester, England; their apartment was serving as a "ricin laboratory." Among them was a 27-year-old chemist who was producing the toxin. Later, on January 5, 2003, British police raided 2 residences around London and found traces of ricin, which led to an investigation of a possible Chechen separatist plan to attack the Russian embassy with the toxin; several arrests were made.

On February 3, 2004, 3 US Senate office buildings were closed after the toxin ricin was found in mailroom that serves Senate Majority Leader Bill Frist's office.

How Biological Agents are Delivered and Detected

Although there are more than 1200 biological agents that could be used to cause illness or death, relatively few possess the necessary characteristics to make them ideal candidates for biological warfare or terrorism agents. The ideal biological agents are relatively easy to acquire, process, and use. Only small amounts (on the order of pounds and often less) would be needed to kill or incapacitate hundreds of thousands of people in a metropolitan area. Biological warfare agents are easy to hide and difficult to detect or protect against. They are invisible, odorless, tasteless, and can be spread silently.

Delivery

Biological warfare agents can be disseminated in various ways.

Through the air by aerosol sprays: To be an effective biological weapon, airborne germs must be dispersed as fine particles. To be infected, a person must breathe a sufficient quantity of particles into the lungs to cause illness. Used in explosives (artillery, missiles, detonated bombs): The use of an explosive device to deliver and spread biological agents is not as effective as the delivery by aerosol. This is because agents tend to be destroyed by the blast, typically leaving less than 5% of the agent capable of causing disease.

Put into food or water: Contamination of a city's water supplies requires an unrealistically large amount of an agent as well as introduction into the water after it passes through a regional treatment facility.

Absorbed through or injected into the skin. This method might be ideal for assassination, but is not likely to be used to cause mass casualties.

Detection

Biological agents could either be found in the environment using advanced detection devices or after specific testing or by a doctor reporting a medical diagnosis of an illness caused by an agent. Animals may also be early victims and shouldn't be overlooked.

Early detection of a biological agent in the environment allows for early and specific treatment and time enough to treat others who were exposed with protective medications. Currently, the US Department of Defense is evaluating devices to detect clouds of biological warfare agents in the air.

Doctors must be able to identify early victims and recognize patterns of disease. If unusual symptoms, a large numbers of people with symptoms, dead animals, or other inconsistent medical findings are noted, a biological warfare attack should be suspected. Doctors report these patterns to public health officials.

Protective Measures

Protective measures can be taken against biological warfare agents. These should be started early (if enough warning is received) but definitely once it is suspected that a biological agent has been used. To read more about protective clothing, see Personal Protective Equipment.

Masks: Currently, available masks such as the military gas mask or high-efficiency particulate air (HEPA) filter masks used for tuberculosis exposure filter out most biological warfare particles delivered through the air. However, the face seals on ill-fitting masks often leak. For a mask to fit properly, it must be fitted to a person's face.

Clothing: Most biological agents in the air do not penetrate unbroken skin, and few organisms stick to skin or clothing. After an aerosol attack, the simple removal of clothing eliminates a great majority of surface contamination. Thorough showering with soap and water removes 99.99% of the few organisms that may be left on the victim's skin.

Medical Protection: Health care providers treating victims of biological warfare may not need special suits but should use latex gloves and take other precautions such as wearing gowns and masks with protective eye shields. Victims would be isolated in private rooms while receiving treatment.

Antibiotics: Victims of biological warfare might be given antibiotics orally (pills) or through an IV, even before the specific agent is identified.

Vaccinations: Currently, protective vaccines (given as shots) are available for anthrax, botulinum toxin, tularemia, plague, Q fever, and smallpox. The widespread immunization of nonmilitary personnel has not been recommended by any governmental agency so far. Immune protection against ricin and staphylococcal toxins may also be possible in the near future.

BACTERIA

ANTHRAX

Anthrax bacteria occur worldwide. The organisms known as *Bacillus anthracis* may ordinarily produce disease in domesticated as well as wild animals such as goats, sheep, cattle, horses, and swine. Humans become infected by contact with infected animals or contaminated animal products. Infection occurs mainly through the skin and rarely by breathing spores or swallowing them. Spores exist in the soil and become active when the organisms in the carcass are exposed to air. Apart from biological warfare, anthrax in humans is rare. In the United States, only 127 cases of anthrax appeared in the early years of the 20th century and dropped to about 1 per year during the 1990s.

Signs and Symptoms

Skin anthrax (cutaneous): Infection begins when the spores enter the skin through small cuts or abrasions. Spores then become active in the host (human or animal) and produce poisonous toxins. Swelling, bleeding, and tissue death may occur at the site of infection.

More than 95% of the cases of anthrax involve the skin. After a person is exposed, the disease first appears in 1-5 days as a small pimple-looking sore that progresses over the next 1-2 days to contain fluid filled with many organisms. The sore is usually painless and it may have swelling around it. Sometimes the swelling affects a person's entire face or limb.

Victims may have fever, feel tired, and have a headache. Once the sore opens, it forms a black area of tissue. The black appearance of the tissue injury gives anthrax its name from the Greek word *anthrakos* meaning coal. After a period of 2-3 weeks, the black tissue separates, often leaving a scar. With adequate treatment, less than 1% of people infected with skin anthrax die.

Inhalation anthrax: In inhalation anthrax, the spores are inhaled into the lungs where they become active and multiply. There they produce massive bleeding and swelling inside the chest cavity. The germs then can spread to the blood, leading to shock and blood poisoning, which may lead to death.

Historically known as woolsorter's disease (because it affected people who work around sheep), inhalation anthrax can appear anywhere within 1-6 days, or as long as 60 days after exposure. Initial symptoms are general and can include headache, tiredness, body aches, and fever. The victim may have a nonproductive cough and mild chest pain. These symptoms usually last for 2-3 days. Some people show a short period of improvement. This is followed by the sudden onset of increased trouble breathing, shortness of breath, bluish skin color, increased chest pain, and sweating. Swelling of the chest and neck may also occur. Shock and death may follow within 24-36 hours in most people with this type of infection.

Anthrax is not spread from person to person. Inhalation anthrax is the most likely form of disease to follow a military or terrorist attack. Such an attack likely will involve the aerosolized delivery of anthrax spores.

Mouth, throat, GI tract (oropharyngeal and gastrointestinal): These cases result when someone eats infected meat that has not been cooked sufficiently. After an incubation period of 2-5 days, victims with oropharyngeal disease develop a severe sore throat or sores in the mouth or on a tonsil. Fever and neck swelling may occur. The victim may have trouble breathing. GI anthrax begins with nonspecific symptoms of nausea, vomiting, and fever. These are followed in most victims by severe abdominal pain. The victim may also vomit blood and have diarrhea.

Diagnosis

Doctors will perform various tests, especially if anthrax is suspected. With skin anthrax, a biopsy is taken of the sore (lesion), and lab tests are performed to look at the organism under a microscope and confirm the diagnosis of anthrax.

The diagnosis of inhalation anthrax is difficult to make. A chest x-ray may show certain signs in the chest cavity. Cultures (growing the bacteria in a lab and then examining them under a microscope) are minimally helpful in making the diagnosis. Blood tests may also be performed.

GI anthrax also is difficult to diagnose because the disease is rare and symptoms are not always obvious. Diagnosis usually is confirmed only if the victim has a history of eating contaminated meat in the setting of an outbreak. Once again, cultures generally are not helpful in making the diagnosis.

Meningitis (brain swelling) from anthrax is difficult to distinguish from meningitis due to other causes. A spinal tap may be performed to look at the person's spinal fluid in identifying the organism.

The most useful microbiologic test is the standard blood culture, which is almost always positive in victims with anthrax throughout their bodies. Blood cultures should show growth in 6-24 hours and if the laboratory has been alerted to the possibility of anthrax, biochemical testing should provide a preliminary diagnosis 12-24 hours later. However, if the laboratory has not been alerted to the possibility of anthrax, there is the chance that the organism may not be identified correctly. Rapid diagnostic tests for anthrax and its proteins include polymerase chain reaction (PCR), enzyme-linked immunosorbent assay (ELISA), and direct fluorescent antibody (DFA) testing. Currently, these tests are only available at national reference laboratories.

Treatment

Inhalation anthrax: As previously stated because inhalation anthrax moves quickly throughout the body, doctors will begin antibiotic treatment right away even before a firm diagnosis is made through lab testing.

Ciprofloxacin (Cipro), doxycycline (Vibramycin), and penicillin are FDA-approved antibiotics for treatment of anthrax. Experts currently recommend ciprofloxacin or other drugs in the same class for adults who are assumed to have inhalation anthrax infection. Penicillin and doxycycline may be used once organism culture sensitivities are known. Traditionally, ciprofloxacin and other antibiotics in that class are not recommended for use in children younger than 16-18 years because of a weak theoretical link to permanent joint disorders. Balancing these small risks against the risk of death and the possibility of infection with a resistant strain of anthrax, experts recommend that ciprofloxacin nonetheless be given to children in appropriate doses.

Because there is a risk the infection will recur, victims are treated with antibiotics for at least 60 days.

Skin Anthrax: Treatment of skin anthrax with antibiotics generally prevents the disease from progressing to the entire body although the black tissue and scar continue to form. Although previous guidelines have suggested treating skin anthrax with 7-10 days of therapy, recent recommendations suggest treatment for 60 days in the setting of bioterrorism, thus assuming the person may also have been exposed to inhalational anthrax.

In pregnant women, experts recommend that ciprofloxacin be given after exposure as a preventive medication following exposure to an anthrax attack.

Prevention

After exposure, the antibiotics ciprofloxacin, or doxycycline may be prescribed by a doctor and the medications are usually taken for 60 days. A vaccination series to protect against anthrax consists of 6 injections given over a period of 18 months, followed by booster shots every year.

If a biological warfare attack is expected or may have occurred, people who have not had the vaccine may be given ciprofloxacin or doxycycline for at least 4 weeks.

PLAGUE

Plague is another infection that can strike humans and animals. It is caused by the bacteria *Yersinia pestis*, which has been the cause of 3 great human pandemics in the 6th, 14th, and 20th centuries.

Throughout history, the oriental rat flea has been largely responsible for spreading bubonic plague. After the flea bites an infected animal, the organisms can multiply inside the flea. When an infected flea attempts to bite again, it vomits clotted blood and bacteria into the victim's bloodstream and passes the infection on to the next victim, whether small mammal (usually rodent) or human.

. Although the largest outbreaks of plague have been associated with the rat flea, all fleas should be considered dangerous in areas where plague may be found. The most important vector (a vector is an animal that can transmit the disease) in the United States is the most prevalent flea of rock squirrels and California ground squirrels. The black rat has been most responsible worldwide for the continuing spread of plague in urban epidemics.

Signs and Symptoms

People infected with plague may suddenly develop high a fever, painful lymph nodes, and have bacteria in their blood. Some victims with the bubonic form of the disease may develop secondary pneumonic plague (a disease similar to pneumonia). Plague is contagious and when the victim coughs, plague can spread. Pneumonic plague is the most severe form of the disease and if untreated, most people die. As few as 1-10 organisms are enough to infect humans or other animals including rodents. During the early phase, the germs usually spread to lymph nodes near the bite, where swelling occurs. The infection then spreads to other organs such as the spleen, liver, lungs, skin, mucous membranes, and later, the brain.

In the United States, most victims with human plague have the bubonic form. If the organisms were used as a biological warfare agent, it most likely would be spread through the air and inhaled by victims. The result would be primary pneumonic plague (epidemic pneumonia). If fleas were used as carriers of disease, bubonic or septicemic (blood infection) plague would result.

Bubonic Plague: Swollen lymph nodes (called buboes) develop 1-8 days after exposure. Their appearance is associated with the onset of sudden fever, chills, and headache, which often are followed by nausea and vomiting several hours later. The buboes become visible within 24 hours and cause severe pain. Untreated, septicemia (blood poisoning) develops in 2-6 days. Up to 15% of bubonic plague victims develop secondary pneumonic plague and thus can spread illness from person to person by coughing.

Septicemia Plague: Septicemia plague may occur with bubonic plague. The signs and symptoms of primary septicemic plague include fever, chills, nausea, vomiting, and diarrhea. Later, bleeding in the skin may develop, hands and feet may lose circulation, and tissue may die.

Pneumonic Plague: Pneumonic plague may occur primarily from inhaling organisms in the air or from exposure to infected blood. Victims typically have a productive cough with blood-tinged sputum within 24 hours of symptom onset.

Diagnosis

The diagnosis of bubonic plague may be made if the victim has painful lymph glands and other common symptoms, especially if the victim has been exposed to rodents or fleas. But if the victim is not in an area where plague is present and symptoms are typical of other illnesses, the diagnosis may be difficult.

The doctor may view under a microscope a sample of sputum from a productive cough or the fluid from a swollen lymph gland. Samples may grow in the laboratory and indicate plague within 48 hours and blood tests may also be performed.

Treatment

Victims of suspected plague will be isolated for the first 48 hours after treatment begins. If pneumonic plague is present, isolation may last for 4 more days. Since 1948, streptomycin has been the treatment of choice for plague but other antibiotics may be given.

If treated with antibiotics, buboes typically become smaller in 10-14 days and do not require drainage. Victims are unlikely to survive primary pneumonic plague if antibiotic therapy is not begun within 18 hours of the beginning of symptoms. Without treatment, 60% of people with bubonic plague die, and 100% with pneumonic and septicemic forms die.

Prevention

Fleas always must be targeted for destruction before the rodents, because killing rodents may release into the environment massive amounts of infected fleas, which will be hungry for a blood meal and, in the absence of rodents, the fleas will seek out any warm-blooded animal including humans and infect them. Pesticides have been successful in getting rid of rats and other animal hosts. Public education about how plague spreads is an important part of prevention.

People who have been exposed to pneumonic plague and those who have been exposed to organisms in the air may be treated with antibiotics such as tetracycline or doxycycline for 6 days.

Contacts with victims who have bubonic plague do not need preventive medication. But people who were in the same environment as those who are infected may need preventive antibiotics. A previously FDA-approved plague vaccine is no longer manufactured. It was useful against the bubonic form of plague but not the more serious pneumonic (lung) form of plague, which is the kind most often expected in a terrorist incident. A new vaccine effective against all varieties of plague is under development.

Only those at high risk for plague should be given the vaccine. This might include military troops and personnel working in areas where plague exists and lab personnel working with the organism. The current vaccine against bubonic plague by flea bite does not have the same effectiveness against the organisms released in the air.

CHOLERA

Cholera is an acute and potentially severe gastrointestinal disease (stomach and intestines) caused by the bacteria *Vibrio cholerae*. This agent has been investigated in the past as a biological weapon. Cholera does not spread easily from human to human, so it appears that major drinking water supplies would have to be profusely contaminated for this agent to be effective as a biological weapon. Cholera normally can infect water or food that becomes contaminated by human bowel waste. The organism can survive for up to 24 hours in sewage and as long as 6 weeks in certain types of relatively impure water containing organic matter. It can withstand freezing for 3-4 days, but it is killed readily by dry heat, steam, boiling, short-term exposure to ordinary disinfectants, and chlorination of water. The toxin causes a person's intestines to create massive amounts of fluid that then produces thin, grayish brown diarrhea.

Signs and Symptoms

Depending on how many organisms a person drinks or eats, the illness could begin within 12-72 hours. The symptoms start suddenly with intestinal cramps and painless (rice-water appearing) diarrhea. Vomiting, feeling ill, and headache often accompany the diarrhea, especially early in the illness. Fever is rare. If untreated, the disease generally lasts 1-7 days. During the illness, the body loses great amounts of fluid, so it is important during recovery to replace fluids and balance electrolytes (such as sodium and potassium). Children may experience seizures and cardiovascular imbalances severe enough to cause heart problems. The rapid loss of body fluids often leads to more severe illness. If not treated, up to half of children with cholera may die.

Diagnosis

The doctor may examine a sample of the stool under a microscope to confirm the diagnosis. Symptoms alone are usually enough to identify cholera.

Treatment

Fluids and electrolytes need to be replaced because the body has lost large amounts of fluids through the vomiting and diarrhea.

Doctors may encourage the person to drink, but if someone continues to vomit or has frequent stools, an IV may be used to replace the fluid lost.

Antibiotics such as tetracycline or doxycycline shorten the duration of diarrhea and reduce fluid losses. The antibiotics ciprofloxacin or erythromycin also may be used for a few days.

Prevention

A live vaccine is available for use in those considered to be at risk for exposure. The vaccine is protective for only about half of those immunized, and protection lasts for no more than 6 months. The vaccination schedule is an initial dose followed by another dose 4 weeks later, with booster doses every 6 months.

An inactivated oral vaccine is safe and provides rapid short-term protection. It requires 2 doses and has about 85% efficacy lasting 2-3 years for 2 different types of cholera.

TULAREMIA

Tularemia is an infection that can strike humans and animals. It is caused by the bacterium *Francisella tularensis*. The disease causes fever, localized skin or mucous membrane ulcerations, regional swelling of lymph glands, and occasionally pneumonia.

G.W. McCay discovered the disease in Tulare County, California, in 1911. The first confirmed case of human disease was reported in 1914. Edward Francis, who described transmission by deer flies via infected blood, coined the term *tularemia* in 1921. It has been considered an important biological warfare agent because it can infect many people if dispersed by the aerosol route.

Rabbits and ticks most commonly spread tularemia in North America. In other areas of the world, tularemia is transmitted by water rats and other aquatic animals.

The bacteria are usually introduced into the victim through breaks in the skin or through the mucous membranes of the eye, respiratory tract, or GI tract. Ten virulent organisms injected under the skin from a bite or 10-50 organisms breathed into the lungs can cause infection in humans. Hunters may contract this disease by trapping and skinning rabbits in some parts of the country.

Signs and Symptoms

Tularemia can be divided into 2 forms: the ulceroglandular (75% of cases) and typhoidal (25% of cases). Victims with the ulceroglandular type have sores on the skin or mucous membranes, large lymph nodes, or both. Those with typhoidal tularemia have smaller lymph nodes and no skin sores. After 3-6 days, people with the ulceroglandular form of the disease develop a group of symptoms: fever, chills, headache, cough, and muscle aches. They may also have chest pain, vomiting, joint pain, sore throat, abdominal pain, diarrhea, shortness of breath, back pain, or neck stiffness.

A sore up to an inch across may appear on the skin in about 60% of people and is the most common sign of tularemia. If the bite associated with infection was from an animal carrying the disease, the sore is usually on the upper part of a person's body, such as on the arm. If the infection came from an insect bite, the sore might appear on the lower part of the body, such as on the leg. Enlarged lymph nodes are seen in about 85% of victims and may be the initial or the only sign of infection. Although enlarged lymph nodes usually occur as single lesions, they may appear in groups. Enlarged lymph nodes may come and go and last for as long as 3 years. When swollen, they may be confused with buboes of bubonic plague. Sore throat and other complications may occur in up to 25% of people with tularemia. People with either type of tularemia may develop pneumonia. They may have a productive or nonproductive cough and possibly chest pain, shortness of breath, and vomit blood.

Diagnosis

Tularemia can be diagnosed by growing the bacteria in the laboratory from samples taken of blood, ulcers, sputum, and other body fluids. Blood tests may not be helpful.

Treatment

Victims with tularemia who do not receive appropriate antibiotics may have a prolonged illness with weakness and weight loss. Treated properly, very few people with tularemia die. A 14-day course of streptomycin is effective treatment for tularemia. Gentamicin is also effective. Although tetracycline and chloramphenicol have also been found effective, they are associated with significant relapse rates.

Although laboratory-related infections with this organism are common, human-to-human spread is unusual. Victims do not need to be isolated from others.

Prevention

An antibiotic given after exposure to tularemia is difficult, because the ideal drug, streptomycin, must be given by injection. Tetracycline is effective after exposure to an aerosol of tularemia if given within 24 hours of the exposure and taken for 14 days.

A vaccine has been developed and used in humans since 1940. In the 1960s, a more purified vaccine was developed. Extensive studies have demonstrated that the vaccine protects humans against the organism released into the air. Immunization with the vaccine prevents the typhoidal type and lessens the effects of the ulceroglandular form of tularemia.

BRUCELLOSIS

Brucellosis is an infection of domesticated and wild animals that can be transmitted to humans. It is caused by an organism of the genus *Brucella.* The organism infects mainly cattle, sheep, goats, and other similar animals causing death of developing fetuses and genital infection. Humans, who usually are infected incidentally by contact with infected animals, may develop numerous symptoms in addition to the usual ones of fever, general illness, and muscle pain.

The disease often becomes long-term and may return, even with appropriate treatment. The ease of transmission through the air suggests that these organisms may be useful in biological warfare.

Each of 6 different species may tend to infect certain animal species. Four are known to cause illness in humans. Animals may transmit organisms during a miscarriage, at the time of slaughter, and in their milk. Brucellosis is rarely, if ever, transmitted from human to human.

Certain species can enter animal hosts through skin abrasions or cuts, the eye membranes, the respiratory tract, and the GI tract. Organisms grow rapidly and eventually go to the lymph nodes, liver, spleen, joints, kidneys, and bone marrow.

Signs and Symptoms

Victims may have a fever or a long-term infection or just a local inflammation. The disease may appear suddenly or develop slowly anywhere from 3 days to several weeks after exposure. Symptoms include fever, sweats, fatigue, loss of appetite, and muscle or joint aches. Depression, headache, and irritability occur frequently. In addition, infection of bones, joints, or the genitourinary tract may cause pain. Cough and chest pain also may be noted. Symptoms often last 3-6 months and occasionally for longer than a year. Different species of the organism can cause different symptoms from skin sores to low back pain to liver disease.

Diagnosis

The doctor will want to know about any exposure to animals, animal products, or environmental exposures in making the diagnosis. Military troops exposed to a biological attack and who have fever are likely candidates for this illness. Environmental samples may show the presence of this organism in the attack area. Laboratory tests and cultures of blood or body fluid samples including bone marrow may be performed.

Treatment

Therapy with a single drug has resulted in a high relapse rate, so a combination of antibiotics should be prescribed. A 6-week course of doxycycline along with streptomycin for the first 2 weeks is effective in most adults with most forms of brucellosis.

Prevention

Animal handlers should wear appropriate protective clothing when working with infected animals. Meat should be well cooked, and milk should be pasteurized. Laboratory workers need to take appropriate cautions in handling the organism.

In the event of a biological attack, the standard gas mask should protect adequately from airborne species. No commercially available vaccine exists for humans.

Q FEVER

Q fever is a disease that also affects animals and humans. It is caused by the bacteria *Coxiella burnetii.* A sporelike form of the organism is extremely resistant to heat, pressure, and many cleaning solutions. This allows the germs to live in the environment for long periods under harsh conditions. In contrast, the disease it causes in humans is usually not harmful, although it can be temporarily disabling. Even without treatment, most people recover. The organism is extremely infectious. The potential of the organism as a biological warfare agent is related directly to its ability to infect people easily. A single organism is capable of producing infection and disease in humans. Different strains have been identified worldwide.

Humans have been infected most commonly by contact with domestic livestock, particularly goats, cattle, and sheep. The risk of infection is increased greatly if humans are exposed while these animals are giving birth to young. Large numbers of the germs may be released into the air as an animal gives birth. Survival of the organism on surfaces, such as straw, hay, or clothing, allows for transmission to other people who are not in direct contact with infected animals. People can become infected by breathing the organisms.

Signs and Symptoms

Humans are the only hosts that commonly develop an illness as a result of the infection. The illness may begin within 10-40 days.

There is no typical pattern of symptoms, and some people show none at all. Most people appear mildly to moderately ill.

Fever (can go up and down and last less than 13 days), chills, and headache are the most common signs and symptoms. Sweating, aches, fatigue, and loss of appetite are also common. Cough often occurs later in the illness. Chest pain occurs in a few people. Sometimes there is a rash. Other symptoms such as headache, facial pain, and hallucinations have been reported.

Sometimes problems in the lungs are seen on chest x-rays. And some people may seem to have acute hepatitis because of their liver involvement. Others may develop a heart condition called endocarditis.

Diagnosis

Blood tests may help in making the diagnosis of Q fever.

Treatment

Tetracycline has been the main drug used since the 1950s. When initiated within the first few days of the illness, treatment significantly shortens its course. Other antibiotics, such as erythromycin and azithromycin, are also effective.

People with chronic Q fever who develop endocarditis may die, even with appropriate treatment.

Prevention

Although an effective vaccine (Q-Vax) is licensed in Australia, all Q fever vaccines used in the United States are under study. Q fever can be prevented by immunization.

SMALLPOX

Variola (the virus that causes smallpox) is the most notorious of the poxviruses. Smallpox was an important cause of illness and death in the developing world until recent times. In 1980, the World Health Organization (WHO) declared that smallpox had been completely wiped out. The last case was noted in Somalia in 1977.

Variola represents a significant threat as a biological warfare agent. Variola is highly infectious and is associated with a high death rate and secondary spread. Currently, the majority of the US population has no immunity, vaccine is in short supply, and no effective treatment exists for the disease. Two WHO-approved and inspected repositories remain: One is at the Centers for Disease Control and Prevention in the United States; the other at Vector Laboratories in Russia. It is widely believed that clandestine stockpiles exist in other countries such as Iraq and North Korea.

Variola virus is highly infectious when released into the air. It is environmentally stable and can retain its ability to infect people for long periods. Infection through contaminated objects such as clothing is infrequent. After a person is exposed to aerosolized virus, the virus multiplies in the person's respiratory tract. After a period of 7-17 days, variola is spread through the bloodstream to lymph nodes where it continues to multiply.

Variola then moves into smaller blood vessels near the surface of the skin where the inflammatory changes occur. The classic smallpox rash then begins. Two types of smallpox generally are recognized.

Variola major, the most severe form, may cause death in up to 30% of unvaccinated people who develop it. (3% of people vaccinated people may also develop variola major).

Variola minor, a milder form of smallpox, produces death in 1% of unvaccinated people.

Signs and Symptoms

The symptoms of variola major occur after a 7- to 17-day incubation period. They begin acutely with high fever, headache, chills, aches, vomiting, abdominal and back pain. During the initial phase, 15% of people develop delirium (hallucinations), and 10% of light-skinned people may develop a fleeting rash.

After 2-3 days, the rash develops on the face, hands, and forearms and extends gradually to the trunk and lower part of the body. The sores progress all at once into fluid-filled sacs. The distribution of the rash is important in making the diagnosis of smallpox.

A greater number of lesions will appear on the face arms and legs compared to the trunk. People with smallpox are most infectious on days 3-6 after the fever begins. Virus is spread to others through coughing and sneezing or by direct contact.

With the milder form of smallpox, variola minor, the skin sores are similar but smaller and fewer in number. People are not as ill as those who have variola major.

Diagnosis

Most doctors have never seen a case of smallpox and may have difficulty diagnosing it. Other viral illnesses with rash, such as chickenpox or allergic contact dermatitis, can look similar. Smallpox is different from chickenpox because of the distribution of the lesions and because they are all at the same stage of development everywhere on the body. With chickenpox, sores may be forming while others are scabbing over.

The failure to recognize mild cases of smallpox in people with partial immunity permits rapid person-to-person transmission. Exposed people may shed virus through coughing without ever showing the signs and symptoms of the disease.

The doctor may look at scrapings of tissue under a microscope but will be unable to tell the difference between smallpox and monkeypox or cowpox. Advanced PCR techniques have been developed and may provide for more accurate diagnosis in the near future.

Treatment

People with smallpox are usually isolated from people without smallpox for 17 days. Anyone exposed to either weaponized variola or people infected with smallpox must be vaccinated immediately; this may lessen or prevent the illness if done within 4 or 5 days of infection.Treatment of smallpox is mainly to help relieve symptoms. The antiviral agent, cidofovir, may be effective in treating symptoms.

Prevention

Smallpox vaccine is used to prevent people from getting smallpox. The vaccine is given as a type of shot, but a 2-pronged needle is used to place the medication into the skin. This leaves a permanent scar, which many adults may still have from smallpox inoculations given to them when they were babies.

Once the shot is given, a small fluid-filled pimple usually appears 5-7 days later. A scab forms over the site during the next 1-2 weeks. Common side effects include low-grade fever and swollen lymph glands. People with weakened immune systems should not have the smallpox vaccination. This includes people with HIV, anyone with a history of eczema, and pregnant women.

MONKEYPOX

The monkeypox virus is a naturally occurring relative of variola, which is found in Africa. The first case of human monkeypox was identified in 1970, but fewer than 400 cases have been diagnosed since. Some concern exists that monkeypox may be weaponized, however, human monkeypox is not as potent as smallpox. Pneumonia due to monkeypox may cause death in about half of people who develop it.

VIRAL ENCEPHALITIDES

The viral encephalitides, Venezuelan equine encephalitis (VEE) virus, western equine encephalitis (WEE) virus, and eastern equine encephalitis (EEE) virus, are members of the Alphavirus genus and are regularly associated with encephalitis. These viruses were recovered from horses during the 1930s. VEE was isolated in the Guajira peninsula of Venezuela in 1930, WEE in the San Joaquin Valley of California in 1930, and EEE in Virginia and New Jersey in 1933.

Although natural infections with these viruses occur following bites from mosquitos, the viruses are also highly infectious when spread through the air. If intentionally released as a small particle aerosol, this virus may be expected to infect a high percentage of people exposed within a few miles.

VEE virus has the capacity to produce epidemics. Outcomes are significantly worse for the very young and the very old. Up to 35% of people infected may die. WEE and EEE typically produce less severe and widespread disease but are associated with death rates as high as 50-75% in those with severe illness.

Signs and Symptoms

VEE: After an incubation period of 2-6 days, people with VEE develop fevers, chills, headache, aches, sore throat, and sensitivity to light (eyes). They may become mildly confused, have seizures or paralysis, or go into a coma. For those who survive, their nervous system functions usually recover completely.

EEE: The incubation period for EEE varies from 5-15 days. Adults may have certain early symptoms up to 11 days before the onset of nervous system problems such as mild confusion, seizures, and paralysis. Signs and symptoms include fever, chills, vomiting, muscle rigidity, lethargy, slight paralysis, excess salivation, and difficulty breathing. Children frequently develop swelling on their face and near their eyes. Up to 30% of survivors of severe disease have permanent nervous system problems such as seizures and various degrees of confusion (dementia).

WEE: The incubation period is 5-10 days. Most people have no symptoms, or they might develop a fever. Other symptoms include nausea, vomiting, headache, a stiff neck, and drowsiness. Up to 90% of victims younger than 1 year have seizures. Typically, adults recover completely. Children, especially newborns, may have lasting nervous system problems.

Diagnosis

Laboratory tests, including nasal swab samples, may show any of the 3 viruses.

Treatment

No specific treatment is available. Doctors will help control symptoms. For some people that may include medications to control fever and seizures or help breathing.

Prevention

A vaccine for VEE can be given as an injection for those at high risk, such as laboratory field personnel. About 20% of those who receive the vaccine fail to respond to it, meaning they would not be protected by the vaccine. An additional 25% of those vaccinated develop high fever, chills, and feel sick enough to be in bed. A different vaccine was developed for those who did not develop protection from the initial activated vaccine. It is an inactivated vaccine, which produces only mild tenderness at the injection site. Shots are given at 2- and 4-week intervals until the person responds and develops antibodies as protection.

The EEE vaccine is inactivated and given as an injection (1 to start and another 28 days later). There are no serious side effects or long-term problems with this vaccine. Boosters are required.

VIRAL HEMORRHAGIC FEVERS

Viral hemorrhagic fevers are caused by 4 families of viruses.

Arenaviridae (Lassa, Argentine, Bolivian, Brazilian, Venezuelan hemorrhagic fevers)

Bunyaviridae (Rift Valley, Crimean-Congo, Hantaan)

Filoviridae (Marburg, Ebola)

Flaviviridae (Yellow, Dengue, Kyasanur Forest, Omsk HFs)

The best known of the viral hemorrhagic fevers is Ebola virus. First recognized in Zaire in 1976, the virus has been linked to 3 outbreaks in Africa. Up to 92% of people who contract Ebola will die. A related virus was discovered in Reston, Virginia, in 1989 in association with an outbreak of illness among monkeys imported from the Philippines. No human cases occurred with this outbreak.

These viruses are each characterized by an acute generalized illness that includes feeling quite ill (flulike illness) with profound exhaustion and often associated internal bleeding. All agents are highly infectious via the aerosol route, and most are stable as respiratory aerosols. Thus, they possess characteristics that may make them attractive for use by terrorists.

The agents that produce viral hemorrhagic fever are all simple RNA viruses. They are able to survive in blood for long periods, which means they can infect people who are around animals slaughtered domestically. These viruses are linked to the rodent or insect that helps to spread them, which helps in searching for a diagnosis.

The specific viral hemorrhagic fever that develops depends on many factors such as the strength of the virus, its strain, and the route of exposure.

Signs and Symptoms

All viral hemorrhagic fevers primarily target blood vessels. They damage the blood vessels and produce internal bleeding. Victims may have fever, aches, exhaustion, infected eyes, low blood pressure to severe shock, and bleeding in tiny blood vessels such as in the eye. More severe cases will have serious problems with the nervous system, liver, and lungs.

Depending on the type of virus, symptoms can include deafness, severe internal bleeding, kidney failure, rash, black (bloody) vomit, and other life-threatening symptoms.

Diagnosis

It is important for the doctor to know a person's travel history in making a diagnosis of viral hemorrhagic fever. These agents are linked tightly with their natural geographic area and the ecology of the species and vectors found in that specific locale. Victims often recall exposures to rodents (Arenavirus, Hantavirus), mosquitoes (Rift Valley fever virus, yellow and dengue fever viruses), or even slaughtered horses (Rift Valley fever virus, Crimean-Congo virus).

Laboratory tests may be helpful. Testing can be conducted at the CDC in Atlanta or the US Army Medical Research Institute of Infectious Disease (USAMRIID) at Fort Detrick in Frederick, Maryland.

Treatment

Treatment for viral hemorrhagic fevers is largely directed at easing the discomfort of the symptoms. Victims benefit from being placed in a hospital setting immediately. Air transport is not advised. Sedative and pain-relieving medications are helpful, but aspirin and similar drugs should not be given because of their tendency to make bleeding worse.

Doctors will also not usually use IV lines or catheters because of bleeding problems. The treatment for bleeding is controversial. Generally, mild bleeding is not usually treated, but severe bleeding requires appropriate replacement therapy (blood through an IV line).

Specific treatment with ribavirin has been used and is currently under investigation as a therapy for Lassa fever, Hantavirus, Crimean-Congo, and Rift Valley Fever. Treatment is most effective if begun within 7 days. Ribavirin has poor activity against the filoviruses and flaviviruses.

Prevention

The only established and licensed virus-specific vaccine against any of these viruses is the yellow fever vaccine. It is mandatory for those traveling into areas of Africa and South America where the disease is commonly found. Current trials are underway for further vaccines and antibody therapies.

TOXINS

STAPHYLOCOCCAL ENTEROTOXIN B

Staphylococcal enterotoxin B (SEB) is one of the best-studied and, therefore, best-understood toxins.

Staphylococcal enterotoxin is one of the most common causes of food poisoning. Nausea, vomiting, and diarrhea normally occur after someone eats or drinks contaminated food. The toxin creates different symptoms when exposure is through the air in a biological warfare situation. Only a small, inhaled dose is necessary to harm people within 24 hours of inhalation.

Signs and Symptoms

After exposure, signs and symptoms begin in 2-12 hours. Mild-to-moderate exposure to SEB produces fever, chills, headache, nausea, vomiting, shortness of breath, chest pain, body aches, and a nonproductive cough. Severe exposures can lead to a toxic shock -type picture and even death. Depending on the severity of exposure, the illness may last 3-10 days.

Diagnosis

Diagnosis of SEB can be difficult. Laboratory tests and a chest x-ray may be performed. Nasal swabs may show the toxin for 12-24 hours after exposure.

Treatment

Doctors provide care to relieve symptoms. Close attention to oxygenation and hydration are important. People with severe SEB may need help breathing with a ventilator. Most victims are expected to do well after the initial phase, but the time to full recovery may be long.

Prevention

No approved human vaccine exists for SEB, although human trials are ongoing. Passive immunotherapy agents have demonstrated some promise when given within 4 hours of exposure, but such therapy is still being tested.

RICIN

Ricin, a plant protein toxin derived from the beans of the castor plant, is one of the most toxic and easily produced of the plant toxins. Although the lethal toxicity of ricin is about 1000-fold less than botulinum toxin, the worldwide ready availability of castor beans and the ease with which the toxin can be produced give it significant potential as a biological weapon.

Since ancient times, more than 750 cases of ricin intoxication have been described. Ricin may have been used in the highly published killing of Bulgarian exile Georgi Markov in London in 1978. He was attacked with a device in an umbrella that implanted a ricin-containing pellet into his thigh.

Signs and Symptoms

The toxicity of ricin varies greatly with the way it is given. Ricin is extremely toxic to cells and acts by inhibiting protein synthesis. Inhalation exposure causes primarily breathing and lung problems. If eaten, ricin causes symptoms in the GI tract. If injected, the reaction takes place in that area.

Following inhalation exposure of ricin, toxicity is characterized by the sudden onset of nasal and throat congestion, nausea and vomiting, itching of the eyes, itching, and tightness in the chest. If exposure is significant, after 12-24 hours severe breathing problems may set in.

In animal studies, death occurs 36-48 hours after severe exposure. Ingestion of ricin is generally less toxic because it is not absorbed well and may degrade in the digestive tract. Out of 751 ingestions recorded, only 14 resulted in a death.

At low doses, injection exposures produce flulike symptoms, body aches, nausea, vomiting, and localized pain and swelling at the injection site. Severe exposure results in tissue death and GI bleeding, as well as widespread liver, spleen, and kidney problems.

Diagnosis

The diagnosis of ricin poisoning is made on the basis of symptoms and whether exposure was possible. In biological warfare, exposure is likely to occur by inhalation of a toxin aerosol. Victims may have certain signs on a chest x-ray. The diagnosis can be confirmed by lab tests on samples from a nasal swab. Ricin can be identified for up to 24 hours after exposure.

Treatment

Treatment is mainly to relieve symptoms. If exposure was by inhalation, the person may need help breathing. Those who ingested the poison may need to have their stomachs pumped (gastric lavage), or they might be given activated charcoal to soak up the material.

Prevention

Currently, no vaccine is available for ricin exposure. Test vaccines have proven effective in animals. Other drugs are being studied as well.

BOTULINUM TOXIN

Botulinum toxins are the most deadly toxins known. Because botulinum toxin is so lethal and easy to manufacture and weaponize, it represents a credible threat as a biological warfare agent. When used in this manner, exposure is likely to occur following inhalation of aerosolized toxin or ingestion of food contaminated with the toxin or its microbial spores. Iraq admitted to active research on the offensive use of botulinum toxins and to weaponizing and deploying more than 100 munitions with botulinum toxin in 1995. All 7 subtypes (A-G) of botulinum toxin act in similar ways. The toxin produces similar effects whether ingested, inhaled, or via a wound. The time course and severity of illness vary with route of exposure and dose received. Symptom onset is slower after inhalation exposure.

Signs and Symptoms

Symptoms may occur hours to several days after exposure. Initial signs and symptoms include blurred vision, dilated pupils, difficulty swallowing, difficulty speaking, an altered voice, and muscle weakness. After 24-48 hours, muscle weakness and paralysis may cause the person to be unable to breathe. Varying degrees of muscular weakness may occur.

Diagnosis

Paralysis may indicate the presence of this exposure. Laboratory tests generally are not helpful. Infection by inhalation can be diagnosed from nasal swabs up to 24 hours after exposure.

Treatment

The most serious complication is respiratory failure. With attention to symptoms and help breathing, sometimes with a ventilator, death occurs in fewer than 5% of cases. For confirmed exposures, an antitoxin is available from the CDC. This antitoxin has all of the disadvantages of horse serum products, including the risks for shock and serum sickness. Skin testing is performed first by injecting a small amount of the antitoxin into the skin and then monitoring the person for 20 minutes.

Prevention

A toxoid (inactivated toxin that produces immunity) has been used in volunteers and occupationally at-risk workers. It is available through the CDC. It was used to immunize US military troops during the Persian Gulf War. The current schedule for immunization is at 0, 2, and 12 weeks with an annual booster.

MYCOTOXINS

The trichothecene mycotoxins are highly toxic compounds produced by certain species of fungi. Because these mycotoxins can cause massive organ damage, and because they are fairly easy to produce and can be dispersed by various methods (dusts, droplets, aerosols, smoke, rockets, artillery mines, portable sprays), mycotoxins have an excellent potential for weaponization.

Strong evidence suggests that trichothecenes ("yellow rain") have been used as a biological warfare agent in Southwest Asia and Afghanistan. From 1974-1981, numerous attacks resulted in a minimum of 6310 deaths in Laos, 981 deaths in Cambodia, and 3042 deaths in Afghanistan. When taken from fungal cultures, the mycotoxins yield a yellow-brown liquid that evaporates into a yellow crystalline product (thus, the "yellow rain" appearance). These toxins require certain solutions and high heat to be completely inactivated.

Signs and Symptoms

After exposure to the mycotoxins, early symptoms begin within 5 minutes. Full effects take 60 minutes. If skin exposure occurs, the skin burns, becomes tender, swollen, and blisters. In lethal cases, large areas of skin die and slough (fall off).

Respiratory exposure results in nasal itching, pain, sneezing, a bloody nose, shortness of breath, wheezing, cough, and blood-tinged saliva and sputum. If ingested, the person feels nausea and vomits, loses appetite, feels abdominal cramping, and has watery and/or bloody diarrhea. Following entry into the eyes, pain, tearing, redness, and blurred vision occur.

Systemic toxicity may occur and includes weakness, exhaustion, dizziness, inability to coordinate muscles, heart problems, low or high temperature, diffuse bleeding, and low blood pressure. Death may occur within minutes to days depending on the dose and route of exposure.

Diagnosis

Diagnosis of an attack of trichothecene mycotoxin depends on the symptoms and identifying the toxin from biological and environmental samples. Many people with these symptoms may report being in a yellow rain or smoke attack.

Initial laboratory tests are not always helpful. Currently, a rapid identification kit for any of the trichothecene mycotoxins does not exist. Gas-liquid chromatography has been used in the past with great success. However, chromatographic methods lack great sensitivity, and presently alternative methods of detection are under investigation.

Treatment

Treatment is mainly to help with symptoms. The immediate use of protective clothing and mask during a mycotoxin aerosol attack should prevent illness. If a soldier is unprotected during an attack, the outer clothing should be removed within 4-6 hours and decontaminated with 5% sodium hydroxide for 6-10 hours. The skin should be washed with copious amounts of soap and uncontaminated water. The eyes, if exposed, should be washed out with large amounts of normal saline or sterile water. US military personnel can use a skin decontamination kit effectively against most chemical warfare agents, including the mycotoxins.

No specific therapy exists for a trichothecene exposure. After appropriate skin decontamination, victims of inhalation and oral exposures may be given superactivated charcoal orally. Activated charcoal removes mycotoxins from the GI tract. Some victims may need help breathing with a ventilator. Early use of steroids increases survival time by decreasing the primary injury and shock-like state that follows significant poisoning.

Prevention

No vaccine exists for trichothecene mycotoxin exposure. Currently, 2 topical skin protectants as well as vaccines are in advanced development but have not been approved yet for use in humans.

Chapter

16

Terrorism and Chemical Warfare

RISK OF EXPOSURE

Injury from chemical weapon agents, known as CWAs, may result from industrial accidents, military stockpiling, war, or a terrorist attack.

Industrial accidents are a significant potential source of exposure to chemical agents. Chemicals such as phosgene, cyanide, anhydrous ammonia, and chlorine are used widely. These chemicals are frequently transported by industry. The accidental release of a methylisocyanate cloud (composed of phosgene and isocyanate) was implicated in the Bhopal, India, disaster in 1984.

Chemical weapons first were used in 1915, when the German military released 168 tons of chlorine gas at Ypres, Belgium, killing an estimated 5,000 Allied troops.

Two years later, the same battlefields saw the first deployment of sulfur mustard. Sulfur mustard was the major cause of chemical casualties in World War I.

CWAs have been used in at least 12 conflicts since, including the first Persian Gulf War (Iraq-Iran War). The Iraqi military also used chemical weapons against the Iraqi Kurds during the second Persian Gulf War.

Civilians also have been exposed inadvertently to chemical weapons many years after weapon deployment during war. Some 50,000 tons of mustard shells were disposed of in the Baltic Sea following World War I. Since then, numerous fishermen have been burned accidentally while hauling leaking shells aboard boats. Leaking mustard shells also have injured collectors of military memorabilia and children playing on old battlefields.

Although a number of international treaties have banned the development, production, and stockpiling of chemical weapons, these agents reportedly are still being produced or stockpiled in several countries.

Within the last decade, terrorists deployed chemical weapons against civilian populations for the first time in history. The release of sarin in Matsumoto, Japan, in June 1994 by the extremist Aum Shinrikyo cult left 7 dead and 280 injured.

The following year, the Aum Shinrikyo cult released sarin vapor in the Tokyo subway system during morning rush hour, leaving 12 dead and sending more than 5,000 casualties to local hospitals. Several characteristics of chemical weapon agents lend themselves to terrorist use.

Chemicals used in CWAs are widely available, and recipes for CWA production may be found on the Internet.

CWAs are transported easily and may be delivered by a variety of routes.

Chemical agents often are difficult to protect against and quickly incapacitate the intended targets.

Most civilian medical communities are inadequately prepared to deal with a chemical terrorist attack.

TYPES OF CHEMICAL WEAPON AGENTS

Chemical weapon agents are hazardous substances. Major categories of CWAs include the following:

Nerve agents (such as sarin, soman, cyclohexylsarin, tabun, VX)

Vesicating or blistering agents (such as mustards, lewisite)

Choking agents or lung toxicants (such as chlorine, phosgene, diphosgene)

Cyanides

Incapacitating agents (such as anticholinergic compounds)

Lacrimating or riot control agents (such as pepper gas, chloroacetophenone, CS)

Vomiting agents (such as adamsite)

Physical Properties: CWAs generally are stored and transported as liquids and deployed as either liquid aerosols or vapors. Victims usually are exposed to agents via 1 or more of 3 routes: skin (liquid and high vapor concentrations), eyes (liquid or vapor), and respiratory tract (vapor inhalation). In general, some liquids may be harmful whether inhaled into the lungs or absorbed into the skin. Vapors can be affected by winds. Even a slight breeze can blow a nerve agent vapor away from its intended target. The effects of vapor are enhanced when used within an enclosed space.

Clinical Effects: Depending on the agent and the type and amount (concentration) of exposure, CWA effects may be immediate or delayed. Large inhalation exposures to nerve agents or mustards are likely to kill people immediately. Small exposures on the skin to nerve agents and mustards are more dangerous than they seem at first. People exposed to such agents need to be carefully observed for slowly developing or delayed effects. A chart of signs and symptoms is available from the North Carolina Statewide Program for Infection Control and Epidemiology.

Medical Management: Ideally, emergency personnel will wear personal protective equipment, decontaminate the victims immediately, provide medical support to the victims and provide specific antidotes to counteract the harmful effects.

Personal Protective Equipment: First responders to a chemical attack are at serious risk themselves from the chemically contaminated environment (known as the hot zone). They can come in direct contact with the CWA or inhale the vapor. They are also at risk if they handle skin and clothing of victims if a liquid chemical agent was used. Vapors pose little added risk for anyone outside the hot zone.

Decontamination: Decontamination is the physical process of removing the remaining chemicals from people, equipment, and the environment. Residual hazardous chemicals on those who have been exposed directly are a source of ongoing exposure to others and pose a risk of secondary exposure to first responders and emergency care personnel. Immediate decontamination is a major treatment priority for those with CWA exposure. Initial decontamination involves removing all contaminated clothes and jewelry from the affected person and then washing the body thoroughly with warm water and soap.

Hot water and vigorous scrubbing may actually worsen the effects by increasing chemical absorption into the skin.

Vapor exposure alone may not require decontamination. But if it is not known whether the exposure was to a vapor or liquid, or if exposed people have symptoms, they should undergo decontamination.

Ideally, decontamination will take place as close as possible to the site of exposure to minimize duration of exposure and prevent further spread. Hospitals receiving contaminated people may establish an area outside the Emergency Department in which to perform initial decontamination before people and equipment are allowed entry. Portable decontamination equipment with showers and run-off water collection systems are commercially available. All hospitals should have the capacity to safely decontaminate at least 1 person.

Supportive and specific therapy: Doctors will first make sure exposed victims are able to breathe. For many chemical warfare agents, doctors can only treat the symptoms they produce. But specific, well-established antidotes are available for nerve agent and cyanide exposures. Lab tests are not widely available in hospitals to rapidly confirm exposure to chemical agents.

Nerve Agents

The 5 nerve agents, tabun (GA), sarin (GB), soman (GD), cyclohexylsarin (GF), and VX, have chemical structures similar to the common organophosphate pesticide Malathion. These agents initially stimulate and then paralyze certain nerve transmissions throughout the body and cause other toxic effects such as seizures.

Physical properties: Under temperate conditions, all nerve agents are volatile liquids, which means they can evaporate quickly. The most volatile agent, sarin, evaporates at about the same rate as water. The least volatile agent, VX, has the consistency of motor oil, which makes it 100-150 times more toxic than sarin when victims are exposed on their skin. A 10 mg dose applied to the skin may cause death in up to half of unprotected people. All nerve agents rapidly penetrate skin and clothing. Nerve agent vapors are heavier than air and tend to sink into low places (for example, trenches or basements).

Signs and symptoms: Nerve agents produce various signs and symptoms depending on the agent someone might be exposed to, its concentration, and length of exposure.

Liquid exposure: Liquid agents easily penetrate skin and clothing. Symptoms may begin anywhere from 30 minutes to 18 hours after skin exposure. A small droplet on the skin, for example, may cause local sweating and muscle twitching, followed by nausea, vomiting, diarrhea, and generalized weakness. Even with decontamination, signs and symptoms may last for hours. In contrast, people with severe liquid exposures may show no symptoms (for 1-30 minutes) but rapidly may suffer abrupt loss of consciousness, convulsions, generalized muscular twitching, paralysis, secretions (from the nose, mouth, lungs), difficulty breathing, and death.

Vapor exposure: Vapor inhalation produces poisonous symptoms within seconds to several minutes. Effects may be local or throughout the body. Exposure to even a small amount of vapor usually results in at least one of the following categories of symptoms:

(1) in the eyes, blurred vision, eye pain, red eyes;

(2) runny nose; or

(3) difficulty breathing, shortness of breath, excessive productive coughing.

Respiratory tract: Nerve agents act on the upper respiratory tract to produce runny nose, drooling, and weakness of the tongue and throat muscles. High-pitched, distressed breathing can occur. A great deal of phlegm production and narrowing of the airways can occur. If untreated, the combination of symptoms rapidly progresses to respiratory failure and death.

Cardiovascular system: Nerve agents also act on the heart and may produce abnormal heartbeats, more likely to be too fast rather than slow.

Central nervous system: Nerve agents produce a variety of signs and symptoms throughout the central nervous system. People may lose consciousness (sometimes within seconds of exposure) and have seizures. Symptoms such as headache, dizziness, numbness or tingling, anxiety, insomnia, depression, and emotional instability also have been reported.

Musculoskeletal system: Nerve agents initially stimulate and then paralyze muscles. With minimal exposure, exposed people may complain of vague weakness or difficulty walking.

Eyes: Nerve agent liquid or vapor readily penetrates the eye tissues and may cause the pupils to contract, blurred and dim vision, headache, redness, tears, pain, nausea, and vomiting. Although contraction of the pupils is the most consistent clinical finding after vapor exposure to nerve agents (this occurred in 99% of people exposed in the Tokyo sarin attack), it may not occur or occur later if the exposure is on the skin. In severe cases, the pupils of the eye may remain narrowed up to 45 days.

Diagnosis: Routine testing is not reliable in identifying nerve agents in blood or urine. So doctors will make their treatment decisions based on the signs and symptoms a person shows and on information about the type of chemical exposure, if known.

Treatment: Treatment of victims exposed to nerve gas is similar to the treatment of those poisoned by organophosphate insecticides.

Atropine sulfate: Victims with symptoms require immediate treatment with atropine. Atropine helps people breathe by drying secretions and opening their airways to allow them to breathe more freely. Atropine also blocks other effects of poisoning, such as nausea, vomiting, abdominal cramping, low heart rate, and sweating. Atropine, however, does not prevent or reverse paralysis. Adults and children will be given appropriate doses of atropine by IV or injection. Another medication, pralidoxime chloride, may also be given. With adequate decontamination and appropriate initial therapy, serious signs and symptoms of nerve agent toxicity rarely last more than a couple of hours.

Mark I kit: The Mark I kit was designed for military self-administration in the field. It consists of 2 spring-loaded devices to inject yourself, containing atropine and pralidoxime, respectively. These antidote kits are not yet available for civilian use.

Prognosis: Peak toxic effects occur within minutes to hours and go away within 1 day. People who were exposed but show no symptoms are usually observed for at least 18 hours because some signs and symptoms can show up later.

Mustards

Sulfur mustard has been used as a chemical weapon since World War I. Nitrogen mustard, a derivative of sulfur mustard, was one of the first chemotherapy agents but never has been used in warfare. These agents cause blistering of exposed surfaces. Both mustard agents rapidly penetrate cells and generate a highly toxic reaction that disrupts cell function and causes cell death. The chemical reaction is both temperature dependent and aided by the presence of water, which explains why warm, moist tissues are affected more severely. Actively reproducing cells, such as skin and blood cells, are most at risk.

Physical properties: Mustards are oily liquids with odors of mustard, onion, garlic, or horseradish. Highly soluble in oils, fats, and organic solvents, mustards quickly penetrate skin and most materials, including rubber and most textiles. Sulfur mustard is considered a persistent agent with low volatility at cool temperatures but becomes a major vapor hazard at high temperatures. Exposure to mustard vapor, not mustard liquid, is the primary medical concern. More than 80% of mustard casualties in World War I were caused by exposure to mustard vapor. Mustard vapor is 3 times more toxic than a similar concentration of cyanide gas; however, mustard liquid is also quite toxic. Skin exposure to as little as 1-1.5 teaspoons of liquid (7 g) is lethal to half of those exposed.

Signs and symptoms: Mustards injure the skin, eyes, respiratory tract, GI tissues, and blood system. The pattern of toxicity depends partly on whether the person is exposed to liquid or vapor. Liquid exposure primarily damages the skin, producing an initial rash followed by blistering similar to a partial-thickness burn. Vapor exposure damages the upper respiratory tract (skin usually is not affected). Mustards penetrate cells in less than 2 minutes, yet signs and symptoms usually are delayed 4-6 hours (the range can be from 1-24 hours). The time it takes to show symptoms is shorter with high-concentration exposures, such as those occurring at increased room temperature and humidity.

Skin: Chemical burns caused by mustard often appear deceptively superficial at first. Earliest symptoms are itching, burning, and stinging pain over exposed areas. Moist, thinner skin is affected more severely. Affected areas appear red and swollen. If contamination is more extensive, superficial blisters occur within 24 hours of exposure. Most burns are partial thickness, but full-thickness burns with deep blisters may result from exposure to higher concentrations. Blister fluid does not contain active mustard and is not toxic.

Eyes: Eyes are especially sensitive to the effects of mustard. Symptoms begin 4-8 hours after exposure. Earliest symptoms include burning pain, a feeling that something is in the eye, sensitivity to light, tearing, and blurred vision. Permanent corneal scarring and blindness may occur with severe exposures, but is rare.

Respiratory tract: Mustards primarily damage tissues in the upper airway through a direct inflammatory effect. Following a period of 2-24 hours after exposure, symptoms may appear. Early symptoms include sinus congestion, a sore throat, and hoarseness. Later, cough, shortness of breath, and trouble breathing may develop. People with severe and extensive contact with mustard gas may develop respiratory complications up to several days after exposure.

Gastrointestinal tract: Rarely, mustard damages rapidly growing cells of the intestinal tract. GI involvement results in abdominal pain, nausea, vomiting, diarrhea, and weight loss.

Blood system: Rarely, mustards cause unpredictable loss in the production of bone narrow. Certain specialized cells begin dying 3-5 days after exposure reaching its worst point in 3-14 days, depending on the severity of exposure.

Diagnosis: Diagnosis of mustard exposure is based on what the doctor observes from the person's signs and symptoms. No laboratory tests are useful.

Personal protective equipment: Liquid mustard contamination poses a risk for emergency care personnel. Ideally, they will be wearing appropriate personal protective gear.

Decontamination: Immediate decontamination within 2 minutes of exposure is the most important intervention for people who have skin exposure to mustard, because it rapidly becomes fixed to tissues, and its effects are irreversible. Even if an exposure takes place and a person shows no obvious sign and symptoms, decontamination is still urgent. Remove clothing immediately and wash the skin with soap and water. Eye exposure requires immediate washing out with a large amount of saline or water.

Decontamination after the first few minutes of exposure does not prevent further damage later but at least prevents spread of the chemical to other parts of the body and protects emergency care personnel from further contact exposure.

Treatment: Treatment of mustard exposure is based on symptoms. Because the effects of mustards typically are delayed, people with complaints immediately after exposure may have an additional injury.

For those with signs of upper airway obstruction, doctors may treat by using a tube in the person's throat or perform surgery to open the airway.

Mustard-induced burns are especially painful. Doctors will use strong pain relievers. Adequate burn care is essential, because skin lesions heal slowly and are prone to infection. Severe burns may require removal of dead tissue, irrigation, and placement of antibiotics, such as silver sulfadiazine, directly on the burned area. The victim may need a tetanus shot.

Severe eye burns may be treated with daily irrigation, topical antibiotic solutions, topical corticosteroids, and drugs that dilate the pupil. Petroleum jelly may be applied to prevent eyelids from sticking together. More severe corneal injuries may take as long as 2-3 months to heal. Permanent visual problems are rare.

Although no antidotes currently are available to treat mustard toxicity, several agents are under investigation.

Victims with bone marrow suppression following mustard exposure may be treated with medication to stimulate the bone marrow, such as granulocyte colony-stimulating factor.

Prognosis: Victims with significant respiratory tract burns usually require admission to the hospital's intensive care unit. Also, victims with several skin burns will be admitted to the burn unit for burn care, pain relief, and supportive care. Blood cell counts will be monitored for 2 weeks following significant exposures. Most people recover completely. Only a small fraction have long-term eye or lung damage. About 2% of those exposed to sulfur mustard in World War I died, mostly due to burns, respiratory tract damage, and bone marrow suppression. Sulfur mustard is known to cause cancer, yet a single exposure causes only a small risk.

Bibliography

Alexander I. Oparin: *Origin of Life*, Dover Publications, NewYork, 1936.

Allison, Graham, *Nuclear Terrorism: The Ultimate Preventable Catastrophe*, New York: Times Books, 2004.

Basrur, Rajesh M., and Hasan-Askari Rizvi, *Nuclear Terrorism and South Asia*, Albuquerque, NM: Sandia National Laboratories, February 2003.

Bukharin, Oleg, *The Threat of Nuclear Terrorism and the Physical Security of Nuclear Installations and Materials in the former Soviet Union*, Monterey, CA: Center for Russian and Eurasian Studies, Monterey Institute of International Studies, 1992.

Charles Darwin: *The Origin of Species by Means of Natural Selection*, The Modern Library, New York, 1971.

Douglas J. Futuyma: *Science on Trial*, Pantheon Books, New York, 1983

Hoffman, B.: *Inside Terrorism,* New York: Columbia University Press, 1999.

Imam Ghazzali's Ihya Ulum-Id-Din: *The Book of Religious Learnings*, Islamic Book Service, New Delhi, 2001.

John L. Esposito: *Islam: The Straight Path*, Oxford : Oxford University, England, 1991,

Kegley, C. W.: *The new global terrorism: Characteristics, causes, and controls,* Upper Saddle Creek, NJ: Prentice Hall, 2003.

Kelly, R. J., & Maghan, J.: *Hate crimes: The global politics of polarization,* Carbondale, IL: Southern Illinois University Press, 1998.

Kressel, N.: *Mass hate: The global rise of genocide and terror,* New York: Plenum Press, 1996.

Laquer, Walter: *The New Terrorism: Fanaticism and the Arms of Mass Destruction*, Oxford: Oxford University Press, 1999.

Levin, J.,: *The violence of hate: Confronting racism, anti-Semitism, and other forms of bigotry,* Boston, MA: Allyn & Bacon, 2002.

Levitas, D.: *The terrorist next door: The militia movement and the radical right,* New York: Thomas Dunne Books, 2002.

Maniscalco, P. M., & Christen, H. T.: *Understanding Terrorism and Managing the Consequences,* Upper Saddle River, NJ: Prentice-Hall, 2001.

Reich, W., & Laqueur, W.: *Origins of Terrorism: Psychologies, Ideologies, Theologies, States of Mind,* Washington, DC: Woodrow Wilson Center Press, 1998.

Sidney Fox, Klaus Dose: *Molecular Evolution and The Origin of Life,* W.H. Freeman and Company, San Francisco, 1972.

Simonsen, C. E., & Spindlove, J. R.: *Terrorism today: The past, the players, the future,* Upper Saddle Creek, NJ: Prentice Hall, 2000.

Stout, C.: *The psychology of terrorism,* Westport, CT: Praeger, 2002.

Whitaker, D. J.: *The Terrorism Reader,* New York: Routledge, 2001.

White, J. R.: *Terrorism: An introduction: 2002 update,* Belmont, CA: Wadsworth, 2002.

Index

□□□